Spring 86

UNWRAPPING SWISS CULTURE

A JOURNAL OF
ARCHETYPE
AND
CULTURE

Fall 2011

SPRING JOURNAL
New Orleans, Louisiana

CONTENTS

BOOK REVIEWS

Honoring James Hillman (1926-2011)

Just a few days before I was to send this issue of *Spring* to press, I learned the sad news of James Hillman's death, a huge loss to the *Spring* community and to all those who knew him personally and who were influenced, inspired, challenged, and provoked by his highly original mind, wit, and extensive body of writings.

As many of you know, Hillman had a long history with this journal. The Analytical Psychology Club of New York, who founded *Spring Journal* in 1941, turned the editorship of it over to Hillman in 1970, while he was living in Zürich. A graduate of the C.G. Jung Institute in Zürich, Hillman went on to serve as Director of Studies and moved *Spring* to Zürich, where it remained for a number of years. In the very first volume of *Spring* that Hillman edited, he published his own seminal paper "Why 'Archetypal Psychology'?", a prelude to his magnum opus *Revisioning Psychology*. A long-time participant in the Eranos conferences in Ascona, Switzerland, Hillman drew on that sensibility in editing *Spring*, emphasizing "image oriented" thought. Under Hillman's editorship, *Spring* focused on inaugurating the new field of archetypal psychology.

Spring Journal helped celebrate James Hillman's life and work by publishing in 2008 the book *Archetypal Psychologies: Reflections in Honor of James Hillman*, edited by Stanton Marlan, who brought together the work of 29 leading scholars, practitioners, and new voices as a testament to the fecundity and influence of archetypal psychology around the world. Stan presented this volume to Hillman three summers ago at a special event in Pittsburgh in Hillman's honor, and *Spring Journal* was privileged to have had the opportunity to help pay tribute to him in this way.

My deepest condolences go out to Margot McLean and other members of James Hillman's family, and to his many friends and colleagues.

Nancy Cater, J.D., Ph.D., Editor
Spring: A Journal Of Archetype and Culture
New Orleans, Louisiana

Unwrapping Swiss Culture

INTRODUCTION

NANCY CATER

This issue of *Spring* is devoted to an exploration of Swiss culture. What slumbers in the soul of Switzerland, the home of C.G. Jung? Drawing on legend, history, and recent events, the contributors illuminate Switzerland's mystical-magical roots, examine its archetypes and cultural complexes, and venture into the unconscious underlying the contemporary Swiss self-image.

Spring is honored to have Stacy Wirth, M.A., and Isabelle Meier, Dr. phil., both Jungian analysts at the International School for Analytical Psychology in Zürich (ISAPZURICH), serve as Guest Editors of this volume.

Stacy graduated from the C.G. Jung Institute Zürich (2003) after earning her M.A. in the psychology of art from Antioch University (1997). Her bachelor's studies in dance and anthropology were completed at Mills College in California (1977). In 1991 she shared the Zürich Mayor's Counsel Culture Prize for dance. Since 2004 she has served on the Association for Graduates of Analytical Psychology (AGAP) Executive Committee, and became co-president in 2010. She is a training analyst of ISAPZURICH, where she is also Co-Chair of the Jungian Odyssey Committee. She conducts her private analytical practice in Zürich.

Isabelle Meier, Dr. phil., is a graduate of the C.G. Jung Institute Zürich, with a private practice in Zürich as a psychotherapist. She is further trained as a Guided Affective Imagery therapist. As a faculty member of ISAPZURICH, she serves as a training analyst, supervisor, and Co-Chair of the Jungian Odyssey Committee. She co-edited *Seele und Forschung* [Soul and Research] (Bern: Karger Verlag, 2006), and is in the Core-Edition of the German edition of the *Journal of Analytical Psychology*. Her special area of interest lies in the links of imagination, complexes, and archetypes.

We hope you enjoy discovering more about the psyche(s) of the Swiss!

In Memoriam

Mario Jacoby (1925-2011)

It is with great sadness that we acknowledge the death of our dear friend, mentor, and colleague, Mario Jacoby. While his death was not unexpected, it is nevertheless a shock for all of us who came to know him well as training candidates in Zürich and then as analysts and colleagues. We will remember his warmth, humor and wit, wisdom, intelligence, kindness, generosity of spirit, and soulful presence. He has touched us all deeply.

—Stacy Wirth and Isabelle Meier

Balancing Between Two Cultures: An Uneasy Swiss Posture

LUCIENNE MARGUERAT

A Swiss Divide

The *Röstigraben*—the "hash brown potato trench"—is a saying and image that the Swiss use to express the feeling of division between Switzerland's German-speaking east and French-speaking west. Why a "*Rösti*" trench? A simple meal of fried potatoes, *Rösti* is a specialty of the German Swiss kitchen. The image thus aptly conveys the sense of a cultural rift that runs between the German Swiss and the French Swiss as deeply and incalculably as the palate's likes and dislikes. As we shall later see, since World War I the *Röstigraben* has been a part of Swiss identity—and it lays bare a disturbing

Lucienne Marguerat, lic. phil., was born and raised in Lausanne, in the French Swiss Canton of Vaud. She earned her degree in sociology at the University of Geneva, and then moved to Zürich, where she worked for twenty years as a computer specialist. She later entered training in Analytical Psychology at the C.G. Jung Institute in Zürich, and was awarded her diploma in 1992. She maintains a private practice in Zürich, and is a lecturer, training analyst, and supervisor at the International School of Analytical Psychology Zürich (ISAPZURICH), where she directed the Counseling Service from 2005-2008.

This paper is based on her talk entitled, "A cheval sur deux cultures. Une posture mal aimée mais bien suisse," which she presented at the 2009 Annual General Assembly of the Swiss Society for Analytical Psychology (SGAP).

incongruity in the vision of Switzerland as a nation that prides itself on its harmonious unification of four different languages and cultures.[1] Thus the *Röstigraben* is a political embarrassment and at the same time a reality that is time and again denied. It crops up when controversy surfaces between east and west, for instance, in connection with our frequent national votes.

Switzerland's twenty-six cantons are divided into four ethno-cultural realms, which cluster geographically according to four official languages and their links to other European countries: the German, the French, the Italian and the Rhaeto-Romansh.[2] Of the two cultural regions forming the *Röstigraben*, the German Swiss look toward Germany, Austria, and Lichtenstein—and the French Swiss toward France, Luxemburg, and Belgium. Until uniting under the Confederation, these two ethnic groups (like the others) had kept their discrete identities and followed different destinies according to their origins: The German Swiss descended from the Alemanni, an alliance of southern Germanic tribes—and the French Swiss from the Burgundians, the inhabitants of a colonized area of Gaul (now French Burgundy).

The Old Swiss Confederacy was, according to legend, founded in 1291 by three Alemannic communities: Uri, Schwyz, and Unterwalden. By 1353 eight Alemannic groups had joined to form a loose alliance of sovereign territories. From this time the Confederation grew gradually to become today's Switzerland, which was established in 1848 with the adoption of its first Federal Constitution. The last of twenty-six cantons joined in 1979.

However, until about 1800, the population consisted primarily of German-speaking, Alemannic descendants. The exception was Fribourg which had joined the Confederation in 1481, and contributed a considerable number of French-speakers. But not until the beginning of the nineteenth century did the cantons of pure Burgundian descent join the alliance—doing so because they favored the cantonal autonomy granted under Swiss governance, as opposed to the monarchical rule of France. By this time the German Swiss cantons were already united solidly by a long-shared history of conflict and compromise.

The ethnic dividing line runs from south to north, cutting the Cantons of Valais and Fribourg down their centers, and snapping a patch of the Jura hills away from Canton Bern. The entire French-speaking region encompasses about twenty percent of Swiss territory. Merely four of Switzerland's twenty-six cantons are entirely French-speaking: Geneva, Vaud, Jura, and Neuchâtel. Two cantons, Valais and Fribourg, are bilingual in French and German, and the Canton of Bern contains a French-speaking enclave. Of nearly eight million Swiss citizens, about 1.5 million are French speakers; this is about twenty percent, or one in five of the total population. By comparison, seventeen cantons claim German as their only official language. For my later consideration of culturally-based political power, it is important to note that the number of German-speaking cantons increases to potentially twenty-one when we take into account the four cantons that claim German as one among other official languages (French, Italian, and/or Rhaeto-Romansh). By this count, some 4.6 million Swiss citizens are officially German speakers, which is sixty-four percent or three in five of the total population.

To make matters more complex, the vast majority of so-called "German speakers" favor their mother tongue, Swiss German, which—lacking a standard grammar and written form—is difficult to learn, if not from the "street." Moreover Swiss German consists of more than thirty dialects[3] that are often incomprehensible to others—be they speakers of Standard German or French, Italian, Rhaeto-Romansh, or any other of many languages spoken in this country.[4] In the German Swiss cantons, Swiss German is used in daily conversation, and Standard German is generally used for purposes of writing, education, public broadcasting, etc. As we shall see, both Standard German and Swiss German also creep into use under other, perhaps less expected, circumstances.

Such measurements as those above illustrate the minority status of the French Swiss in relationship to the German Swiss, and they point to the unequal terms of coexistence between these two cultures. Indeed, coexistence would have been a mission impossible had it not been for the economic power that French Switzerland gained by the rise of banking and tourism, and by the prestige brought by the establishment of international organizations such as those in Canton Geneva, like the Red Cross.

Dark Sides of Democracy

As will be mentioned again in this issue, Switzerland is the oldest surviving federal democracy, following only the United States. Our country runs on a multi-party system, and it comes closer than any other country in the world to having a direct democracy. This permits our citizens and cantons a high degree of "sovereignty," as we call the right to political self-determination. Among the ways this is accomplished at the federal level is by the "initiative" and the "referendum." These two instruments, respectively, enable individual citizens to directly submit motions to amend the Constitution, and to challenge constitutional laws that have been approved by the Parliament. When the Parliament moves to amend our Constitution, the motion must be approved by a double majority: that of all voting individuals nation-wide; and that of all the cantons, each of which have one vote. Highly cherished is the Swiss ideal of consensus, which can serve to avert the will of a crushing majority: matters are debated until the conflicted parties reach an acceptable compromise that can be formulated for a decisive vote. This democracy, on the whole, was designed to insure the greatest possible independence of the individual citizens and cantons.

However, our system of governance reflects an ideal, and things do not always end up according to this high standard. When political interests congeal in parliament along cultural lines as they often do, the result is not only the division of east and west, the German Swiss and French Swiss. The French Swiss de facto become deprived of viable political power at the federal level, because they inevitably remain a statistical minority, with little influence alongside the German Swiss. This state of affairs amounts to a silencing of the minority, and thus paradoxically sustains the illusion of a Swiss national discourse that successfully upholds harmony between cultures.[5] Our diversity in such matters as taste, language, and emotional attachments could be seen as an asset—and yet we seem often at a loss as to how to exploit this wealth of difference in a constructive manner. Apparently, even in government, we Swiss ward off the threat of cultural difference by denying its reality.

Institutionalized denial of the cultural divide affects the mind: To present a political demand as being a French Swiss matter becomes tantamount to claiming a non-existing right. Thus rather than risk confrontation on behalf of the French Swiss region as a whole, French Swiss politicians tend to lay low, representing only their own cantons and local concerns. As a Swiss scholar puts it, "The French Swiss are excellent citizens, careful and respectful. Their handicap: their wish to please and their fear of fighting."[6] As a result, the French-speaking cantons of western Switzerland never have shown much solidarity or cooperation among themselves, and to this day, they remain challenged to develop a singular voice that conceives and defends larger regional projects in parliament. This is why many innovators in the French-speaking region feel victimized, and give up on their progressive efforts.

Let us hope that the new signs of economic vigor and technical creativity, which have been emerging over the last twenty years, will help the French Swiss to develop more self-confidence. For example, in 2006 the cantons Vaud and Geneva undertook a joint project, through which they have been promoting the economic and cultural development of the region that lies along the Lake of Geneva on the Swiss side.[7] The Jura region around Neuchâtel has been most important in building up the Swatch Group. After its establishment by a merger in 1983, the founder Nicolas Hayek led the Swatch Group to expand from watch-making to the manufacture of microelectronics and hybrid cars. The Technical University of Lausanne (EPFL), rated as one of the best international institutes world-wide, is a partner to the project Solar Impulse, the prototype of an airplane driven by solar energy.

THE *RÖSTIGRABEN*

Watching Swiss national political debates, one might think that to speak of cultural division is to point at a mirage. For not only does our cultural division remain denied, but its existence is obscured by the political party lines that define and shape dispute. In other words, there are few visible signs of the German Swiss and French Swiss going for each others' throats. Politicians are trained to be respectful and cautious, especially toward ethnic minorities. German Swiss representatives in the National Council try to avoid injuring the sensibilities of their French Swiss counterparts; to show good will, they may even try to speak French. The French Swiss, in turn, take great care not to expose their German-speaking colleagues' language blunders, and they rush to appease ill feelings that may be roused.

Does the *Röstigraben* exist? Or is the cultural divide a phantom born of unquiet minds or a construction of the media? The problem is that the aim for harmony built into our governing structures succeeds generally to conjure away the *appearance* of conflict, but leaves actual conflict alive and unresolved.

As it is, the French Swiss typically take recourse to humor and irony to cope with their frustration. Younger generations of French Swiss who move to Germanic cantons soon realize that their years of studying Standard German in school leave them ill equipped to understand the various dialects of Swiss German that are spoken instead of Standard German, and so they switch to the more common ground of English. It is no secret that meetings of the federal government permit communications in Standard German, French, and Italian. Yet minorities wishing to be heard are best advised to be fluent in Standard German. When they join sub-committees mandated to accomplish legislative work, the few French speakers grow accustomed to being left out when debates heat up and the German Swiss revert to their Swiss German dialects.

One might think that since things have been running smoothly for some years now, resentments have subsided, and the two sides finally have accepted one another. But the last decades tell another story. The two mentalities can clash quickly and unexpectedly, revealing another Switzerland, no longer at peace but torn apart. At this writing, I have spent forty years as a French Swiss residing in Germanic Zürich. I would like to relate a time when I witnessed the two cultures come to a terrible clash:

It was frightening to experience the rage that flared up in December 1992, when opinion polarized over the referendum for Switzerland's accession to the European Economic Area (EEA).[8] Crucially, the referendum was linked to a proposal for the nation's integration into the then-forming European Union (EU). To achieve a "yes," the referendum required the double majority I mentioned earlier—a majority by the vote of the people *and* by the vote of the cantons. As opinion divided along the cultural rift, two French-speaking members of the government's executive threw themselves passionately into the pro-EEA battle. It became a question of identity: on each side, it was "us" against "them." The French Swiss finally experienced a peculiar and deeply unsettling loss: When it came to the vote of the people, the French Swiss voted an overwhelming "yes" to the EEA by a margin of three to one—while a nation-wide "yes" of the cantons was defeated only by a hairline margin of 50.3% to 49.7%.[9] In the cantonal vote seven cantons—among them all six French-speaking cantons—said "yes;" however this was five short of the twelve cantons that were required to form a majority vote. Thus, the Germanic cantons exerted a thumping majority and a rebuff of the crystal clear "yes" that was resounded by all six French cantons and nearly 50% of the people nation-wide! In the face of this massive opposition, the French Swiss fell into a raging frenzy, some "talk[ing] heatedly of secession" from the Confederation.[10]

The pain was unrelieved by the fact that several German Swiss contingents had favored accession—the city of Zürich, Canton Basel, and Canton Basel Land, for example. For the French Swiss, it all boiled down to the feeling, "You see? They don't understand us. They force their way of thinking on us." Taken completely by surprise, German Swiss parliamentarians rubbed their eyes. For weeks following the vote, appeasing declarations were issued, numerous national meetings convened, and committees for cultural exchange established. The German Swiss on the whole created the impression of a fat cat puzzled at having hurt its darling mouse. Tempers finally cooled, but it had been a hot winter.

What triggered the explosion of rage and despair in the French Swiss? Historians explain the polarization as resulting from the referendum's abstract phrasing, "Are you for, or against acceding to the Economic European Area?"[11] This, they say, was destined to provoke antithetical ideas about the EEA and the EU. On that issue, the *Röstigraben* materialized, as emotionally charged as ever.

French Swiss citizens associate the EU largely with the ideal of a peaceful and egalitarian union of states, such as that which was extolled following World War I and II by the renowned politicians of France, Aristide Briand, Jean Monnet, and Robert Schuman. Thus, the French Swiss viewed the prospect of joining a strong French-speaking community (France, Luxemburg, and Belgium) with confidence and enthusiasm. Many German Swiss, on the other hand, felt that the requirement to adopt EU legislation would threaten Switzerland's historic autonomy. Ultra-right wing isolationists stoked the opposition, asserting stridently that the expanding EU amounted to nothing less than a new Third Reich.

As I see it, in their rage the French Swiss expressed bitter disappointment in crushed hopes, and burning humiliation in being overcome by the majority. The denial and smashing of their deeply cherished desire for a larger French-speaking union was, at this point, profoundly destabilizing—simply too much to bear. This is where Thomas Singer and Samuel L. Kimbles would recognize the case of a group becoming swamped by the highly charged affect of a cultural complex, which produces a simplistic view of the world: "we," the victims, and "they," the perpetrators.[12] Such group complexes often bespeak a background of trauma, with a perpetrating group pegged as the cause of feelings of discrimination, oppression, and inferiority on the victims' side.[13]

Such highly destructive emotions take over when the group spirit is threatened and felt to require defense at any cost. Individual group members—such as those of the French Swiss minority—are beset by the rushing-in feeling of "once-again," comparable to a re-traumatization that shakes one's identity to the core. I had shared the pro-EEA enthusiasm. Finding myself on the losing side was to feel as though I had received slap in the face. After twenty years of living in Zürich, I was sharply reminded of my standing as an outsider in the German Swiss world.

The Deepest Divide

The trauma that engulfed Switzerland, and gave rise to the fissure that came to be known as the *Röstigraben*, was occasioned by World War I (1914–1918)—for then, as the nation declared neutrality toward the outside, it had never come so close to falling apart within. With Germany's invasion of Belgium, and for the War's duration, the French Swiss favored the Allies while opposing virulently the pro-German bias prevailing in German Switzerland. Among the German sympathizers were some of Switzerland's highest state officials. A most renowned sympathizer was Ulrich Wille, the Commander in Chief of the Swiss Army, who had a background of Prussian military training and marriage into the Bismarck family.

The French Swiss consequently accused their government of supporting Germany through silence and passivity. Several scandals confirmed their claim, and moreover disclosed the breaching of Swiss neutrality by covert negotiations of Swiss officials with the Germans and other belligerents. For instance, two of General Wille's "staff officers were caught and tried for passing secrets to the Germans and Austrians."[14] The "most spectacular violation of neutrality occurred . . . at the very top of the political hierarchy . . .," when,

> Federal Councilor Arthur Hoffmann, Head of the Political Department (Swiss Foreign Office) had to resign in 1917 . . . when his secret attempt to bring about a separate peace between Germany and the new revolutionary regime in Russia became known.[15]

Protest from the French Swiss grew ever more acute, whereupon they in turn were accused of being unpatriotic, and of undermining national defense, polarizing the nation, and trying to draw it into the War. As the Swiss media reported on the growing protest, their alleged collusion and poisoning of the atmosphere was met with the imposition of nation-wide censorship. A number of Swiss intellectuals—such as Carl Spitteler and Gonzague de Reynold of the "The Society for a New Helvetia" (*Nouvelle Société Helvétique*)—soon began to promote Swiss national unity over and against German nationalism. Yet when the Allies won the War, the *Röstigraben* remained within Switzerland as a gaping wound, roughly comparable to the wound remaining after the Civil War in the United States.

After merely twenty years of peace, Hitler provoked the outbreak of World War II. The Swiss government moved immediately to instill feelings of national solidarity, determined by this means to prevent a re-divided nation as well as to defend the country's boundaries. Thus Switzerland hastened to distinguish itself from the Axis Powers by re-asserting its armed neutrality. Bearing in mind the schism provoked by General Wille and his kind during WWI, the parliament elected a new Commander in Chief—Henri Guisan, an amiable French Swiss country gentleman, whose deep enmity for Nazi Germany was well known. To consolidate themselves as "not German," the German Swiss were urged to speak their Swiss German dialects rather than Standard German. For official purposes of education, government, public media, and the like, Standard German was supplanted by Swiss High German, which differs from the Standard in a variety of ways, for instance in grammar, and even meaning.[16]

In the meantime the Third Reich extolled the "natural nation" unified by one ethnic group, one language, one religion. By contrast, Switzerland took pride in being the *Willensnation*—the "nation of will," built by the will of the people to unify the plurality of ethnic cultures, languages, and religions.

Who Are "the Swiss," Really?

Despite the inland solidarity achieved during WWII, the French minority and German majority continue to differ in their relationship to the nation as a whole. The Swiss in general feel more deeply tied to the places where they live, with their hearts bound more to their cantons than to Switzerland. Whatever feeling of national patriotism remains, it is not of the same substance for the German Swiss and French Swiss.

At a gut level the French Swiss find it difficult to identify with the traditional symbols that explain the Confederation's origins: The legendary time is 1291. The legendary place is Rütli Meadow, which actually does lie in the German Swiss canton of Uri. Here, it is said, the original Swiss Confederacy was founded when the (Germanic) communities of Uri, Schwyz, and Unterwalden swore an oath of alliance in defense against the Austrian Habsburg dominators. Around the same time, legend has it, Wilhelm Tell, a humble farmer from the region of Uri, murdered the cruelest Habsburg bailiff, named Gessler. With this, Tell is said to have ignited the uprising of the people that liberated the land.

This heavily Germanic imagery speaks little to the French Swiss. It leaves them with loose emotional bonds to their country, and the unlikely tendency to claim the epithet, "we, the Swiss." Their feeling of being Swiss arises, if at all, in injured reaction to being labeled by the French as "*les petits Suisses*"—"the little Swiss"— the brand name for an unripened or young French cheese sold in miniature portions.

The matter of national identity is far less troublesome for the German Swiss, most of whom remain firm in the unconscious assumption that their populace, its concerns, and jurisdictions comprise "the Swiss." They do so not out of ill will, but because their cultural unity creates a collective blind spot, which results in the de facto exclusion of others.

Mutual Prejudice

Mutual prejudice in Switzerland abounds in inverse proportion to the balance of power. The French Swiss are prone to say of the German Swiss, rather nastily, "They like us, but we don't like them." A rich palette of slurs furthers this all-but-well-meaning sentiment. The French Swiss describe the German Swiss variously as *Totos* (dodo); *Köbis* (pig-headed); *Bourdons* (bumbler); *Schnoques* (worthless old bag); *Fritz* (during both World Wars, a derogatory name for German ground troops). As "Teutons"—Germanic tribesmen—the German Swiss are said to be compulsively hard working, deadly serious, and callously efficient. In other words they are held out as being boring, humorless, authoritarian, and fans of military discipline. Their accent when speaking French is something that the French Swiss never tire of ridiculing.

The German Swiss might, at most, drop a smile and critical remark about their French Swiss compatriots by calling them the "Welsh," which arouses mixed feelings of (condescending) affection and insult. Although it may not be commonly known, the origin of the emotional tone can be found in the etymology: "Welsh" originally meant "Celtic;" it evolved to mean "incomprehensible foreigner/ language,"[17] and it later came to refer to speakers of the Romance languages, including French. Thus, when speaking of the "Welsh," the German Swiss (unconsciously) acknowledge their compatriots' French roots but also imply the stereotypical attributes: an odd charm, humor, an endearing accent—and an "incomprehensible" lack of discipline and responsibility.

Needless to say, both images—the Welsh and the Teutonic—contain germs of truth, without picturing the complete reality. Relevant, psychologically speaking, are the French Swiss and the German Swiss projections onto each other of a pair of enemy combatants: the irresponsible French anarchists versus the obedient Teutonic brutes. Both sides ordinarily deny their holding of such caricatures of one another. Yet the many jokes and stories, practically unchanged over generations, reveal the stereotypes' tenacity. Here is one of my favorites:

> An American, a Frenchman, and a Swiss from Bern are arguing about who has the most difficult language. The American: "We write 'life' but don't pronounce 'e.'" "That's nothing!" says the Frenchman. "We write 'Bordeaux' and say 'Bordoo!'" "That's nothing compared to us," says the man from Bern. "We write 'pardon?' and say, 'HEY [what are you doing?!]'"

Another joke I like, for its libidinal innuendo:

> Two Swiss men, a [Germanic] one from Bern and the other from [French] Geneva, had first met in the military service. One day they bump into each other in Bern. The man from Geneva asks, "Well, Müller, how are you doing?" Müller knows that with his compatriots from Geneva one has to be cautious, lest he make of fool of himself. So he answers: "I'm doing alright, alright . . . just about . . . once a month!" The man from Geneva replies, "Hey, Müller, that's not what I meant. I meant how are you doing at home?" Says the man from Bern, "Oh! . . . Well at home, not . . . any . . . more!"

Built into the feeling of belonging, especially among minorities, is a certain mistrust of "the other." Indeed as a minority member, I have often felt the shift from relaxed involvement with my own group, to its rigid closing of ranks against "the other." At the slightest offense to its collective values, the minority mind seems to spot an overpowering "other" popping up like a Jack-in-the-Box, and with it, an age-old outrage and frustration. Here we see the forcefulness of the cultural complex when feelings of vulnerability flare up among members of a minority group.

The theory of the cultural complex explains the intrusion of compulsive emotion with the fact that, once the cultural ego feels threatened, complexes take over, washing away all ambiguity to fill the psyche with absolute certainty. Following John Weir Perry's theory of the complex,[18] we can say that the cultural complex, too, splits perception into two extremes: "our side" clings to ego-syntonic contents (the fragile, dependent, considerate victim)—and "their side," to which emanates the projection of the dystonic (the brutal, abusive, unfair perpetrator). The dynamics of polarization/projection/aggression take hold when threat is perceived to those collective values and symbols that largely comprise one's sense of self.

Seen from this perspective, the group shadow manifests itself in projections onto the alleged perpetrators.

What might the shadow figures, in our case, reveal of each side? The ugly "Teuton" could embody the unconscious desire of the French Swiss for power and domination, which we seem bound to deny, to maintain self-esteem in the face of our dependency. As a matter of fact, rather than mustering the power to compete with those who are seemingly stronger, we French Swiss emphasize our affirmed qualities such as flexibility, individuality, and originality. We ensure our economic and political survival by living the clichés, and denying abilities that would enable us to confront the "others."

The French Swiss, or the "Welsh" as infantile anarchist, might personify feelings of leisure and playfulness in which the German Swiss have difficulty in indulging. In this vein, the values prized most consciously by the German Swiss would be those such as industriousness, responsibility, common sense, and respect for traditions. Extending these values to political process in their best effort to serve the common good, the German Swiss often forget that they themselves do not constitute all of Switzerland, and find themselves rather at a loss to understand protest coming from the other side.

Balancing Between Two Cultures

As a French-speaking Swiss, I moved more than forty years ago from Geneva to Zürich, compelled by my love for a man who was living in Zürich. My first twenty years in Zürich were spent trying to assimilate into the German Swiss culture. I finally let go of the idea of belonging one hundred percent. By now, the question of which "side" I belong to is no longer an issue, and I am fond of switching from one culture to the other. I have learned to love and admire the melody of the German language, its subtlety, and wonderful logic. I enjoy reading the dialect-colored German of Swiss writers. Now that I speak the Zürich dialect and can access the German Swiss sense of humor, I take great pleasure in the expressivity of the words and idioms. And it no longer aches—to the contrary, it is great fun—to stroll like a tourist through Lausanne, my home town, absorbing the switch in language, manners, place, food. Although this posture between two somewhat antagonistic cultures was uncomfortable at the start, today I would not wish to give up either.

Some of the barriers to my assimilation were obviously due to my cultural bias. My inability to roll the "r" on my tongue, as the people in Zürich do, was possibly due to my resistance to and the last remnant of an initial dislike of the dialect. To this day I am incapable of pronouncing those words in the Zürich dialect that are adapted from French: for instance, "*ägsküsi,*" for "*excusez,*" "excuse me;" or "*märsi,*" for "*merci,*" "thank you." The difficulties I encountered in reading German poetry were humbling, initially tedious. It was as though the emotional ground of the German language could not possibly be *learned* but had to be *experienced.* Does this mean that the emotional resonance of language—residing in its words, rhythm, and music—belongs to the deepest folds of culture? Do we acquire the *feel* for a language and culture primarily through early intimate exchange with our caretakers? These are, at any rate, conclusions I draw from my limitations.

My belonging to the two cultures should not imply that I feel equally at home in both. The real place of my roots reveals itself in my struggle with the German language and the upsetting political loss of 1992. As much as I feel at ease in Zürich, I know now in my bones that "home" abides in my French mother tongue, in French language literature, and the rhymes and songs of my childhood, spent in Lausanne.

What also became clear in my adjustment process was how profoundly "Swiss" I am after all—how Swiss *all* we Swiss are, whether on this side or that—and how decidedly different from the Germans or the French. Personal experience from the Zürich side of the *Röstigraben* gives me pause to wonder: Can my people at "home" come to apprehend the common grounds of our Swiss identity? It saddens me that the sustaining need to assert cultural difference *against* others may amount to a high price for upholding our minority identity.

NOTES

1. Sandro Guzzi, "Kleine Heimat, grosser Raum. Überlegungen zu politischer Integration und lokalem Widerstand aus historischer Sicht," in *Traverse. Zeitschrift für Geschichte,* No. 3 (1994): pp. 144-158.

2. The Rhaeto-Romansh language and people descend from the old Romans and are often oriented toward Italy. Although counted as

one of Switzerland's four official languages, Romansh is not integrated in the federal discourse.

3. Richard J. Watts, "The Ideology of Dialect in Switzerland," in *Language Ideological Debates*, ed. Jan Blommaert (Berlin: Mouton de Gruyter, 1999), p. 71.

4. Some 0.5 million Swiss are Italian speakers, making up about 6.5% of the population. Those speaking Rhaeto-Romansh number around 35,000, composing about 0.5% of the population. About 653,000 others speak mother tongues such as Spanish, Serbo-Croatian, Portuguese, Turkish, English, and Albanian. Statistics from "Bevölkerung, Sprache, 2000," Platformst@las, *Statistischer Atlas der Schweiz*, ed. Schweizerische Eidgenossenschaft, Bundesamt für Stastistik (© Bundesamt für Statistik, Thema Kart 2009-2011), at www.statistik.admin.ch (accessed December 3, 2010).

5. See for instance, François Cherix, *La Question Romande, Enquête sur une Suisse Romande entre Attentisme et Projet* (Lausanne: Favre, 2009).

6. Werner De Schepper, quoted in *ibid.*, p. 105, my translation.

7. This joint project is called "arc lémanique," which derives from the French name for the Lake of Geneva, Lac Léman. The project name translates roughly as "The Lemanic Arc," or "The Arc of the Lake of Geneva."

8. The European Economic Area (EEA) came into force in 1994 as a trade union of nations endorsing the European Union's (EU) free movement of people, goods, services, and capital. After rejecting accession, Switzerland entered into bilateral agreements and treaties that have, thus far, allowed its enjoyment of the benefits of membership without losing sovereignty.

9. Harnish McRae, "Fury of the French Minority," Tuesday, 8 December 1992, Geneva (Reuter), *The Independent* (©independent.co.uk), p. 21, at http://www.independent.co.uk/news/world/europe/fury-of-french-minority-1562241.html (accessed 4 July, 2011).

10. *Ibid.*

11. Martin Zbianden, "Die Unterschiede in der Perzeption der Europäischen Integration zwischen der Deutschschweiz und der Romandie," in *Traverse,* pp. 40-63, my translation.

12. Thomas Singer and Samuel L. Kimbles, "Introduction," in *The Cultural Complex: Contemporary Jungian Perspectives on Psyche and Society,*

eds. Thomas Singer and Samuel L. Kimbles (Hove, New York: Brunner-Routledge, 2004).

13. *Ibid.*, p. 7.

14. Jonathan Steinberg, *Why Switzerland?*, 2nd edition, reprinted (Cambridge: University of Cambridge Press, 2001), pp. 54-55.

15. *Ibid.*, p. 55.

16. Charles V. J. Russ, "The Characteristics of High German in Switzerland," *The German Language Today: A Linguistic Introduction* (London: Routledge, 1994), pp. 73-80.

17. Pól Ó Dochartaigh, "Julius Pokorny and Celtic Swiss Identity," in *Beziehungen und Identitäten: Österreich, Irland und die Schweiz. Connections and Identities: Austria, Ireland and Switzerland, Wechselwirkungen 6*, eds. Gisela Holfter, Marieke Krajenbrink, Edward Moxon-Browne (Bern: Peter Lang, AG, Europäischer Verlag der Wissenschaften, 2004), p. 129.

18. John Weir Perry, "Emotions and Object Relations," *Journal of Analytical Psychology*, Vol. 15, no. 1 (1970): 1-12.

Between Ticino and Northern Switzerland Stand Not Only the Alps

ELENA KRINKE

Translation by Isabelle Meier and Katy Remark
Gabrielle Rossi, Historical Consultant

Introduction

The Canton of Ticino, being among the youngest and smaller "children" in the Swiss family, often seems to "behave" like the last child—the one who oscillates between the neglect and the indulgent spoiling of its "mother," the Swiss Confederation. Ticino, lying at Switzerland's southernmost tip, is both separated from and joined to this "family" of other Cantons by the Alps. Ticino's relationship

Elena Krinke, Dr. med., was born in 1964 in Czechoslovakia. When she was four years old her family was forced to flee Czechoslovakia as political refugees. They found asylum in Switzerland in the Canton of Ticino, where Elena Krinke has lived ever since. She studied medicine at Fribourg and Bern and worked as a hospital physician in Lugano and Bellinzona before she went on to earn her diploma as an Analytical Psychologist at the C.G. Jung Institute Zürich, Kusnacht. She lives and conducts her private analytical practice in Ticino in Bellinzona. Not last for the reason of her family history, she is especially interested in the phenomenon of forced emigration, and the transcultural and intercultural issues associated with it.

to the *whole* of Switzerland has been described by the historian Orazio Martinetti as that of "the rascal to his step-mother."[1] In Martinetti's parlance, Ticino would be not only a mischief-maker but also a "stepchild," whose "real mother" is Italy: the country by which Ticino is nearly surrounded and to which our ancestors once belonged. And Italy is of course, too, the country from which the Ticinesi inherit their mother-tongue, Italian. True to its rogue spirit, among all the Swiss cantons, Ticino is the only one that claims nothing but Italian as its official language—a fact that makes of the Ticinesi one of Switzerland's smallest official cultural minorities, the Italian Swiss.[2]

Coming with Ticino's position as such is a separation/union dualism that permeates our canton's history and current situation. This same dualism fuels an acute conflict of opposites and psychology of ambivalence in the Ticinesi search for self-identity.

The Alps: North and South, Connect and Disconnect

In early adulthood I moved from the Canton of Ticino to the German part of Switzerland to begin my university studies. During the six years I lived there, my positive experiences were intermingled with difficulties in the realms of cultural difference and language. Indeed among all of the Swiss—and I propose that the language difference contributes to the Ticinesi's feeling of being small—we Italian speakers most lack our compatriots' language reciprocity. This is because, as explained by the sociologist Carol Schmid, "in contrast to French and German, which meet on more or less equal terms [in Switzerland],"

> Italian . . . is spoken by relatively few French- and German-speaking Swiss. Thus the Italian Swiss must be fluent in either French or German, or both, for any career that transcends the purely local level.[3]

What I have learned is this: While multilingualism is an admirable quality and forms a foundation for strength, it can also be a double-edged sword in that it is taken for granted that the Italian speakers will switch to their compatriots' native tongues. Moreover: From the standpoint of the Ticinesi, once you master Standard German, you fail at *Schwyzerdütsch,* the Swiss German dialect, whose speakers form the ultimate club of belonging in the north.[4] Since the time of my youth and even to this day, I have repeatedly found Switzerland's minority languages to be typically neglected in clubs and associations that designate themselves as "national," that is, as representing the interests of *all* Swiss. This goes for instance in professional, cultural, and political associations—and even among national insurance companies. It is as if assumed that German is the common language—and this, as if simply forgetting the existence of Switzerland's several cultural minorities.

Germanic and French Switzerland in the north, beyond the alpine barrier (or we say, the "*oltralpe*"), hold the promise of everything the Ticinesi could long for: advanced education, employment opportunity, and thus a better economic situation. Yet between the cultures on each side of the Alps there is a wealth gap, which contributes to the Ticinesi the sense of a love/hate relationship toward our "parent" that looms beyond the Alps, and which can (if not always) fuel an inferiority complex. We Ticinesi must overcome this and various other difficulties if we want to go north. Naturally there are many different ways to react to or deal with obstacles, according to one's available psychological resources. Accordingly, a variety of individual responses emerge among the Ticinesi.

For instance some of us feel ourselves to be victims of the alpine geography and its limiting circumstances, and so we withdraw into ourselves and our inferiority complex, remaining isolated from the rest of Switzerland. Others of us *deny* the mountain barrier to equal education, employment, and wealth. Denying all of this, we disavow simultaneously a conflicted aspect of our identity. Still others treat this "mountain" as an obstacle to be overcome. These latter Ticinesi arise to the challenge to learn, and to expand their geographic horizons while retaining an identity with roots in Ticino. The latter is the hero's way, as we find it in fairy tales and myths. The image of the hero can mobilize many Ticinesi to become effective at the national level—politically, socially, and culturally.

Yet another reaction is to face the challenge through anger, revenge, and rivalry. Such Ticinesi often exhibit a demanding attitude, revealing an exaggerated sense of entitlement. As this strategy neither solves the problem nor overcomes the complex, the tensions and conflicted relationships remain. Finally, there are others who say, "We Ticinesi are so much more likable, more pleasant, and more sociable than our German Swiss compatriots." In both cases, the individuals defend against their inferiority complex by asserting their superiority, whereby those asserting superiority may be more disposed to finding creative means to overcome the complex.

As a collective, we Ticinesi remain at some level convinced that the Alps divide the Ticino from the rest of Switzerland and stand for a mountain of clichés—and thus obscure the vision of the Swiss north of us, and prevent them from knowing about and understanding our home. Ticino is thus perceived by the other Swiss as offering a wonderful climate and idyllic landscape par excellence—steep valleys, waterfalls, lakes, subtropical vegetation, picturesque villages, rustic stone houses, polenta, and local merlot wine poured from *Boccalini*—the little pot-bellied glazed ceramic pitchers, adorned with colorful painting. There is a certain fascination for the curiosity of the long-standing Ticinesi families—the "*patriziati*" or "patricians," who own lands and buildings, and command certain privilege within their local communities. These are the "pedigreed" citizens, the "special members," who can claim and represent our original lineage.

Missing, however, from this romanticized and one-sided view is the fact that the steep and rocky landscape of Ticino often results in a life of hard labor, danger, poverty. The Alps in this sense have played a role in forced emigration for some who grow up here—as occurred, for example, in the nineteenth century exodus of many Ticinesi to Italy and France, to the rest of Europe, to America, and other countries as well. It is easy to forget that it still may be difficult to forge a living in these rugged climes that are lacking in natural resources. The nineteenth century Industrial Revolution precipitated the near collapse of Ticino's handicraft and other small industries—for example pottery making, silk growing, leather making, and marble work. Twentieth century globalization, allowing less costly production by developing countries, witnessed the complete collapse of our steel manufacture—and the marginalization of our other mainstays and sources of export such as rock mining, chocolate and cheese production, and fishing and agriculture.

On the positive side, at the beginning of the twenty-first century our little-known Canton has become entrepreneurial and competitive in the manufacture of electro-mechanics, chemical-pharmaceuticals, and plastics; we have become strong as well in the management of tourism, international finance, commerce, and transport and communication.[5] This creative and productive awakening was sparked largely by Ticino's founding in 1996 of its first two federally recognized universities, the University of Lugano (USI) and the University of Applied Science (based in Manno), which includes the Vocational University College of Italian Switzerland (SUPSI). We have as well several other accredited institutes of higher learning, such as the Institute for Research in Biomedicine, the Conservatory of Italian Switzerland, and the State School of Hotel and Tourism Management. Ticino is thus now the site of world-renowned research in fields such as oncology and molecular biology. It has produced architects of international repute like Luigi Snozzi, Aurelio Galfetti, Livio Vacchini—and Mario Botta, who designed the San Francisco Museum of Modern Art in the USA. Lugano has grown to become Switzerland's third largest financial center (after Geneva and Zürich). Conversely, the wages in Ticino are below average and the unemployment higher than in the rest of Switzerland. Day-to-day life is marred by ubiquitous shopping centers, significant air pollution, casinos, and brothels.

We Ticinesi are generally viewed as friendly people, multilingual, open, sociable, relaxed, and knowing how to enjoy life—and we may be envied in this regard by other Swiss. On the dark side, however, we are considered to be unreliable, lazy, messy, imprecise, and profiteering. We are not only victims of such stereotypes. We carry a certain responsibility for the perpetuation of these stereotypes in that we do not decisively reject them or set boundaries between the majority who do not enact them and the exceptional few who do. Another ambivalence.

As previously said, our ambivalence is mirrored in the region's geographic and historical realities. The Alps' creation of a geographical divide between the north and south has helped shape Ticino's history and its relations with the rest of Switzerland. For instance, the Alps form a weather barrier, giving Ticino the advantage of a Mediterranean climate and subtropical vegetation—which, being very different than the climate on the northern side of the Alps, contributes an essential component to our tourist industry.

Three historical trails through the Alps run through Ticino: one through the Lukmanier Pass, which was used by the Romans; one through the St. Bernardino Pass (which pass itself lies in the Canton of Graubünden), and one—the most direct yet most difficult—through the St. Gotthard Pass. The scenic St. Gotthard Pass, lying at our northern border in the Alps, links Ticino directly with the Germanic Canton of Uri. In fact since antiquity, the Gotthard has opened up the most direct transit route (now a highway) that links most of Europe from the south to the north, and for centuries Ticino benefited as a manager of trade here. Today Ticino is a key point in modern Europe's main south-north transport axis, thanks largely to the Gotthard Pass, and the tunnel that now runs beneath it, opening the mountain for trains and highway traffic.

The St. Gotthard Pass additionally holds the symbolic value of an archetypal center and source, for it lies in the heart of the Alps and here arise four major and majestic rivers: the Rhine, the Rhone, the Reuss, and the Ticino. Through these rivers the St. Gotthard Pass joins the borders of Switzerland's four language regions and cultures. Thus the geography gives rise to the image of unity in diversity—or expressed otherwise, a common heart and origin that that "fertilizes" Switzerland's cultural richness (to play further with the image).

To follow the symbolic meaning, both psychologically and concretely Ticino may be growing into its own as an important modern crossroad, with borders increasingly open to the comings and goings of many people with many different origins and purposes. And yet, as invigorating as it may sound, this development is met with ambivalence:

The Ticinesi's mountain existence links organically with the psychological issue of boundaries and their experienced qualities, such as opening and closing, belonging and excluding. Our movement *across* psychological borders bears the feeling of advantage, comparable with the actual free flow of traffic, goods, and people (workers, migrants, tourists). But it can just as much contain the feeling of disadvantage, comparable with the real cross-border flow of pollutants and capital crime, such as drug trafficking. At the same time, our spirit is anchored in an archaic tendency to *not* move, that is, to be as unmoving as the Alps that hold our spirit—which can translate psychologically into a tendency to stagnate.

Identity, Or Under What Conditions Does Cheese Mature?

Just as cheese ripens in a delicate and not entirely predictable process, Ticino's identity has been evolving gradually and in phases, leaving us not entirely certain about the outcome: In antiquity the region that would only far later become known as Ticino was inhabited by the Lepontian Celts, and was later integrated into the Roman Empire. In the Middle Ages the region was invaded by the barbaric Ostrogoths, Longobards and Franks. After 1100 AD it came under siege by the southern communities of Como and Milan. In the fourteenth century it fell to the Duchy of Milan. At this stage Bellinzona, now Ticino's capital city, belonged to the Duchy and provided the last defense against the German-speaking Confederation in the north.

Beginning c 1400, the northern confederates had sought to dominate the region by military campaign. In 1478 the canton of Uri seized and subjugated the Valle Levintina (now northern Ticino). By 1515 most of the territory comprising today's Ticino had been conquered in battle or purchased by the confederates and annexed to the Confederation. The subjugated territory was divided into eight colony-like entities (*baliaggi*) and placed under the Confederation's ownership. Of the twelve cantons at the time, Uri, Schwyz, und Nidwalden held the largest swaths. Thereafter, "[f]or more than 250 years," writes the historian Jonathan Steinberg, "these Italian-speaking communities were subject to alien rule by ignorant, corrupt, German-speaking bailiffs."[6] The era was characterized by abuses of law and power, by administrative inefficiency and dysfunction.[7] From 1798-1815 Switzerland fell under the rule of Napolean Bonaparte, whose call for "liberty, equality, fraternity" fired the hearts of the Italian-speakers. It was Napolean who first re-structured Switzerland as a union of cantons with one central federal government, and moved the annexed regions into the Confederation. Ticino itself was thus moved and given sovereign cantonal status in 1803.

Yet Ticino's lack of inner political unity prevailed, dating back to the region's annexation in 1515. As the historian Raffaello Ceschi puts it, the municipalities that comprised this area—the communities, the villages, the cities, and wider districts—failed to muster solidarity among themselves, despite common concerns related to their local populations, economy, and governance.[8] This failed solidarity may be partly explained by the mountain terrain that, even today, can interfere with developing coherence among our scattered and far-flung communities. However I among others am prone to consider the equally influential impact of Ticino's history of annexation. By analogy, two symptoms that characterize colonized peoples are their submissiveness toward the colonizing power, and their subsistence at the economic periphery of the culture. At any rate, these symptoms describe today's Ticinesi collective and they point to our abiding feeling that Ticino was and remains to some extent colonized by the Confederation:

Even after Ticino gained admission to the Confederation in 1803, the Ticinesi continued to experience the German Swiss as governors, because it was the German Swiss who held the majority power in the newly formed federal government. From the standpoint of political "individuation," it bears considering also that Ticino's entry into the Confederation was motivated not by its own will, but at Napolean's command. In other words, the Ticinesi came in lacking the specific will that had served historically to transcend the heterogeneity of the German Swiss (and later, the French Swiss), and bind them in loyalty to the "Nation of Will" (*Willensnation*). And so, prior to Switzerland's creation of the first Federal Constitution in 1848, the Ticinesi continued to view the other Swiss as a group of colonists.

Beginning in 1848 Switzerland gradually grew into the image of a unified state, with Ticino however perceiving it to be more like a thief than a genuine union of partners: With the first Federal Constitution Ticino's "equality" was suddenly realized in the new requirement for all cantons to render customs revenues to the Federal Government. Because Ticino's economy had relied so heavily on its advantage as a trade route, this provision substantially cut into one of its few sources of income. Thus, even as late as the nineteenth century Ticino remained ambivalent in its desire to bind itself to the greater whole. Indeed until World War One, Ticino's Swiss identity remained more an abstract concept than a lived reality. Instead, the Ticinesi identified in spirit with Italy and participated freely in large cross border movements, which were attractive especially for seasonal workers. In other words, Italy and the Italians were not perceived as foreign.

For centuries the Ticinesi economy was unprofitable, with agriculture in particular being difficult to sustain. With the Industrial Revolution the centuries-old tradition of migration to Italy, France, and other European countries for seasonal labor evolved into a state of permanent migration to the USA and Australia, bringing about expectable local population losses. Due to the high customs tariffs imposed on imports by foreign governments, Ticino's export to nearby

Italy of handicrafts and other goods became unprofitable as did export to northern Switzerland and beyond due to the high cost of transport through the Alps. The novelist Plinio Martini painted a vivid picture of the resulting isolation:

> The Canton of Ticino, surrounded in the north by the Alps and in the south by the [Italian] border, is like a cheese that has not gotten enough air and become wormy: the worms are the lawyers, the consultants, the helpers of the consultants, the helpers of the helpers, and behind that is the mafia.[9]

The construction of the north-south railway in 1882, connecting southern and northern Europe, initially brought the hope of reduced transport costs and relief from isolation in general. But this too proved to be a disappointment, for the transport tariffs collected by the Ticinesi were fixed and had to be surrendered to the federal government, the owner of the railroads. This arrangement again cut into profits and hindered the canton's competition in the wider Swiss market. Moreover train transit itself contributed to local population loss, in making it easier for more Ticinesi to leave home.

On the other hand, the railways benefited tourism in Ticino, bringing to the now decreased local population a number of German Swiss. Despite their relatively small proportion the German Swiss built up a strong political and economic force, and took into their fold and idealizing gaze the Ticinesi and all things "Italian." However, with the rise of Fascism, the German Swiss grew disinclined to identify with "Italianness." And now for the first time in their history the Ticinesi themselves began to feel more Swiss than Italian. In other words in the face of Fascism, Swiss identity gained favor by its association with democracy, freedom, and respect for the laws that protect these values.

Yet the eve of World War One witnessed the start of a long debate on the question of Ticino's identity, in national parlance known as the "'*questione ticinese*'"—the "'Ticino question.'"[10] The Ticinesi had begun to look askance on the German Swiss living in Ticino, for their population was growing and as the linguist Kenneth D. McRae notes, "they showed considerable cultural tenacity and resistance to assimilation."[11] They deprived the Ticinesi of work by occupying federal public service positions (including the railroads), and by making (Swiss-)German the preponderant language of these workplaces. They founded private

German-language schools, cultural associations, and newspapers. This was all to the effect of the German Swiss barricading themselves into an exclusive, closed colony. Meanwhile, Ticino was underrepresented in the offices of the Federal Administration.

An anonymous author of 1923 offered a clear analysis of the situation, listing the financial problems engendered by emigration, the closed geographical environment, the plague of lawyers, abuses of power, and favoritism. This author remarked, "[I]t is a chaotic and fragmented set of experiences, which is, not last, a cause of our weakness."[12] Another hurdle to the achievement of a strong and autonomous cultural identity for the Ticinesi was their dependence on German and French Switzerland for higher education until 1996, when Ticino established the previously mentioned universities.

Towards Cultural Bio-Diversity

Let us recall Ticino as being like the youngest child in the Swiss family, the neglected *and* spoiled one. To paraphrase Orazio Martinetti, Ticino has behaved like "an Italian rascal that both dodges and longs for his German Swiss step-mother."[13] But Ticino remains bound to Switzerland, and the historian Silvano Gilardoni concludes that, in what we might call "the psychology of the rascal," there has lurked a healthy, self-preserving instinct and creative potential. In Gilardoni's own words:

> The political, economic, social conditions in Switzerland appeared to be favorable for the citizens of the Canton of Ticino . . . . The Canton could retain its old institutions—for example, the importance of long-established [patrician] families, the fragmentation in small communities and so on. This allowed the survival of the regionalist atavistic instincts of the valleys.[14]

This understanding does not diminish the fact that Ticino's history and current situation are characterized by conflicting experiences that develop the canton's ambiguous identity—the opening and closing, the including and excluding, the moving and the stagnant. Our struggle with such dualities is reflected, symptomatically, in the abundance of publications on the "*questione ticinese.*" As established by the historian Georg Kreis, Ticino's intense interest in the question of identity is unmatched by any other Swiss canton.[15]

Ticino *does* stand between two worlds. Geographically and culturally bound to Italy, it is more recently connected by history, politics, and economics to the north, that is, to Germanic Switzerland. As we have noted, the search for identity between these two worlds is shaped by an acute conflict between cultural opposites. Adopting the nomenclature for uncoordinated eyes, Oscar Mazzoleni and Remigio Ratti call this our "strabismus culture,"[16] meaning that we Ticinesi are unable to align into one identity the two images that lie in our field of vision.

In the eyes of Ticinese, the close relationship with German Switzerland in the north was born under the sign of oppression, and this feeling of negativity remains. Journalist Silvano Toppi accordingly observes the "range of historic baggage" that Ticino still carries on its back: "a speculative and parasitic mentality, improvisation, servility and lack of resolve."[17] The challenge remains to follow the path from oppressed object to autonomous subject. A next step would be to move, collectively, toward ownership of a creative and original identity—and this in turn would require common recognition of the need to abdicate the victim stance.

With such a step Ticino would begin to enter as an element of Switzerland's "biodiversity," enriching the biological system, as it were, with the variety of species required to sustain ecological balance, genetic diversity, and potential. In this picture, the Ticinesi might see themselves as being in line with the seemingly unimportant or even disadvantageous species whose characteristics are discovered to enhance the ecosystem's potential to positively adapt to unforeseen environmental changes. Science has indeed observed the negative effects of profit-oriented monocultures for instance, which in the long term lead to impoverished systems with threatened futures. Which is all to say, I see in cultural variety the "biodiversity" in which differences, including those belonging to minorities, are responses to specific conditions of life and hold the potential to constructively expand human potential itself. We recognize the same "non-monolateral" principle in the individual psychological goal of expanding consciousness by the integration of undervalued aspects of the personality.

A positive sign in the direction I am considering came in 2008 with the strike of the railroad mechanic shops in Bellinzona. Since opening in 1884, these shops have been a meaningful part of Ticino's history, in particular as they have linked our canton directly to the Confederation. The strike was provoked by the federal government's decision to save costs by shutting down all of the mechanic shops and laying off their 400 employees—a substantial number for our small canton. During the one-month strike, in an historically unprecedented show of solidarity, the mechanics were supported by the Ticinese government, political parties, trade unions, churches, and general populace. In the process masses of people mobilized to participate in recurring demonstrations, to assert their positions, and to host related cultural events. It was all motivated by the recognition that not only the loss of 400 jobs was at stake—but just as much, a threat to basic life values. On one hand there was concern about Ticino's position within the Confederation and the canton's relationship to the rest of Swiss, including the question of solidarity. On the other hand there were concerns about the right to work, about short-term profit versus long-term outcomes, about the absence of creative problem solving, and about the need to defend the human or "soft factor" in the work world.

Well-backed by their fellow Ticinesi, the mechanics dealt with the crisis in exemplary fashion: While protesting, they undertook the research required to develop concrete alternatives to a shut-down. They discovered the source of the economic problem to be not in "Ticinesi laziness" (as had been asserted)—but rather, in the federal management whose profit-orientation came at the expense of cultivating respect for and motivation in the local personnel. Their research further revealed that such symptoms signaled the management's long-standing neglect to invest in long-term modernization. They succeeded in motivating university-based scientific research that confirmed the feasibility of a proposal to convert the mechanic shops into large, sophisticated, and attractive centers for technological production, repair, and research. The model was ascertained to hold profitability not only for Ticino and Switzerland as whole, but also for Europe in general. So persuasive was the movement that the Federal Minister of Transportation was compelled to convene a "round table" of mediation with all parties involved. The outcome thus far has been the cancellation of the shut-down and the preservation of jobs. Unfortunately, however, the changes required for a new future have not yet been put in place, and so the mechanics shops are threatened by silent dissolution while others in

Europe pick up their innovative model. Yet they have not surrendered hope, for they remain actively involved in production processes and the round table negotiations go on.

Conclusion

Much remains to be done. Ticino need outgrow the role of "rascal" or rogue state—and the rest of Switzerland the role of stepmother. In fact, the journalist Joëlle Kunz noted the conspicuous gap standing between northern Switzerland's motherly compassion for Ticino, and Ticino's lack of political influence. As she put it, Ticino is tenderly embraced as the "flower in the buttonhole" of the nation—a thing nice to look at, but neglected in its potential to develop.[18] Ideally, we Ticinesi will advance from our "strabismus" to three-dimensional vision, not only to heal the split in our self-image, but also to gain the quality of depth in our identity. Ticino would then contribute significantly to its own identity-building as well as to Switzerland's renown for sustaining its cultural plurality, its "diversity in unity." Such a development would improve our chances of psychological survival and adaptation to the reality of life's constant changes.

NOTES

1. Orazio Martinetti, *La matrigna e il monello* (Locarno: Dadò, 2001), p. 77, trans. Isabelle Meier and Katy Remark.

2. Eds.' note: Italian is also an official language for the eastern Canton of Graubünden, which is, however, a trilingual canton. In Graudbünden the Italian speakers are the minority; (Swiss) German is the majority language, followed by Rhaeto-Romansh, the language of Switzerland's smallest official minority.

3. Carol L. Schmid, *Conflict and Consensus in Switzerland* (Berkeley: University of California Press, 1981), p. 32.

4. Eds.' note: For readers unfamiliar with this language dilemma, it is important to understand: The German-speaking Swiss, Switzerland's majority, generally conduct their schooling and official communications (written and broadcasted) in Standard German—yet their mother tongue and day-to-day language is the Swiss German dialect. This "mother dialect" consists in fact of at least thirty different

regional dialects, which are not immediately comprehensible to speakers of Standard German. Because Swiss German has no standard grammar or written form, it is not generally taught, but learned "on the street." Thus, those who speak or learn Standard German in order to function in the Germanic regions of Switzerland are additionally challenged to learn Swiss German if they want to attain a more intimate sense of belonging.

5. Arnoldo Coduri, *Turnkey Logistics: Made in Ticino* (Bellizona: Republic and Canton of Ticino, Department of Finance and Economy, Economy Division, undated), p. 7, downloadable brochure: http:// www.marinamasoni.ch/joomla/pubblicazioni/TurnkeyLogistics.pdf (accessed July 22, 2011).

6. Jonathan Steinberg, *Why Switzerland?*, 2nd ed., reprinted (Cambridge: The University Press, 2000), p. 12.

7. Eds.' note: See *Ibid.*, pp. 73-128; and Thomas Maissen, *Geschichte der Schweiz* (Baden: hier+jetzt, Verlag für Kultur und Geschichte, 2010), pp. 7-204. The Confederation's drive to expand its holdings by military campaign and subjugation ceased by and large in 1515, when the confederates were defeated by the French at the bloody battle of Morignano. Along with Ticino five other territories gained cantonal status in 1803, and in 1815 three more were admitted. After Napolean's defeat by the greater European powers, Switzerland was recognized as an officially neutral nation, and began to consolidate under the boundaries and laws that evolved to characterize the nation today.

8. Raffaello Ceschi, "Buoni Ticinesi e buoni Svizzeri. Aspetti storici di una duplice identità," eds. Remigio Ratti e Marco Badan, *Identità in cammino* (Locarno, Dadò, 1986), p. 17f.

9. Plinio Martini, *Il fondo del sacco* (Bellinzona: Casagrande, 1970), p. 79, trans. Isabelle Meier and Katy Remark.

10. Kenneth D. McRae, *Conflict and Compromise in Multilingual Societies: Switzerland*, second printing (Ontario, Canada: Wilford Laurier University Press, 1998), p. 214.

11. *Ibid.*, p. 215.

12. Anonymous author, in *Adula*, quoted in Silvano Gilardoni, *Italianità ed elvetismo nel Canton Ticino* (Bellinzona: Archivio Storia Ticinese no. 45-46, 1971), p. 42, trans. Isabelle Meier and Katy Remark.

13. Orazio Martinetti, *La matrigna e il monello*, p. 77.

14. Gilardoni, *Italianità ed elvetismo*, p. 77, trans. Isabelle Meier and Katy Remark.

15. Georg Kreis, "La non-identità come normalità. Riflessioni critiche sulla questione dell'identità," in Mazzoleni e Ratti, *Identità,* p. 112.

16. Mazzoleni e Ratti, "Come e perchè studiare l'identita," in Mazzoleni e Ratti, *Identità*, p. 13, trans. Isabelle Meier and Katy Remark.

17. Silvano Toppi, "Cambia tutto e cambia poco," in Basilio Biucchi, *Un paese che cambia* (Locarno: Dadò, 1985), p. 11, trans. Isabelle Meier and Katy Remark.

18. Joëlle Kunz, "Sulla passionale indifferenza fra il Ticino e la Svizzera," in Mazzoleni e Ratti, *Identità*, p. 136.

The Swiss as Hobbits, Gnomes, and Tricksters of Europe

ISABELLE MEIER

Translation by Andrew Fellows

I begin with a striking statement about Swiss character by C.G. Jung:

> Here, where nature is mightier than man, none escapes her influence, the chill of water, the starkness of rock, the gnarled, jutting roots of trees and precipitous cliffs—all this generates in the soul of anyone born there something that can never be extirpated, lending him that characteristically Swiss obstinacy, doggedness, stolidity, and innate pride which have been interpreted in various ways—favorably as self-reliance, unfavorably as dour pigheadedness.[1]

Isabelle Meier, Dr. phil., first studied general history and philosophy, and later psychology, at the University of Zürich where she completed a doctorate in psychology. She trained at the C. G. Jung Institute in Zürich and also is certified as a Guided Affective Imagery psychotherapist. She is a lecturer, training analyst, and supervisor at ISAPZURICH, and has been Co-Chair of the Jungian Odyssey Committee since 2007. She maintains a private practice in Zürich and is a published writer.

This article is based on the lecture, "*Die Schweizer: Hobbits Europas*" ("The Swiss: Hobbits of Europe"), delivered at the *Drei-Ländertagung* (Conference of Analytical Psychologists and Jungian Clubs of Switzerland, Germany, and Austria) in Berlin, 4-9 September 2008.

Anyone who wants to understand the Swiss from a depth-psychological perspective should take Jung's remarks on Switzerland into account:

> From the earth-boundness of the Swiss come all their bad as well as their good qualities: their down-to-earthness, their limited outlook, their non-spirituality, their parsimony, stubbornness, dislike of foreigners, mistrustfulness, as well as that awful *Schwizerdütsch* and their neutrality. Switzerland consists of numerous valleys, depressions in the earth's crust, in which the settlements of man are embedded. Nowhere are there measureless plains, where it is a matter of indifference where a man lives; nowhere is there a coast against which the ocean beats with its lore of distant lands. Buried deep in the backbone of the continent, sunk in the earth, the Alpine dweller lives like a troglodyte, surrounded by more powerful nations that are linked with the wide world, that expand into colonies or can grow rich on the treasures of their soil. The Swiss cling to what they have, for the others, the more powerful ones, have grabbed everything else. Under no circumstances will the Swiss be robbed of their own. Their country is small, their possessions limited. If they lose what they have, what is going to replace it?[2]

Jung bound the Swiss soul to the earth, the land, and the smallness of the country, and he emphasized the deep-rooted resentment at outside interference, which would immediately make every Swiss man or woman bristle. The Swiss resist any interference in their national affairs absolutely, Jung says, and he continues:

> If it be true that we are the most backward, conservative, stiff-necked, self-righteous, smug, and churlish of all European nations, this would mean that in Switzerland the European is truly at home in his geographical and psychological centre. There he is attached to the earth, unconcerned, self-reliant, conservative and backward . . . occupying a neutral position between the fluctuating and contradictory aspirations and opinions of the other nations . . . .[3]

Jung describes the Swiss character type as strongly colored by the sensation function and as a people who stick to what they have. He does not in any way deny the typical national vices and the ugliness of the earthy Swiss character, but he wants to find some sense in it. This is because he believes that the Swiss national character was not established throughout centuries by accident, but that it is "a meaningful response to the dangerously undermining influence of the environment."[4] What is it, then, that has been reflected in the Swiss collective consciousness throughout the centuries? What sort of image has coalesced out of Switzerland and in its inhabitants?

Who and What is Switzerland?

Geographically, Switzerland is a landlocked country and a distinctly mountainous region. While almost half of the country is higher than 1,000 meters (3,300 feet), the majority of the population lives in the flattest third of the land. Switzerland is not a nation in the usual sense of having a common language and a common culture. On the contrary, it is characterized by the cultural diversity inherent in its four language regions: German, French, Italian, and Raeto-Romanic. There is no confessional unity either—Protestants slightly outnumber Catholics, and Jews and Muslims live alongside Christians, agnostics, and atheists. Switzerland is, moreover, a watershed: At the Gotthard, the magical mountain pass at the center of the country, four rivers arise and run to the north, south, east, and west: the Rhine to the North Sea, the Inn to the Black Sea, the Rhone to the Mediterranean Sea, and the Ticino to the Adriatic Sea. Therefore, Switzerland has been called Europe's moated castle. Since the country has no direct access to the sea, its foreign trade relies on the ability to transport goods across international boundaries.

Foreign trade matters because Switzerland is poor in commodities. Almost a quarter of its land is completely non-productive, being covered with lakes, glaciers, and rocks. Another quarter is covered with forest, and another consists of mountain meadows and alpine pastures, so that less than 30 percent of its land is available for agriculture and industry. Industrial resources such as coal and iron are lacking. Switzerland possesses the capacity to produce food only for three fifths of its population and must rely on imports, which makes the country highly dependent on foreign countries and international economies. Explorers in search of a territory for nation building certainly would not have sought out this region.

At the same time, lying at the heart of Europe, Switzerland offers vital commerce routes for other European countries. Historically, such commerce was especially dependent on the Gotthard Pass, originally accessible only by a narrow and treacherous trail. Access to the Gotthard was improved in 1230 with the construction of the *Teufelsbrücke*, or Devil's Bridge, which spanned a deep gorge and the dangerous River Reuss. Inhabitants near to this route came to play pivotal roles in the conduct of interregional trade. It is this rugged and mythic landscape that gives rise to the stubborn Swiss soul.

Politically speaking, the stubborn resolve and provincialism of the Swiss as *frumen edle puren*—pious, noble peasants[5]—began to consolidate with the building of the Devil's Bridge. In 1291, the inhabitants of small communities and representatives of alpine cooperatives hailing from three areas around the Gotthard—Uri, Schwyz, and Unterwalden—entered into an alliance for mutual defense against foreign attack. They swore an oath of mutual support and bound themselves to one another in a written pact, standing together as *Eidgenossen*, or Confederates. At the same time, as legend has it, another decisive event occurred nearby. A mountain herdsman from Uri named Wilhelm Tell stubbornly refused to bow down before Hermann Gessler, the despotic bailiff acting on behalf of the foreign Count of Habsburg in central Switzerland. For defying orders, Tell was forced to use his crossbow and arrow to split an apple that had been placed on his son's head. Although he succeeded, Tell was shackled and shipped away, swearing vengeance for the brutal punishment. Later, Tell ambushed Gessler on an overgrown path of thick forest, shot and killed him with an arrow, and thereby freed the land from foreign oppression. The oath of alliance among Cantons Uri, Schwyz, and Unterwalden, along with Wilhelm Tell's political act of liberation, tell not only of the practical establishment of the Swiss Confederation. They also form the legend of the Confederation's founding and symbolize the forces that have imbued the Swiss with their particular national attitude and emotional tenor for hundreds of years.

As noted by the historian J.R. von Salis, the stubbornness of the Swiss was viewed skeptically by neighboring countries:

> It cannot be overlooked that this provincialism of a small people living in the heart of the European continent, surrounded by great nations, at times led to some irritation of the big and powerful against a weak and small one who took the liberty of sticking to his own views.[6]

For five centuries, alliances were repeatedly made in the heartland of Switzerland to provide mutual assistance against attacks, mutual conciliation, and mutual interest. The alliance system was very heterogeneous and could include city-states, abbeys, village republics, single estates, and places. Later, cities such as Zürich, Lucerne, and Bern joined the Confederation. The people of the original Switzerland discovered their ability to defend the Alps, and their freedom, against their enemies, such as those from Austria and Burgundy. These Confederates gained a reputation for being brave, terrifying warriors who were fiercely determined and who relentlessly and defiantly defended their territory and drove away strangers with halberd and spiked mace. Because of this reputation for fierce fighting, the Confederation soon became the recruiting area for mercenary soldiers to serve in many surrounding countries. The Swiss were sought-after mercenaries who sold their service as fighters to France, Germany, and Austria, also to the Pope (who is protected by the Swiss Guard to this day). This in turn provided a vital source of revenue for the Swiss.

The alliance system was extended over time as more cities and areas became included in it. Slowly Switzerland grew organically to become a diverse federal republic. In contrast to the surrounding countries, this country was never a monarchy; there were no princes and no aristocracy who deserved this name. Some of the cities, like Basel, still boast old quasi-aristocratic families, but they live modestly and do not dwell on huge estates. No Swiss government was ever overthrown, nor did the nation ever own any overseas colonies because it never subscribed to imperialist politics. The land belonged mostly to middle and small farmers. Swiss industry was decentralized, so no slums and no numerically strong proletariat could emerge. The ancient craftsmen were required in the production of high-quality products as before. In the 19th century, democracy developed even among Europe's monarchies. Switzerland is thus proud to be the "oldest democracy in the world," dating its democratic tradition back 1291. The compulsion to find workable political compromises has been practiced in Switzerland for centuries. In 1848 the federal state, which is governed by the magic formula,[7] came into being, and its constitution replaced the agreements of the earlier federal confederation while the individual cantons were able to retain many of their original powers. Direct democracy as well, by which Swiss citizens can have influence on legislation through a referendum system, has been in force since then.

A strong national identity arose in the 19th century, in large part through the liberation stories of Wilhelm Tell (especially in the form of the theatrical version by Friedrich Schiller), which was based in myth and was regularly performed at the federal shooting festivals that take place throughout Switzerland annually. This is important because a sense of identity, community, and collective consciousness, especially about wars, came into being in other countries too, even though offensive war has never been instigated by Switzerland. Wilhelm Tell belongs to the national collective memory and represents the national myth of the brave, freedom-loving Swiss who, at the foot of the Gotthard, created the "Cradle of the Confederation". 1291 became a symbol of resistance and independence, as 1776 is for American Independence, not any other moment in history, although there could have been others.[8]

At the Vienna Congress of 1815, the powers of Austria, Russia, Prussia, England, Portugal, and France recognized the principle of neutrality of Switzerland. On the one hand, this agreement was reached because Switzerland had always stubbornly insisted on its freedom and independence, playing nations off against each other according to their desires; on the other hand, it emerged as a compromise among the demands of the surrounding great powers, all of which could better live with it than without it. As the historian Tobias Kästli has described the agreement:

> The fact that our country exists as a nation has something to do with European sentimentality toward the homeland of Wilhelm Tell. Alongside all the realpolitic anger over Switzerland, there was an admiration for the "free Confederates." The great powers acknowledged and accepted Switzerland's strong desire for neutrality and independence, and they came to believe that only an independent Switzerland offered a guarantee of reasonably safe and calm conditions in a strategically important part of Europe. This was because a non-neutral Switzerland would have become a constant bone of contention. Austria and France, also the southern German states and indirectly Prussia, would have tried further to assert their strategic interests in Switzerland, to gain an advantage with military alliances and the right to march

> through it, which would have inevitably led to new conflicts. The existence of a neutral Switzerland seemed to be in the interest of a peaceful Europe.[9]

Each great power would have liked to possess the Gotthard for itself, and all other passes of the Alps as well, but none of them would then grant passage to the others. A neutral zone was necessary for European equilibrium. Thus Switzerland remained the guardian of the mighty Alps. Throughout the Alps, the Swiss army built many tunnels and fortifications, to which they would have fled in the case of invasion by the Germans in WWII (the *Réduit*) for instance, and from where they would have destroyed the Gotthard transit axis by means of explosives. That was seen as the last resort. Switzerland maintained its guard over the Gotthard by using its adamantine will. That the mountains actually have something to do with the soul of Switzerland was shown in a representative survey conducted in 1977 by sociologist Hans-Peter Meier-Dallach, who asked: "Suppose we could spread out Switzerland like a tablecloth so that it would be then as big and flat as, for example, Germany. Would you agree that we should do it?" 90% were against it[10], although it would have been economically worthwhile.

Such a history does not suggest an extraverted identity, such as that which can be seen, for example, in the USA with its world mission, but rather an introverted one. This is reflected also in the image that foreigners have of us. We are ridiculed by other nations such as Italy, where there is a saying "*Non fare lo svizzero*" ("don't do it the Swiss way," i.e., "don't be too correct"). The French of the "Grande Nation" call us "*les petites Suisses*" and do not take us very seriously. We are seen as naive, hard-working, cautious, and staid. If possible, we operate by compromise and consensus, otherwise we just hold out. The Germans find us unapproachable, obstinate, and inhibited and they do not understand our indirect manner with each other and complain that in Switzerland the conversation quickly turns to money (as I often hear from my German analysands). We have a deeply rooted aversion to personality cults and a mistrust of leaders. We do not interfere with others, or, as C.G. Jung says, we hold ourselves back from everything, and we obstinately do not want anyone to interfere with us either.

> I have in my time been accused of "Swiss wooden-headed-ness". Not that I have anything against possessing the national vices of

> the Swiss, I am also quite ready to suppose that I am a bigoted Swiss in every respect. I am perfectly content to let my psychological confession, my so called "theories", be criticized as a product of Swiss wooden-headed-ness or queer-headedness . . . . I am proud of my subjective premises, I love the Swiss earth in them . . . and I also admit my so-called "father complex": I do not want to knuckle under to any "fathers" and never shall . . . .[11]

C.G. Jung, as is well known, did not submit to the authority of Sigmund Freud but formed his own psychological views.

We Swiss experience ourselves in our conscious *Selbstbild* (self image) as faithful (Swiss Guards of the Pope!), loyal, quality-conscious, consensus-oriented, tough, stable, not dominating, and courteous. We do not make a big scene about things. Our work ethic is sacred to us. We work on the whole more than the other Europeans.[12] Small objects like the Swiss army knife and the Swatch watch are emblematic of the precision, pragmatism, and conscientiousness of the Swiss.

Like a Hobbit

This cluster of characteristics that typifies the Swiss (most especially the German Swiss) finds an almost perfect representative image in the Hobbits, a literary creation of the British writer and scholar, J.R.R. Tolkien (1892-1973). The character and the realm of the Hobbits are well described in his early work, *The Hobbits*, and these little beings became the most important characters in the later 3-volume work, *The Lord of the Rings*.[13] The Hobbits are a physically small people, very skillful in handiwork, peace-loving, never aggressive with each other, and they live without a king or distinct hierarchies. They stay out of world events as much as possible and are reluctant to cross the Brandywine River, which frames their territory. They live out of sight in caves in a land of Middle-earth, and are not even mentioned in the list of its peoples—the elves, dwarves, and humans.

With the Hobbits, Tolkien created a hero type that resembles fairytale heroes like the *simpleton*, *stupid Hans,* and the *tomfool.* Like them, Hobbits are heroes against their will. They are naïve and limited in vision, and precisely because of this they are strong in character and resistant to temptation. Since they live wholly in the present, they do not foresee the dangers that could face them ahead. The great wizard, Gandalf, on the other hand, sees into the future very well, and this is why he rejects the magic ring of power—he knows he would misuse it to help the weak. Two of the Hobbits, Frodo and Sam, when called to destroy the magical ring of power, set out to do this by themselves. Once they have accepted this task, they feel obliged to see it through. They receive strength from their loyalty to each other, from which they do not deviate, a loyalty which does not exclude a certain stubbornness and rebelliousness. They do not want their country to submit to the more powerful peoples surrounding them. Their intention is pure, they do not want to cheat anybody, and they only want to fulfill their task. In dangerous situations, they rise above themselves. They obtain their wisdom from a healthy common sense and have the cunning of country people at their disposal.

Marie-Louise von Franz describes this Simpleton-hero type as follows:

> [He or she]. . . appears in an infinite number of fairy tales. For instance, a king has three sons and the youngest is a fool whom everybody laughs at; but it is always this fool who becomes the hero in the story. Or there is a peasant who has three sons, two are all right, but the youngest only sits by the stove and scratches himself all day, and finally he is the one who becomes the hero, marries the princess, and becomes czar.
>
> So the simpleton is a general figure, not only in fairy tales, but a general mythological motif. He symbolizes the basic genuineness and integrity of the personality. If people do not have in their innermost essence a genuineness, or a certain integrity, they are lost when meeting the problem of evil.[14]

The little heroes, against their will, whether Simpleton, Hobbit, Wilhelm Tell, or more generally the Swiss as a whole, have one thing in common: they think differently and not according to the dominant assumptions of collective consciousness. It is often sensation types—earthy, introverted, often neglected characters who are unequipped with instruments of power but persistently go their own way if necessary—who are ultimately successful. Occasionally one encounters such people in analytical practice. They often suffer from an inferiority complex because they compare themselves with the great and the famous. They would certainly benefit from considerations such as these when they reflect on themselves.

Little Heroes in the Shadow

The possibilities of the small, such as the country of Switzerland, give rise to a capacity for the development of niches. For centuries, Switzerland has been a haven for refugees from France, Italy, and Germany. Jean-Jacques Rousseau (18th c.) sought refuge here, as did Benjamin Constant (18th c.), the Scottish reformer John Knox (16th c.), liberal German fraternities or Italian revolutionaries like Giuseppe Mazzini (19th c.) who later became important in Italian unification, not to mention Vladimir Lenin (20th c.). Revolutionaries of many shades of opinion have fled to Switzerland, and again and again Switzerland has accepted them as political refugees. Anyone who does not command the attention of the great, who indeed cannot talk with them on equal terms, and who also wants to remain free and does not want to participate in international organizations with great power, like the European Union (EU) and the United Nations (UN), has considerable opportunities to keep secrets and to take secret actions. Of course, such a country can become the playground of outcasts as well. Analytically speaking, we may well encounter in this type of realm some shadow aspects of the larger collective.

Already Wilhelm Tell, the illustrious resistance fighter from the mountains and alpine partisan, resorted to actions that looked unfair to the collective of the day. He murdered Gessler in ambush and shot him in the back. Of course, this act looked different to the Swiss who were being oppressed; for them it was heroic and altogether justified. (We are allowed to throw foreign invaders out of the country by all means necessary!) In this case, one man's terrorist is another man's national hero.

The little "heroes" belong, partially at least, to the shadow of the collective at large. The Gnomes, those small creatures who conduct their trade underground in semi-darkness, hoard their treasures, and are miserly. The word "gnome," first used by the Swiss alchemist and physician, Paracelsus, is derived from the Greek *genomos*, meaning earth-dweller. Nowadays, the *Gnomes of Zürich* are well known. They are the bankers of Bahnhofstrasse who carry out secret transactions under the protection of Swiss banking secrecy laws. This expression was originally meant to cast aspersion on them and their practices. The British Labor Prime Minister, Harold Wilson named the Swiss bankers the *Gnomes of Zürich* in 1964 when he accused them of devaluing the British pound through speculation in international financial markets.[15] Since then, this term for Swiss bankers has stuck. They are seen as crafty and not above board, sly manipulators of financial markets who care nothing about the human cost of their nefarious and selfish behavior.

One could see Gnomes, then, as representing the shadow side of the peace-loving and domestically inclined Hobbits. In contrast to Hobbits, they tend to be expansive, smart, open-minded, and extraverted. The fact that Switzerland could become one of the richest countries in the world certainly has something to do with these financial Gnomes. Swiss banks are the epitome of stability and reliability, and the financial centers of Switzerland have a world-wide leading position in asset management.[16] The financial Gnomes meanwhile operate covertly world-wide under the guise of Swiss banking secrecy laws. They guard money for others, exploit the hiding places offered by Swiss tax havens, and transfer funds deftly around the globe.[17] Their underground steel vaults and their numbered bank accounts have a mysterious aura that appears again and again in movies, stories, and reportage. They are linked symbolically with the dark hidden caves of the Alps.

The gold and money of many people in the world end up in Switzerland, and it is quite understandable and reasonable that other countries complain about this. For many people, Swiss banking secrecy is seen as unjust and morally unacceptable (it is therefore currently being revised under pressure from the EU and the USA). This money can be "dirty", as was the case with the unclaimed fortunes of millions of victims of German fascism that were stored in Swiss numbered bank accounts and finally, after massive protests from the USA, had to be paid back to rightful claimants. Another example of shadow activity for financial benefit lies in Switzerland's close economic relations with Nazi Germany during WWII. Although officially neutral, Switzerland provided weapons, approved loans, and made gold transactions possible so that the Third Reich was able to obtain foreign exchange. In return, Switzerland was able to import raw materials from Germany, such as coal, iron, chemicals, mineral oils, etc. Without these imports, Switzerland would not have been able to guarantee its people either bread or work during these years. Much of Switzerland remained largely integrated into the German economy during these years as well, and with the Alpine passes it had an important strategic significance for the German armed forces (again everything hung on the Gotthard!).[18] From the outside, Switzerland was neutral and independent, but in fact it compromised heavily. This shadow hangs over Switzerland to this day. Of course, one can ask what room for maneuver Switzerland had at the time when other small countries like Belgium, the Netherlands, and Denmark were simply overrun and seized.

Another feature of Switzerland that emerges in this reflection, for which C.G. Jung specially wrote an article titled "On the Psychology of the Trickster-Figure"[19] is linked to the *Simpleton, stupid Hans,* or the *tomfool* who, in their stupidity, obtain what others cannot successfully get even with their smartest endeavors. The trickster is goblin-like, plays malicious tricks, is a puerile rogue, and sometimes also suffers from it: "In his clearest manifestations he is a faithful reflection of an absolutely undifferentiated human consciousness . . . ."[20] "He is so unconscious of himself that his body is not a unity, and his two hands fight each other."[21] One could attribute such trickster-like traits to Switzerland. Economic relations with the allied forces were not totally abandoned during the Second World War, and afterwards Switzerland quickly reoriented to the new situation and joined organizations[22] that took the distribution of aid under the Marshall Plan. Later, Switzerland acceded to pressure from the USA in the Cold War and withdrew from well-established economic relations with Russia and Eastern Europe, received NATO ammunition, and generally aligned itself with the Western military block.[23] This could be described as a trickster-like exploitation of the possibilities of a small state, a Machiavellian "free ride"[24] without having to pay money or join major international organizations (like the UN or EU). This results in benefits from others while keeping distant on the grounds of neutrality. With regard to its banking secrecy laws, their characteristics were set up along lines that would permit tax evasion and tax fraud and make use of sophisticated tactics like the delay of negotiations, complaining, craftily turning an argument, and haggling if anyone dared to cast doubt on banking secrecy. It needed heavy pressure from the USA and the EU to make this non-negotiable banking secrecy provision suddenly negotiable in 2009.

On the other hand, a small state also has more positive trickster possibilities than great powers do, since it can set unconventional proposals and initiatives in motion without undue problems. As a small country, it is seen as more naïve and not suspected of only pursuing its own interests. Switzerland played an active role with its diplomats, for instance, in the formation of international institutions such as the Conference on Security and Cooperation in Europe and the European Free Trade Association. Political scientists here speak of the "mediator" possibilities of a small state.[25] It can achieve the "Policy of Good Services", which as a host country it was able to attain by accommodating international organizations such as the League of Nations in Geneva after WWI. Switzerland today represents the USA in Cuba and in Iran, Cuba in the USA, and now Russia in Georgia and vice versa. The Swiss Confederation acts as the messenger and neutral mediator between rival states and contributes to the stabilization of conflicts with this transcendental function.

Conclusion

The geographical and human potentialities of the small mountainous country of Switzerland have shaped the Swiss soul. As C. G. Jung describes it: ". . . the chill of the water, the starkness of rock, the gnarled, jutting roots of trees and the precipitous cliffs—all this generates in the soul of anyone born there something that can never be extirpated . . . ."[26]

The desire for independence and aversion to outside interference, accompanied by unconventional thinking, are and were ineradicable. This is linked to, and indeed is unimaginable without, the Alps, the magical Gotthard with the *Teufelsbrücke* and *Via mala* bridges over it, and the pledge of the early Confederates against enemy insurgents. Here lies even perhaps the Self of the Swiss, the Archimedean point towards which all Swiss have gravitated since time immemorial, and from which they derive their stubborn power in the foundational myth of Wilhelm Tell. However, Switzerland was also aided by the will of the great powers to create a neutral zone in the heart of Europe; otherwise it would have had no chance of independence. It can offer trickster-like niches and negotiate with the great powers without losing face.

In the view of ourselves and others, we are seen as hard-working, industrious, and cautious, and as introverted sensation types. One may think of us with the image of the Hobbits, as reluctant heroes. Orthodox heroes, such as Hercules or Parsifal, are extraverted and fight openly.

Reluctant heroes instead fight secretly and are not even aware that they are heroes, since it is only from their instinctive actions that heroism arises. Wilhelm Tell was one of these, too. However, Gnomes belong to the shadow aspects of these heroes as they craftily and selfishly take advantage of every hiding place to hoard treasures invisibly and without trace. Banking secrecy helped them to collect and to store money and gold in underground vaults and caves. This mentality of retreating into caves and into the "hollows of the earth's crust" is perhaps regrettable, for it prevents differentiated discussion and political maturation. In the end, this attitude is probably molded through the legacy of the landscape and the history of this small country.

NOTES

1. C.G. Jung, "Paracelsus," in *The Spirit in Man, Art, and Literature,* vol. 15 of *The Collected Works of C. G. Jung*, trans. R.F.C. Hull (Princeton, N.J.: Princeton University Press, 1966), § 2. All future references to the *Collected Works* (hereinafter "*CW*") will be by volume number and paragraph number.

2. Jung, *CW* 10, § 914.

3. Jung, *CW* 10, § 920.

4. Jung, *CW* 10, § 924.

5. Christoph Guggenbühl, "Biedermänner und Musterbürger im 'Mutterland der Weltfreyheit.' Konzepte der Nation in der helvetischen Republik," in *Die Konstruktion einer Nation. Nation und Nationalisierung in der Schweiz, 18.-20. Jahrhundert,* eds. Urs Altermatt, Catherine Bosshart-Pfluger und Albert Tanner (Zürich: Chronos, 1998), p. 35. Originally this population—consisting of Celts, Romans, and Germanic peoples—had been part of the Roman Empire.

6. J.R. von Salis, *Schwierige Schweiz. Beiträge zu einigen Gegenwartsfragen* (Zürich: Orell Füssli Verlag, 1968), p. 18, trans. Andrew Fellows.

7. The "magic formula" is an arithmetically defined formula that, by common agreement, allocates the seven executive seats of the Swiss Federal Council among the four ruling parties. The purpose is to prevent any given party from gaining an unfair power advantage over the others.

8. For example, the period between 1789 and 1848, when the Swiss nation was created, or the Revolution of 1847-1848, see Tobias Kästli, *Die Schweizeine Republik in Europa. Geschichte des Nationalstaats seit 1789* (Zürich: Verlag Neue Zürcher Zeitung, 1998), p. 378.

9. Kästli, *Die Schweizeine Republik in Europa,* p. 198, trans. Andrew Fellows.

10. Hans-Peter Meier-Dallach, Moritz Rosenmund, *CH-Cement. Das Bild der Schweiz im Schweizervolk,* p. 40. (Results of a study conducted from 1977 to 1979 with support from the Swiss National Science Foundation at the Sociological Institute of the University of Zürich [Zürich: Eco-Verlag, 1980].)

11. Jung, *CW* 10, § 1026.

12. On average, the Swiss work 40.5 hours per week, whereas people work shorter hours in all 25 EU countries (except for Estonia, Latvia, and Lithuania). See *Arbeitszeit. Tarifarbeitszeit von Industriearbeitern 2004* at http://wko.at/statistik/eu/europa-arbeitszeit.pdf (accessed October 30, 2010).

13. John Ronald Reuel Tolkien, *The Lord of the Rings* (London: HarperCollins, 2002).

14. Marie-Louise von Franz, *Shadow and Evil in Fairy Tales,* rev. edition (Boston, London: Shambhala, 1995), p. 221.

15. Hansard, House of Commons, 5th series, vol. 560, col. 579 at http://en.wikipedia.org/wiki/Gnomes_of_Zürich (accessed October 30, 2010).

16. *Finanzplatz Schweiz. Übersicht über wichtige Themenbereiche und Entwicklungen im Finanzbereich,* 2003 ed. Eidgenössischen Finanzdepartement EFD und Eidgenössischen Departement für auswärtige Angelegenheiten EDA at www.taxjustice.net/cms/upload/pdf/finanzplatz.ch_2003.pdf (accessed October 30, 2010).

17. An example of such a Gnome is the Swiss character in the James Bond film *Casino Royale.* He has brought a safe deposit box filled with money and carries out the secret transaction.

18. Hans-Ulrich Jost, "Identität und nationale Geschichte. Die Schweizergeschichte unter dem Einfluss der Geistigen Landesverteidigung", *Widerspruch, Beiträge zur sozialistischen Politik* no. 13 (1987): 7-20, p. 15, and Jakob Tanner, *Bundeshaushalt, Währung und Kriegswirtschaft. Eine finanzsoziologische Analyse der Schweiz zwischen*

1939 und 1953 (Zürich: Dissertation Universität Zürich, 1986), p. 244.

19. Jung, *CW* 9i, §§ 456-488.

20. Jung, *CW* 9i, § 465.

21. Jung, *CW* 9i, § 472.

22. The OEEC is the Organisation for European Economic Cooperation.

23. Jakob Tanner, "Die Aushöhlung der Neutralität durch ihre Bewaffnung", *Widerspruch, Beiträge zur sozialistischen Politik*, no. 17 (1989): 33-44, p. 35.

24. See Gregor Walter and Michael Zürn, "Regieren jenseits des Nationalstaates: Chancen und Gefahren für kleine und grosse Staaten", in *Der Nationalstaat am Ende des 20. Jahrhunderts. Beiträge im Rahmen der Berner Vortragsreihe: "Die Schweiz im Prozess der Globalisierung"*, ed. Klaus Armingeon (Bern: Haupt, 1996), pp. 149-180. Walter and Zürn discuss, among other things, three possibilities for a small state in the globalization process using the example of Switzerland: to act as a "broker", a "fare-dodger", and a "free-rider".

25. See endnote no. 18, above.

26. See endnote no. 1, above.

SWEET DREAMS: CHOCOLATE AND SWISS IDENTITY

IRENE BISCHOF

TRANSLATION BY ANDREW FELLOWS

Europe has a heart of chocolate—Switzerland.
TV commercial for the Swiss confectionary company, Lindt & Sprüngli[1]

Doesn't this quote conjure up a delicious image suggesting that Switzerland and chocolate belong together? In this article I pursue the idea that—among things typically Swiss such as the Swiss watch and the Swiss Army knife—Swiss chocolate aptly symbolizes some of the consciously valued aspects of our cultural identity.

Recently I had been journeying abroad, and was on my way back to Switzerland, ready to depart from the Berlin airport in my native

Irene Bischof, dipl. psych., was born and raised as citizen of Germany, where she studied psychology at the University of Bonn. She has lived in Switzerland since 1971—long enough that she feels at home in Switzerland and shares in a sense of Swiss identity. She graduated from the C.G. Jung Institute in Zürich, and now works as a Jungian analyst and psychotherapist in her own practice in Switzerland's capital city of Bern. She is currently a member of the board of the Swiss Society for Analytical Psychology (SGAP), and a member of the Association of Graduate Analytical Psychologists (AGAP). Her special interest lies in the area of inter-subjectivity and its meaning for individuation.

home of Germany. At the airport I happened to glance at a rack full of the so familiar Swiss Toblerone chocolate bars stacked to form a row of triangular mountain peaks, packaged in breath-of-yellow cardboard, and adorned in writing with the Swiss national color, red. I said to my friend: "It seems like I'm already back home again!" In that moment I realized that, although I grew up in Germany, decades of living in Switzerland had made me a "real" Swiss. The mere sight of the Toblerone chocolate bar was enough to fill me with warm feelings of home. In the language of analytical psychology this was a typical complex reaction. In my view, Swiss chocolate creates in the Swiss what I call the "positive chocolate complex," a psychological complex residing in the cultural layer of the Swiss psyche, at least as concerns our collective sense of identity.

What is Chocolate and Why Do We Love It?

The story of chocolate begins with the exotic cacao bean, which grows only in the tropics. Cacao beans harvested for the making of chocolate are first fermented, and then dried, cleaned, roasted, peeled—and finally ground into "cocoa liquor" or pure, fluid chocolate. The fluid chocolate is processed to yield cocoa solids, and also cocoa butter, the fine aromatic fat that gives luster and a delicate glaze to chocolate confections; what remains is the "cocoa mass." Chocolate confections (except for white chocolate) contain as basic ingredients, in varying proportions, the cocoa mass, cocoa butter, sugar, and sometimes vanilla; for milk chocolate, powdered or condensed milk is added.[2] From here, the distinguishing features and quality of any given confection rest on highly complex and delicate procedures—and as well, on the confectioner's special recipes.

A large part of humanity finds it wonderful to eat this slightly bittersweet confection, because, as Swiss chocolate manufacturers commonly agree:[3] Good chocolate delivers above all intense oral pleasure. The surface of a high quality chocolate bar shines like silk. It breaks with a faint, hard cracking sound; the fracture surfaces are clean and not crumbly. Its aroma is full and round, but never intrusive. On the tongue Swiss chocolate melts gently; it is neither sticky, nor mushy or grainy—and its flavor is delicate, tender, perfect, unique. The psychologically relevant core aspect of chocolate is thus sensory pleasure derived from the palate, the senses of smell and touch—and even the eye and ear, which all add up to an experience of gratification and joy.

It is well known that many of us today reserve (or mean to reserve) chocolate as a "comfort food" or as a reward, by which chocolate becomes associated with feelings of well being. Research of the last decades has gone far to support the recognition of chocolate's therapeutic properties: Contemporary science holds that the good feeling associated with chocolate consumption results partly from the stimulating effect of theobromine—the substance in chocolate that is chemically related to caffeine. The sugar in chocolate releases serotonin, a brain chemical that works via our neurotransmitters to produce these positive feelings. Moreover, chocolate contains "phenlylethlylamine, the same chemical [the] brain produces when [we] fall in love."[4] Certain substances in cacao are now recognized to lower blood pressure and promote circulation.[5] Other research, still in an early phase, indicates that "polyphenols in . . . chocolate increase the blood flow and oxygen to the brain that in turn could boost [brain] power—especially in the elderly."[6]

Like so many others, we Swiss love to eat chocolate—indeed we have the highest annual per capita chocolate consumption in the world: 12.4 kilograms (27.3 pounds) per person![7]

FROM THE "FOOD OF THE GODS" TO SWISS CHOCOLATE

Whether we realize it or not, with every bite of chocolate we link ourselves to the ancient "food of the gods"—the sacred food extolled in Mayan myths that tell the pre-history of mankind.[8] In Latin this food is called *Theobroma*, and it appears in *Theobroma cacao*, the botanical name of the tropical cacao tree from which the cacao bean is harvested. The word "chocolate" itself is thought to stem from the Aztec for "bitter water," *xocolātl*. Archaeological evidence and research focused between 600 and 400 AD has established that the Mayans of Mesoamerica were the first to cultivate cacao.[9] The Mayans used whole cacao beans both as highly valued currency, and for ritual offerings to the gods. With the ground beans they made a bitter beverage spiced with chili peppers, which was served at ritual ceremonies. The ground beans were also mixed with maize to make a gruel that was part of the ordinary Mayan diet.

Christopher Colombus first brought the cacao bean to Europe, but it remained an exotic item of curiosity until the Spanish conquistadors introduced the chocolate drink around 1528. At the time, and for some two centuries thereafter, chocolate was a luxury for the European aristocracy, who imbibed it as a spicy drink enhanced with other spices, sugar, vanilla, and later with milk. By the mid-seventeenth century, European physicians were touting chocolate's medicinal properties. The first solid chocolate delights—albeit crude ones—appeared in the early nineteenth century, when chocolate also gained acclaim in Europe for its aphrodisiacal powers. Some "female cookbook writers" disparaged the latter development as "decadent, sinful and feminine."[10] An apparently irrevocable wedding of chocolate to Valentine's Day suggests that the "sinful and feminine" have prevailed to this day!

But how did chocolate, whose primary ingredient is the tropical cacao bean, come to be a Swiss specialty? Perhaps it was in Switzerland that the exotic cacao met with the best conditions in which to be transformed into the forms of chocolate we savor today. We Swiss are blessed with abundant high alpine pastures that nurture many cows. Our cows produce such an abundance of milk that plenty is left for such luxury as chocolate making. This happenstance of geography combined with our history of skilled dependence on cattle is further coupled with a Swiss inclination for entrepreneurship and demand for superior quality.

The original Swiss confectioners learned the art of making solid edible chocolate by hand, apprenticing mainly in Italy or France, and returning to Switzerland to open small confectionary shops. François-Louis Cailler, Philippe Suchard, and Rudolf Sprüngli were among these early pioneers whose shops flourished, thanks not last to their own inventiveness and the contributions of their compatriots: In 1819, François-Louis Cailler established a chocolate factory in Geneva, thereby initiating the mass production of chocolate in Switzerland.[11] At this time all the chocolate produced in Europe was the dark type. Momentously, in 1875, Henri Nestlé in Vevey, Switzerland discovered how to make powdered milk; and then, soon thereafter the famous Swiss chocolatier Daniel Peter discovered how to combine powdered milk with solid chocolate to create milk chocolate and to produce the first milk chocolate bars.[12] The next leap came in 1879 with the "mixing conche," an appliance invented by Rodolphe Lindt, the founder of a chocolate factory in Bern. Lindt's conche, named for its shell-like shape, was a tabletop machine that refined the chocolate mixture by agitating it under high heat. Today's industrial conches can process up to ten tons of chocolate in one batch. The flavor of any given chocolate product and its melting quality depend in part on the duration of conching, which already in Lindt's time lasted from six to seventy-eight hours.[13]

In the nineteenth century Swiss discoveries and inventions such as those mentioned above, along with innovations from other countries, made chocolate less expensive to produce and buy. Chocolate was thus "democratized," becoming affordable for the population at large, and a source of quick high-calorie supply in the military.[14] Today chocolate is typically eaten as an inexpensive snack, available to everyone—at least in our latitudes—even to those with little money. Of course the finest Swiss chocolates are luxury items that command high prices, and so are indulged in by fewer people, and less frequently.

Statistics from 2009 show that the chocolate industry in Switzerland employs some 4,000 people[15] and that total annual sales amount to about 1.7 billion Swiss francs (at the time of the study, slightly less that 1.7 billion US dollars). These figures are based on our production of over 170,000 tons of chocolate—60% of which was exported to 140 countries, with Germany, the United Kingdom (UK), France, and the United States as the leading importers.

The Swiss Chocolate Complex

A complex is a coherent and autonomous "personality fragment" or "splinter psyche," characterized by its own set of beliefs, ideas, and images that are linked by specific feeling tones. Complexes thus act as focal points in the human soul; they influence psychological dynamics[16] and also contribute to our sense of identity. As we have noted, for many people chocolate is indeed associated with pleasure, at first glance because of its delicious taste. However in the Swiss, the chocolate complex is broader and deeper because its meanings go straight to the heart of our cultural identity. Let us now "test" this claim, by imagining other associations that chocolate might awaken in the Swiss.

Mountains and Milk

Swiss chocolate readily conjures up the idyllic image of the Swiss as a rugged and industrious folk, at home in the Alps, and rooted in nature, health, and agricultural life. It is probably safe to say that most Swiss (even those who have spent their whole lives in cities) would identify with this image and concede that it belongs to our shared sense of home and self. Using the power of subliminal suggestion, chocolate advertisements mirror and commercially exploit this aspect of the complex as follows: For decades milk chocolate has come in packaging quaintly decorated with pictures of cows, dairymen, mountain flowers, and other alpine motifs—and more recently, striking mountain scenery has come into fashion. Such wrappings typically depict Swiss cows grazing in magnificent alpine meadows, eating healthy grass (which in turn, as we Swiss know, produces plenty of good milk).

Under the sway of the complex's autonomy, we register perhaps less consciously, if at all, a truth that would be somewhat at odds with our conscious self-image. Namely, the powdered milk used to make chocolate no longer comes from alpine cows, because the transport from the mountain heights to the industrial processing sites is too time-consuming and costly. Therefore, to insure freshness and economic manufacturing, the milk used for chocolate is produced and processed into powder mainly in the flat Swiss lowlands, far away from the idyllic alpine landscapes that resonate with our sense of self.[17]

A more recent development in chocolate packaging should certainly not be overlooked. The wrappings of many of the ever more visible and more expensive dark varieties of chocolate are elegant designs consisting of rich, dark-colored backgrounds embellished with gleaming gold pictures and lettering. If packaging mirrors and exploits our sense of identity, what are we to make of this implicit display of wealth? Switzerland now ranks among the countries with the highest per capita income in the world. Yet up to now we have tended to share a sense of discretion about our riches. We have inherited this discretion perhaps from previous generations, who inhibited expressions of wealth for fear that all they had gained could be lost or taken away at any moment. So the question arises: In such lavish packaging might we discern a Swiss collective that is gaining the confidence to integrate into its idyllic, alpine identity an orientation toward wealth and luxury?

Quality and Reliability

It is a widely held notion—and certainly a Swiss belief—that we Swiss produce the best chocolate in the world. In this we have a long tradition of which we are very proud. As a testament to this sentiment, we Swiss celebrated the 100th anniversary of the Swiss Chocolate Federation in 2001 by issuing a postage stamp that smelled and tasted like chocolate![18]

The gold-adorned wrapping around Swiss chocolate resonates—somewhere in the recesses of our souls—as a reminder that our chocolate is our own creation and one of those high quality products that enable us as a small, resource-poor country to match our powerful foreign competitors. We rest assured in the belief that the superior quality of our chocolate is achieved through our procurement of first-class raw materials, careful workmanship, and strict controls. And we take satisfaction in the fact that these standards are subject to democratic legislation that regulates the ingredients. (It is interesting to note that, although nowadays it is permissible in chocolate production to substitute the cocoa butter with up to 5% of other vegetable fat, no Swiss chocolate producer yet has broken with tradition to exploit this possibility.)[19]

Hand in hand with our striving for quality is our time-tested Swiss reliability. If the currently mounting crises in Swiss banking threaten to tarnish our identity in this sense, Swiss manufacturers have upheld our reputation for punctuality and our honoring of contracts. My friends, the Swiss chocolate producers Louise and Peter Gysi, assure me that our chocolate makers have followed in stride—and that this is always a selling point in their favor.

Family Entrepreneurship

The history of Swiss chocolate is the story of creative, risk-taking entrepreneurship cultivated by family tradition. When we shop for chocolate, the wrappers present us with family names that echo the 19th century, and the individuals who personally invented the processing methods, developed recipes, founded companies, created jobs, and opened up markets: Cailler, Peter, Lindt, Sprüngli, and Tobler, among others. Such names personify the craft and subtly convey the reassuring impression that the founders are guarding our interest in quality and tradition.

In many cases the original companies remained in family ownership over several generations. However today—again perhaps somewhat at odds with our ideal—the majority are subsumed under the umbrella of larger concerns. Nestlé, for instance, has for a long time produced Cailler chocolate. Yet no one has thought to change the Cailler name that remains on this chocolate because Nestlé is a huge conglomerate that lacks the personal aura that we favor. The large corporations notwithstanding, chocolate continues to symbolize the entrepreneurial spirit on which we Swiss stake our identity.

In fact, chocolate proves to be an ideal creative material for this purpose, for our chocolatiers have proven themselves capable of taking on the challenge of current trends to produce chocolate in new forms. Take, for instance, the old Swiss chocolate bar as a quick and "democratic" energy snack—now reincarnated as a healthy, organic morsel laced with yogurt, nuts, and mixed grains, offering a fast food to replace a sit-down lunch. On the other end of the spectrum is the luxurious dark chocolate that today's connoisseurs savor like wine, discerning nuances of flavor that arise in the origin of the cacao bean, in methods of roasting, and in the confectioner's unique blend of ingredients. Might our most recent chocolate innovations unite in one symbol a pair of opposites: our adherence to tradition, and our flexibility and openness toward the new?

Mercantile Spirit and Intercultural Relations

We have already noted the popularity of Swiss chocolate around the world. Let us now go beyond the consumer figures to consider chocolate's symbolization of the Swiss as a people with a long-standing mercantile spirit and tradition of intercultural relations. Chocolate as an emblem of our cultural identity in this sense seems to be suggestive of our openness and flexibility, at least where trade is concerned!

The foundation of modern Swiss trade was laid down in nineteenth-century Europe, when worldwide trade routes began to open up, and the quality of transportation was dramatically improving. Soon industrialization would give rise to a middle class with the time and money to invest in leisure. Accordingly, European tourism began to flourish around 1900. In connection with this development we discovered our flare for hospitality, first welcoming to the Alps British mountaineers and then many others—and we began to offer our mountains as a place of convalescence, especially for those afflicted with tuberculosis. It was during this same period that the previously mentioned Swiss discoveries and inventions contributed to the democratization of chocolate. And it was the same condition of improved transport that promoted the growth of our chocolate export and/or establishment of chocolate production in other countries. Thus in the early twentieth century we seized a unique opportunity to establish our country as a land of alluring mountains and the "land of chocolate"—whereupon Swiss chocolate became *the* chocolate par excellence[20] and an international "calling card" for Swiss identity.

Switzerland has not always been a wealthy nation. For a long time the poverty of our country was the driving force behind our cross-border relations. Today the drive arises in the force of globalization, which demands and also encourages contact with other cultures. A "global" outlook turned inward is indeed bound intimately to Swiss identity, because Switzerland long ago vowed to uphold the plurality of cultures that comprise our nation. Thus, within the borders of our small country, it has long been daily fare for the speakers of our four indigenous languages and their respective cultures to encounter one another. And, Switzerland has provided asylum for the religiously and politically persecuted from many countries around the world. Our foreign population today of over 20% suggests our sustaining acceptance of others, even if the integration process often doesn't run smoothly. The situation as it is in our country unquestionably requires our openness toward the "other," an openness that in turn reflects our fascination with things foreign. Perhaps it was a fascination with the exotic cacao bean that contributed to the creative history of Swiss chocolate.

Wrap-Up: Chocolate and Swiss Identity

Who am I? What makes me different from others? What is special about me? These are central questions when it comes to identity. Identity is a product of the interaction between inside and outside, between "I" and "Thou." It emerges not only in my own self-image, but it must also be apprehended and affirmed by others. This is the case for any individual, and it applies likewise for the cultural identity of a nation and its people.

As I have observed, chocolate provides a universally human pleasure in delicious things. Yet the specifically Swiss experience of chocolate goes further, awakening associations to Switzerland's natural assets as well as to several virtues of Swiss character: abundant alpine meadows, healthy herds, and good milk; an entrepreneurial and mercantile spirit; the striving for excellence; reliability, flexibility, and openness to the world. This cluster of images adds up to what I have called the "chocolate complex" and a positively endowed symbol of Swiss identity. Our self-image is affirmed not only by world-wide trade figures, but also by the appreciation of many non-Swiss for our mountains, our watches, our Swiss army knife—and of course, our chocolate.

I suspect that because we Swiss are so strongly identified with our chocolate, we always feel a bit unfaithful and guilty when eating foreign confections. At any rate, my suggestion to this effect is regularly met with affirmative laughter! It all begins with the exotic cacao bean, the ancient "food of the gods." Doesn't this origin lend a mysterious "spice" to chocolate as a symbol of Swiss identity?

NOTES

1. Rossfeld Roman, *Schweizer Schokolade. Industrielle Produktion und kulturelle Konstruktion eines nationalen Symbols*, 1860-1920 (Baden: Hier und Jetzt, Verlag für Kultur und Geschichte, 2007), p. 11.

2. *Chocologie. Geschichte und Gegenwart der Schweizer Schokoladenindustrie*, ed. Verband Schweizerischer Schokolade fabrikanten (Bern: Chocosuisse, 2008), pp. 28-30.

3. *Ibid.*, p. 42.

4. Ernst Small, *Top 100 Food Plants: The World's Most Important Culinary Crops* (Ottowa, Ontario, Canada: NRC Press, 2009), p. 173.

5. Stephanie Lahrtz, "Schokolade: wie gesund ist sie wirklich?," *Neue Zürcher Zeitung*, December 23, 2009.

6. Richard Alleyne, "Red Wine and Chocolate Can Boost Your Brain Power," *The Telegraph* (6 May, 2011), at http://www.telegraph.co.uk/foodanddrink/8495528/Red-wine-and-chocolate-can-boost-your-brain-power.html (accessed 19 September, 2011).

7. Statistics from *Chocosuisse, Facts and Figures*, Association of Swiss Chocolate Manufacturers, at http://www.chocosuisse.ch/web/chocosuisse/en/home.html (accessed 19 September, 2011). The statics I cite here and elsewhere do not account for chocolate produced abroad by licensed subsidiaries using Swiss recipes. A precondition for use of

the "Swiss Chocolate" label is that the product is manufactured entirely in Switzerland.

8. Gabrielle Vail, "Cacao Use in Yucatan Among the Pre-Hispanic Maya," in *Chocolate: History, Culture and Heritage*, eds. Louis Evan Grivetti and Howard-Yana Shapiro (Hoboken, NJ: Wiley & Sons, 2009), pp. 3-4.

9. *Ibid.*, p. 3.

10. Deanna Pucciarelli, "Chocolate as Medicine: Imparting Dietary Advice and Moral Values Through 19th Century North American Cookbooks," in *Chocolate: History*, p. 119.

11. Rodney Snyder, Bradley Foliart Olsen and Laura Pallas Brindle, "From Stone Metates to Steel Mills," in *Chocolate: History*, p. 613.

12. Pucciarelli, "Chocolate as Medicine," p. 120.

13. *Chocologie. Geschichte und Gegenwart*, p. 8ff. See also Pucciarelli, "Chocolate as Medicine,“ p. 120.

14. Roman, *Schweizer Schokolade*, p. 462 ff.

15. *Chocosuisse, Facts and Figures*, Association of Swiss Chocolate Manufacturers.

16. See Verena Kast, *Dynamics of Symbols: Fundamentals of Jungian Psychotherapy*, trans. Susan A. Schwarz (Ontario: Fromm Int. Corp. Publ., 1992).

17. These and other questions related to my topic I have discussed with my friends, the Swiss chocolate producers Louise and Peter Gysi. I thank them sincerely for their information.

18. Small, *Top 100 Food Plants*, p. 174.

19. *Chocologie. Geschichte und Gegenwart*, p. 45.

20. Andrea Franc, *Wie die Schweiz zur Schokolade kam. Der Kakaohandel der Basler Handelsgesellschaft mit der Kolonie Goldküste*, 1893-1960 (Basel: Schwabe Verlag, 2008).

We Indians—Or, the Minor and the Major
An Attempt to Bring Across the Feeling of Being Swiss

GEORG KOHLER

Translation by Stacy Wirth and Dominique Rub

The Indians, that is to say, the Native Americans, never made it to India. However we Swiss did. We are to be found in an incredible number of places on this earth. And nearly always, that which is Swiss in the Swiss is unmistakable—even where Switzerland is not even a known name or place. Of course this resonance

Georg Kohler, Prof. em. Dr. phil., Lic. iur., was born in 1945 in the municipality of Konolfingen, in the Canton of Bern. He is currently Guest Professor at the Technische Universität Dresden. From 1994 to 2010 he held the Chair in Philosophy at the University of Zürich, where he focused especially on Political Philosophy. His own studies in philosophy, literature, and law were completed in Zürich and Basel. From 1984 to 1991 he was a member of the board of directors and publicist for a family firm in Vienna. From 1992 to 1994 he held the Chair as substitute Professor in Political Philosophy and Theory at the Geschwister-Scholl-Institut der Ludwig Maximilian Universität München. He authored, most recently, *Bürgertugend und Willensnation. Über den Gemeinsinn und über die Schweiz* (, 2010). He was co-editor of and contributor to the collections, *Expansion der Moderne* (Zürich, 2010), *Souveränität im Härtetest. Selbstbestimmung unter neuen Vorzeichen* (Zürich, 2010), and *Wozu Adorno? Beiträge zur Kritik und zum Fortbestand einer Schlüsseltheorie des 20. Jahrhundert* (Weilerswist, 2008). In May 2011 he spoke on Jung's *Red Book* at the Museum Rietberg in Zürich.

A version of this essay was previously published under the title, "Wir Indianer. Ein Versuch über das helvetische Lebensgefühl," in *Swiss, made: die Schweiz im Austausch mit der Welt*, ed. Beat Schläpfer (Zürich: Verlag Scheidegger & Spiess, 1998), © Georg Kohler. The current version is translated and reprinted by permission of the author.

can be registered only among those who are intimately familiar with Switzerland, like people who stem from the same tribe, or who have lived long with it.

In the spectrum of Swiss proclivities, the most readily discernable marker is the language. Overheard in passing—for instance in the Congolese capital of Kinshasa, or on Maylasia's Pangkor Island, or in Ipoh on the coast of Maylasia—we immediately register, "There goes one of us." And this we apprehend only for ourselves. After all, who can speak Hopi apart from the Hopi Indians and a few ethnologists? This Swiss-German that the linguists label as "only a dialect" is after all a language—meaning, an all-encompassing medium for the representation of reality, because the dialect binds poignantly to the world and to one another all who grow up with it. This is the case even for those of us Swiss (such as myself) who are raised in homes in which one parent or the other is not Swiss, and so we learn the so-called "high languages" as "mother-tongues."[1]

The image of the world—appearing in the medium of Swiss-German words such as *Buuch* (stomach), *Puur* (farmer), *Bünzli* (a square person), and *Bolizei* (police)—is in fact quite different from a world built upon Standard German expressions such as *Bauch* (stomach), *Bauer* (farmer), *Spiessbürger* (a square person), and *Polizei* (police). A German-speaking Swiss need compare this list of words only one, two, or three times to feel precisely the fundamental difference.[2]

However, that which is easy to feel is equally difficult to conceptualize.

Minor and Major

Basically we are confronted with the difference between "minor" and "major." The Swiss dialect orders us within the small, the graspable, and trusted as well as within the limited. It excludes the "higher" styles and manners of speaking and thinking that are held and developed by our potential audiences—those "major" players and speakers of standard languages. Yet our dialect also includes and conserves something essential: that central and binding feeling of otherness, the feeling we Swiss immediately develop upon our first contact with the world's major languages, and which from this moment onward accompanies and slightly irritates us throughout our lives.

To be Swiss means to be born into the dialectic of foreign broadness and our own definiteness. Out of this results a Swiss spawned urtension that disperses itself freely in many different ways. For instance: in the fanatically patriotic consciousness of being special; or in the melancholic "unease in the small State;" in the cool reduction of idealizations and grand aspirations to nameable utilitarian purposes. Or—and this is the most sovereign form—in the ability to combine both: being a member of the exclusive local elite with being a player on the greater world stages.

Friedrich Dürrenmatt is the exemplary exponent of the latter type: citizen of the village of Konolfingen and preeminent author of the twentieth century, imbued with his origin in the Protestant region of Emmental (which harbors on every second hill a tight-lipped apocalypticist).* Simultaneously Dürrenmatt is a universally comprehensible foreteller of those myths of humanity that resonate in every language. The otherwise so pertinent formulas for artistic productivity in our country—"discourse in the narrows," "outsider poets"—agree in no way with Dürrenmatt's work and its emotional sensitivity.[3] Although he was Swiss, Dürrenmatt's works were never handicapped by this. No Swiss asthma attacks impair his expression.

Dürrenmatt is the exception that confirms the rule that was aptly put by Albert Steffen, the Swiss author who is forgotten today outside of anthroposophical circles: "It is the peculiarity of the Swiss that, as soon as they speak Standard German, they assume somehow a preachy demeanor."** Steffen's truly extensive publications revolve unswervingly

* Eds.' note: Friedrich Dürrenmatt (1921-1990) is counted among the most influential writers of the twentieth century: "During the years of the cold war, arguably only Beckett, Camus, Sartre, and Brecht rivaled him as a presence in European letters. Yet outside Europe, this prolific author is primarily known for only one work, *The Visit*;" a three volume collection of his selected writings in English translation was published by the Chicago University Press in 2006.[5]

** Eds.' note: Albert Steffen (1884-1963) succeeded as the president of the Anthroposophical Society after the death of its founder, Rudolf Steiner. Prior to his engagement with the Society his poems, plays, and other writings had already displayed spiritual leanings. To our best knowledge his literary works are not widely translated in English. In 1937 *Life Magazine* reviewed his play, *The Peace Tragedy*,[6] which had just run in German in Basel and had been translated with a view toward a production the USA. Here Steffen is described as "the brilliant author" handling "one of the greatest themes in modern history:" the "titanic failure" of Woodrow Wilson, "the President of the nation that won the War, to impose on European politicians a just peace." It was further noted that, "Switzerland, neutral site of the League Nations, is one of the few places in Europe where such a play could today be shown." ("Woodrow Wilson Walks a Swiss Stage," in *Life Magazine*, Vol. 2, No. 5 [Chicago: Time Inc., February 1, 1937], p. 52.)

and touchingly around the anti-modern theme, "how humanity can overcome evil." Steffen is indeed the paradigm of the Swiss as "'the good provincial man.'"[4] The latter epithet appears in an essay in which Steffen tries to distinguish the Swiss spirit from the German, and he means it absolutely self-critically.

It would be nothing but the mark of personal narrow-mindedness to fail to recognize the formidable rank that may be claimed by Steffen, this poet of healing. But the friendly, all-too-ready-to-trust, odd harmlessness of his lifelong humanitarian endeavor bespeaks after all a basic feature of the Helvetic disposition: our seeming aloofness from the rest of the world, arising from our decision not to suffer it. I refer to the belief of those of us who have been shielded for centuries from war and radical catastrophe that, in the end, the predominance of the bad will be subverted always. Or to express it in terms of existential smugness: in the end it won't be all that bad (at least if one remains in Switzerland).

This reign of the good is the biased predisposition of Helvetic collective consciousness, the effect of which should not be underestimated. For as much as it is the basis of our virtue, it is as well the barely shakable origin of our essential conceit. As Swiss, we are disinclined to alarmism. Thus we deal in a rather panic-free and non-hysterical manner with the problems of the super-artificial and ever disturbance-prone machine of civilization. Correspondingly, our democracy works with a secure sense for factual issues, without being too heavy on rhetoric. We may also hope that the earth is not the dungeon of soul that the Gnostics hold it to be. It may be not last for this reason that most of our culture's preeminent figures are, at the core, healers and harbingers of potential confidence. (I am thinking now of those who did not emigrate, that is, men such as Johann Heinrich Pestalozzi, C.G. Jung, or Karl Barth).[7]

Yet it must be said: Our fundamental belief in the world's habitability—at least as it has developed in these alpine environs—promotes at the same time our tendency to this dull immobility, defensive encapsulation, and the holier-than-thou attitude that nothing can happen to us anyway, so it would be best to not even begin to venture into anything new. Such are the phantasms ensuring that we become a nation of know-it-alls, where the upper hand remains with those who promise to preserve the status quo.

Admittedly, our clinging to the status quo has been the unchanged case for a very long time. However, it has become increasingly difficult to maintain the correctness of this position. Under pressure from the outer world, the reality that has been long overdue begins to appear as common sense: Switzerland must re-define itself, define itself anew, because the pre-conditions for our old self-image are dying away. The erosion of our grand historical fundaments has been repressed for an excessively long time. Thus, we fail to recall Switzerland's entanglement in the East/West antagonisms of the Cold War—and we forget that in today's geopolitical situation the essence of Swiss neutrality no longer goes unquestioned. Between 1945 and 1990 the old conditions guarded Switzerland from the necessity of fundamental self-analysis. We have been led to recognize—albeit late, perhaps too late—that the world and those nations competing for the advantages of Switzerland's place in it are no longer prepared to concede all that we have held to be our inalienable rights.

The current altercations around our federal banking secrecy provide only the most glaring example. Helvetic tax law rulings, too, are under attack by the United States, and even by the European Union, whose supranational courts now interpret the laws in ways that no longer comply with favored Swiss practice. It is therefore high time to bid farewell to self-delusion. Which, in principle, should not be all too difficult. For in the meantime, a large part of our own population has grown suspicious of Switzerland's image as the Shangri-La of the Alps. It may be bitter and upsetting for many. Yet at the same time—and of this I am convinced—the unavoidable conflicts related to this country's future and self-definition also make visible the vitality of political Switzerland. Since the nineteenth century Switzerland has conceived itself as the *Willensnation*—the "nation created by its own will" and a project anchored in the civic determination of the people. Over and over again the country has renewed itself in conflicts over its myths, and need do so again in a world that has become too tightly networked and too well informed to put up with our Helvetic schizophrenias and rogue shenanigans.

Willensnation—The Nation Created by Its Own Will

The cockiness of the sheltered ones, Dürrenmatt's paramount literary gesture, those suffering the small country, the observers of world history (Jakob Burckhardt![8]), the partisans of democratic autarky, the sad knights of banking secrecy, and so on. As already mentioned, the fundamental Helvetic tension translates into many variations. We remain with the problem of bringing into structured consciousness the reconciliation of our patent narrowness with a super-sized environment. Despite all differences among us, the common factor is the obligation to measure ourselves in proportion to that which we are not, and to deal with the fact that the Other is incommensurably larger. The mastery of a narcissistic wound belongs inevitably to the self-definition of the Swiss. This explains, for one, the curiously neurotic but astonishingly widespread mentality that preposterously rejects all forms of Switzerland's joining into politico-international solidarity and commitments of cooperation. What we see here is the conversion of an imagined offense into obstinate pride: "We might be small, but of this we have made something unique, something the rest of you could never do!"

The unavoidable experience of being small ties in with our remarkably dexterous and sober juggling of the false ideals of nationalism, power, and historical mission—a modus that characterizes some of our nation's rituals. Those who have learned that they belong to a tiny tribe a priori do not mistake themselves as important subjects in matters of world-wide historical impact with significant meaning for humanity. Such disillusionment, on the other hand, opens our sensibility for those lesser values and payable demands that belong to global trade and international financial management. The Swiss penchant for bargaining and money is legendary.

"*Pas d'argent, pas de Suisses*"—"No money, no Swiss," the foreign kings of old were constantly reminded. Their Swiss subjects on the other hand found themselves confirmed by the saying in two ways: in their good conscience of having sealed contracts that avoided the betrayal of their democratic honor, and in their cozy sentience of having sold themselves at a sufficiently dear price.[9] Anon one is again in the midst of the wasp's nest of ambivalence, owing to the Helvetic ur-dialectic of minor and major. We definitely know that we ("we as Swiss") are rich by all comparative socio-economic standards. We are small, *but rich.* At the same time we try to hide this fact because we are all too precisely familiar with the risks of envy and capital accumulation. Thus we are also rich, *but small.*

Admittedly this assertion no longer goes undisputed. The capitalism unleashed after the world economic crisis of 1989 demonstrated at least twice in the first decade of the new millennium that the Swiss elites in charge are no less immune to hubris and megalomania than are Wall Street's investment bankers or Russia's oligarchs. Hair-raising examples materialized in the 2002 collapse of the seemingly invulnerable airline Swissair—and later, in the grandiose bust of the mighty Union Bank of Switzerland (UBS), which had hedged its bets on its very embodiment of the image of reliable Swissness.

The latter events notwithstanding, a general characteristic of being Swiss is reputed to involve the paradox of a high measure of caution and combined with a flair for risk-taking. For this reason our chiefs of interest rates and profit rarely find their way to life's enjoyments and pleasures, not to mention its excessive delights. Instead their bearing is permeated by a subcutaneous dynamic of disquiet, despite or due to the belief that the worst can be avoided. One should do something—there is always something to be done—the deficit of smallness demands it. So seen, it is nothing but consistent when we hold our country—*Confoederatio Helvetica*—not as a gift of nature, but as a labor of intent. We are, after all, the very *Willensnation*—the nation that is most certainly the product of will and the preeminent fruit of our collective energies.

The Rawest Nerve

With this we stray again to contemporary Switzerland's rawest nerve. To that spot where contradictions become taut and the debates hot—and where we are no longer aided by resort to the old, reliable knacks and mediation methods. Because today, in nearly half the population, our constitutional Swiss self-doubt has become fused with an equally deep-rooted inclination to cling to the status quo. For still too many of us, the *Willensnation* serves to entrench frozen forms of communication and action, and its clannish thinking provides reliable guarantee against any sort of fundamental change.

Change is now more necessary than ever. Because, as outlined, over the last twenty years ago a fundamental shift has occurred in the dialectic between our smallness and the Great Ones in the rest of the world. And this has transpired in all areas that are relevant to the continuance of the *Willensnation*. International competition for the privilege of place exposes Switzerland to a political-economic contest that wears and tears at nearly all advantages that were long taken for granted. This cannot be overlooked—one can read about it almost daily. Our democratic structures are groaning under the urgent need for rapid decisions, while the very same structures obstruct far-reaching reform.

In other words: We have witnessed the collapse of the complex value system that reliably buttressed our tribal behavior. It is the falling apart of that basic principle of consensus that for over a half a century efficiently regulated the Helvetic dialectic and its various syntheses. This it did by coordinating the heterogeneity of the many social groups, political clans, hordes of friends, kith and kin, clubs of influence, and local scenes (all of which of course belong to the small tribe). "Disorientation on the basis of dwindling reserves" is therefore the most apt diagnosis for the spiritual state and current mood of the natives of the alpine environs.

How does one escape this critical condition? Where does one find new points of anchor that can provide new self-confidence for Switzerland and its capacities? To pose the questions is to recognize their difficulty. Because in the answers one readily wants to give lies also the core of the problem. Why?

Switzerland as a nation is determined neither by its geography nor by one dominant culture. Rather it is comprised of three to four cultural groups, each with its own distinct language and dialect—none of which are able to radiate large power beyond their immediate regions of influence.[10] Swiss unity, on the other hand, owes itself to a history dominated by the strivings of these dialect groups to *not* belong to their larger cultures of origin (the German, the French, the Italian, the Rhaeto-Romansh). It was this shared negativity that originally sparked the positive impulse to an independent, self-determined national existence. Switzerland's common and binding ground thus amounts to little more than the shared republican statehood that allows us to be small, but still something special. And this is precisely the core of the problem: For some of us this State is nothing more than a burdensome necessity. For others it is the sanctum of time-honored principles that under no circumstances may be re-written. For all, it is threatened in the time of globalized economy.

Switzerland as a "Willensnation"— a nation created by its own will—depends always on the will of its citizens to have their own country. Without the active affirmation and democratic participation of the people who call themselves Swiss, Switzerland cannot long exist as a political unity. It may be that the meaning of such elementary conditions has become lost to some of us. And without doubt, in the course of the last years, the definition of "being Swiss" has become questionable to many of us. Switzerland is a very special nation because its unity, despite its centuries-old existence, is all other than taken as a matter of course.

And yet I remain confident. At least, for the next hundred years. It is a special thing, to be an "alpine Indian."

NOTES

1. From the standpoint of language, the Swiss tribe is known to be diverse. My concern here is limited to the Alemannic, i.e., the Germanic sub-tribe. *Swissness* however is not be identified alone with that which is *Swiss German*. That we in German Switzerland do this nevertheless is the not-so-secret suspicion of our French Swiss compatriots living beyond the Saane River. They are not unjustified, for the claim does indeed exist, so to speak, unconsciously. I myself provide testimony: My comparing of Swiss German and Standard German enlightens an especially conspicuous contrast that is not shared in the same degree by our other native dialects in relationship to their high languages. I hope that my comparison will not be taken as an expression of Alemannic arrogance, but rather as a symptom par excellence of being Swiss German—indeed of being Swiss, and sharing with all of my compatriots this basic feeling of belonging to very small, very different clans.

2. How, for heaven's sake, shall we translate into French or Italian—i.e., to our other national languages—the apprehension of life's most

diverse experiences as mediated through dialects? I have no idea, and hope for the help of experts. Yet my compatriotism disinclines me to eliminate this passage. For it demonstrates *in actu* the complex challenge that we Swiss face in the effort to hold together, even nominally at the level of language. We require constantly an "endnote system" to keep one another abreast of and identified with our tribal particularities.

3. Eds.' note: With "discourse in the narrows" ("*Diskurs in der Enge*") and "outsider poets" ("*Dichter im Abseits*") the author paraphrases titles by the Swiss writers Paul Nizon and Dieter Fringeli respectively, who deal with the phenomenon of the Swiss literary outsider. For more on this topic in English see for example, Jonathan Steinberg, "Chapter 4: Language," in *Why Switzerland?* 2nd ed., reprinted (Cambridge: Cambridge University Press, 2003).

4. Albert Steffen, quoted in Dieter Fringeli, "Der therapeutischen Dichter Albert Steffen," in *Dichter im Abseits. Schweizer Autoren von Glauser bis Hohl* (Zürich: Artemis Verlag, 1974), pp. 49-63.

5. For his works in English, see Friedrich Dürrenmatt, *Volume 1: Plays, Volume 2: Fictions, Volume 3: Essays, in Selected Writings of Friedrich Dürrenmatt*, trans. Joel Agee (Chicago: The University of Chicago Press Books, 2006).

6. Albert Steffen, *Peace (The) Tragedy*, a play in five acts, trans. Margaret Lloyd, © January 1937, D47167, 522 in *Catalogue of Copyright Entries*, Part 1, Group 3, Dramatic Compositions, Motion Pictures, New Series, Vol. 10, No. 1 (Washington, D.C.: Library of Congress Copyright Office, 1937), p. 21.

7. Eds.' note: The Zürich-born Johann Heinrich Pestalozzi (1746-1847) founded a liberal, psychologically oriented system of education for primary school, focused on the child's inner dignity, innate spontaneity, and propensity for self discovery. Karl Barth (1886-1968), raised in the Swiss capital of Bern, is the Protestant theologian and professor known world-wide for his rejection of liberal church dogma. Among his essential contributions was a critical understanding of beliefs that had made the Church vulnerable to and accepting of Nazism.

8. Eds.' note: Jacob Burkhardt (1818-1897) was the Swiss historian of art and culture who is credited with being a major contributor to the original discipline of cultural history. His best known work, originally published in 1860, is *The Civilization of the Renaissance*

in Italy, trans. S.G.C. Middlemore, 1878 (Teddington, Middlesex: The Echo Library, 2006).

9. From historical distance it appears that the murky view, "no money, no Swiss," refers as well to payments made for the recruitment of farmers' sons into mercenary army service during the Late Middle Ages and Renaissance. The only choice was between poverty and the misery of the mercenary soldier. Even under later conditions of democracy, such circumstances prevailed, i.e., until the epoch of revolution, beginning around 1800. However the unmistakable contentment to cite "no money" remained characteristic irrespective of the time and conditions, and thus expresses the Swiss penchant to bargain and strike deals.

10. There can be no Swiss literature, as there is for instance German literature, philosophy, music, and so on—but merely contributions from Switzerland to the respective "high" cultures. In this sense it is always askew to contrast "Swiss" and "German" cultural production. The two benchmarks lie at completely different levels. The difference can be discerned in the example of assimilation: The larger cultures, such as the German, English, and French, continuously produce authors whose origins are in other cultures and languages; one thinks for instance of Joseph Conrad, E.N. Cioran, V. Nabokov, Paul Celan. For Switzerland such assimilation is out of the question. Although foreign authors do sometimes reside here or even take up citizenship (Thomas Mann, Herman Hesse, Patricia Highsmith, and again Nabokov), no matter how long they remain they will never become representatives of Swiss literature.

The Cultural Unconscious in French-Speaking Switzerland: the Legacy of Calvin

Yvonne Kocher

Translation by Barbara Whitaker and Kristina Schellinski

Cultural Unconscious, Cultural Complex, and Identity

The concepts of the cultural unconscious and the cultural complex were developed by the American Jungians Joseph Henderson,[1] Thomas Singer, and Samuel Kimbles.[2] Henderson notes,

> [t]he cultural unconscious, in the sense I use it, is an area of historical memory that lies between the collective unconscious

Yvonne Kocher, lic.psych., was born in Frauenfeld near Zürich; she wasraised as a Protestant in La Chaux-de-Fonds, a city in the French Swiss Canton of Neuchâtel. She holds a degree in psychology from the University of Geneva, and a diploma from the C.G. Jung Institute, Zürich, Küsnacht. She worked for fifteen years as a clinical psychologist and psychotherapist at the Institutions Universitaires de Geriatrics at the University of Geneva. She conducts private practice as an analytical psychologist in Geneva, and as well, in Lutry (Lausanne). She is a training analyst of the C.G. Jung Institute in Zürich and a lecturer at the "Antenne romande", a branch of the Institute that offers lectures in French Lausanne and Geneva.

> and the manifest pattern of culture. It may include both these modalities, conscious and unconscious, but it has some kind of identity arising from the archetypes of the collective unconscious, which assists in the formation of myth and ritual and also promotes the process of development in individuals.[3]

In 1963 the Austrian ethologist Konrad Lorenz extended his own study of ritual behavior in animals to humans, observing that we, like animals, tend to inhibit aggression for the sake of assuring group cohesion.[4] Lorenz further noted that we humans achieve this inhibition/cohesion by transmitting values through ritual and other codified behavior, such as customs and manners.

Transmitted values form the basis of our cultural identity and ways of understanding the world. That is, we are formed psychologically by the culture that has surrounded us since birth, and of which we are only partially conscious. Becoming more conscious of these fundamental values may hopefully enhance our self-knowledge and promote an acceptance of our neighbors' cultural differences, be they near or far away.

However, insofar as we experience the transmission of these values emotionally and rather unconsciously, we grow quietly in the conviction that our values alone are the true and eternal ones. Those who deviate are met with aggression and exclusion. Thus differences between groups are the origin of incomprehension, mistrust, mockery, devaluation—and can even lead to hatred and fanatical wars. Accordingly, group differences are the basis of cultural complexes that cause misunderstandings between the German- and French-speaking Swiss—and that express themselves in the mockery visible in stereotypes that the French-speaking Swiss project upon the German-speaking Swiss, and vice versa. For example, the French Swiss are prone to view the German Swiss as compulsive workers—while the German Swiss tend to view the French Swiss as being superficial and lacking a sense of responsibility.

Swiss Romandy and Cultural Identity

Let us begin to explore French-speaking Switzerland, which is commonly known in this country as *Suisse Romande*, or Swiss Romandy. The region is comprised of the six cantons of Geneva, Neuchâtel, Vaud,

Jura, Valais, and Fribourg. We inherit these names from the Romans, who colonized the Helvetic Celts—the Celts themselves being among the tribes that settled in the region, beginning in the first century B.C. After the fall of the Roman Empire the Alemanni, a Germanic tribe, settled in the east up to the River Sarine, amidst the ruins of the French-Roman cities. The west was settled by the Burgundians, who spoke Roman, a Latin-derived language. Therefore, the River Sarine, flowing not far from Fribourg, forms the geographical divide between the German- and French-speaking cultures of this area.

Now, when I ask those close to me about their identities as French-speaking Swiss, they answer: Above all I feel I am a *Genevois*, or a *Vaudois*, or a *Neuchâchtelois*, or a *Fribourgois*, or a *Valaisan*. In other words, the identities of individuals in Swiss Romandy are rooted in their own cantons. At the same time, however, all six of the cantons in Romandy are francophone, meaning not only that their citizens are French-speaking, but also that they feel culturally attached to France. Despite their common underpinnings, each of the six French-speaking cantons has its own history, mindset, and customs. The citizens in turn express themselves in ways that are unique to each canton—for example, in accents, turns of phrase, and vocabulary. The literary author Denis de Rougemont goes so far as to say that,

> [i]n a very complex interaction of allegiances and loyalties, [one's own] canton represents the fatherland, in the most classical (and most romantic) sense of the word.[5]

Without doubt: there are six different ways of feeling and being a French-speaking Swiss. Yet it is remarkable that, when I asked those around me about their feelings of identity, none of them mentioned their common background of Christianity—much less did they mention the Catholicism or Protestantism that so permeates the history and culture of Romandy. This omission can be taken as a basic clue about the cultural unconscious in the region.

Consciously speaking, my own cultural identity is rooted in the Canton of Neuchâtel, more precisely in the Jura Mountains that form the canton's upper region and austere landscape of pine trees and pastures. Today, Neuchâtel is the home to a working class devoted to the watch industry and precision mechanics. It is the region of my paternal lineage and childhood; here I went to school, formed my first friendships, and married—and this is where I felt at home! A difference in attitude can be detected between the citizens living in the upper part of the canton and those living in the lower part, in the *city* of Neuchâtel. The difference reflects the diverging interests of a socialist working class versus an intellectual elite—an elite, which in the case of the city of Neuchâtel, descends from aristocratic French Protestants who received asylum here during the Reformation in the sixteenth century.

Toward the Cultural Unconscious

In mentioning the Reformation I allude to the thread that will run through the rest of my essay, namely that the Protestant Reformation of the sixteenth century emerges as an essential component of the cultural unconscious in Romandy—and this, despite the fact that three of our six cantons are predominantly Roman Catholic. My focus will be on Romandy's opening to Protestantism, and particularly to the Calvinist branch, which fundamentally influenced secular life and thus transformed the Romand culture as whole.

To better follow this idea, it should be helpful to clarify from the start that Christianity is the religion of Switzerland's majority; of this majority today, roughly half are Roman Catholic and half Protestant. I wish to clarify also that throughout, I will be using interchangeably such terms as "Protestant" and "Protestant Church," and "Reformist" and "Reformed Church." Although these terms could refer to the variety of Protestants and Protestant Churches that evolved over time, here they refer primarily to the Protestantism that materialized directly out of the Reformation, and again, especially Calvinism.[6]

Against the background of the Reformation is a history in which Catholicism had become entrenched as the de facto religion of the land—and this, resulting from the spreading of Christianity throughout Europe beginning with the rule of the Roman Empire. The Catholic dominance, thus asserted long before there was even a notion of "Switzerland," prevailed until the sixteenth century, when it was deposed by the Protestant Reformation. The Reformation was far from being a gentle process. Writing about it in Switzerland specifically, the American Jungian analyst Murray Stein emphasizes that,

> [t]he Protestant spirit was not ever a tolerant one. It draws sharp, hard lines and distinctions. In its heyday, it was famous for persecuting and banning heretics. The Catholic Counterreformation with its grand inquisitors mimicked this style and perhaps even took it a step or two further.[7]

In Switzerland (as in the rest of Europe) the benefits of the Reformation came at the steep price of battle and destruction, leaving a long legacy of conflict between Protestants and Catholics, examples of which will be given in later pages.

My studies at the Jung Institute in Zürich awakened my interest in the history of religion, and since then I have tried to understand the religious tendencies in different human groups, and among them, my own. After many detours, I stumbled upon a book by the theologian Bernard Reymond, the title of which translates roughly to, *The Protestant Religion in French-speaking Switzerland.*[8] This book deals with the Calvinist Protestant faith in which I was raised—and from which I believed I had distanced myself long ago. But as I discovered, the Protestant values described in this book are exactly the ones that continue to orient me today!

Hindsight suggests that it was my reading of Reymond's book that led me to the threshold of the cultural unconscious. For I suddenly realized (stupefied by my own naiveté) that the *secular* Zeitgeist reigning in my native canton, Neuchâtel, bespeaks a set of religious values that do indeed form the foundation of my identity. Transmitted by my Protestant family, my school, my catechism classes, the scouts, songs, and local customs, these values have determined a number of my character traits, my behavior, and my choices in life.

In line with what Joseph Henderson calls "the cultural unconscious," Calvinist Protestantism reveals itself to be the underpinning of the spirit and culture of modern Romandy. To paraphrase Bernard Reymond, in French-speaking Switzerland Protestantism is above all a social fact, a way of life rather than a strictly religious movement.[9] From the sketch artist Rodolphe Töpffer[10] to the previously mentioned Denis de Rougemont, from the Blue Cross to the Red Cross, from the mountain chalets to the banks—the Reformist spirit is alive, and the French-speaking Swiss encounter it every day. Protestantism in Romandy is, in Reymond's sense, a "civilization,"

> . . . a certain spirit, a mindset which is shared in a region, by all members of a human group. But it is also very concrete achievements, such as the standard of living, economy, industry, art and culture.[11]

In the course of the sixteenth century three of the six cantons that now comprise Romandy entered into this "civilization" by adopting the doctrines of the Reformation, thus contributing to what would become the Reformed Church and the reformed cantons, Geneva, Neuchâtel, and Vaud. The other three cantons—Jura, Valais, and Fribourg—remained loyal to the Roman Catholic Church. The three reformed cantons are therefore bound together not only in their faith per se—but also in their shared history of reform, which imbues all of Romandy with a particular character.

Ulrich Zwingli, a Swiss theologian who subscribed to Martin Luther's teachings in 1523, promoted the Reformation in German-speaking Switzerland.[12] Guillaume Farel, a Frenchman living in Neuchâtel, introduced the Reformation to Romandy. To advance the cause in Geneva, Farel recruited a fellow Frenchman, Jean Calvin, who was a theologian and lawyer. Some years later the two were joined by Pierre Viret, a native of Canton Vaud who preached mainly in Lausanne. Loyal to the *spirit* of Luther's Reformation, these three men held the common goal of reforming the Roman Catholic Church.

In Swiss Romandy Reformist values took root in a Latin civilization and were fertilized by Calvin's powerfully persuasive personality and ideas. Calvin eventually departed from Luther and Zwingli to develop his own theology. In doing so he influenced the whole European Reformation, notably with his major work, *Institutes of the Christian Religion*.[13] This scholastic monument sent major waves throughout the reforming world, as it articulated the ideas of the Reformation in lucid, comprehensible French. Moreover Calvin was a talented polemic speaker who made a great impression on his audience—particularly when preaching from the height of his pulpit at the St. Pierre Cathedral in Geneva.

Calvin presided over his flock with an iron hand, buttressed by the doctrines of the Reformed faith. An exemplary man of serious disposition, Calvin was honest, upright, modest, and frugal. History remembers him for his suffocating control of the faith and morals of the people of Geneva. From Calvin's point of view, it was only by the genuine labor of reformed Christian education that the entire city could be governed by the fear of God.[14] With the exception of two years, Calvin reigned over Geneva with undisputed authority—from 1536 until his death in 1564—making of this city the "Protestant Rome." Still today, Geneva is often called the "City of Calvin."

Crucially, the Reformation introduced the freedom of religious choice between Catholicism and Protestantism. Protestantism in turn transformed society by engendering changes in the collective mentality and life style, and by stimulating cultural and economic development.[15] Among the influences in this transformation were the many Italian and French refugees who fled religious persecution in their home countries to gain asylum in the three reformed cantons of Romandy. In particular there were the previously mentioned French Protestants, some eight thousand of whom found asylum here between 1549 and 1587. They imported an elite culture and knowledge that contributed specifically to the expansion of banking and the establishment of new craft industries. Especially notable was their contribution of expertise in watch making, which took root in Geneva and in parts of the Jura Mountains located in the Cantons of Neuchâtel and Vaud.

Under the influence of the Protestant virtues of work and social responsibility, the reformed cantons grew rapidly richer. The Catholic cantons on the other hand—Fribourg, Valais, and Jura—remained more traditional and poorer. Some Catholics gradually emigrated to the reformed cantons, where they found better work and pay. While the Catholics soon became the majority, they nevertheless came under the sway of Reformist values. Since the mid-twentieth century the influx of Italian, Spanish, and Portuguese workers has again changed the proportion of Catholics and Protestants, yet the spirit of the Reformation remains present to this day.

Calvinism: Remaining Inner Values

Along with many people of Romandy, I have shared in the understanding of Calvin as an original Reformist who especially embodied the austere and intolerant theologian. However as said, my readings led me to the startling discovery that surviving Calvin himself is the legacy of a far more nuanced and widely influential *Calvinism.* My perception of this Calvinism began to emerge as I encountered it in the works of a number of well known Protestant Romand authors, as well as in commentary about them. This was particularly the case as I read articles published in conjunction with the "Year of Calvin" in 2009—an event that was celebrated despite the fact that Protestant institutions are in crisis, the churches are quite empty, and the details of Calvin's life and enduring impact are little known.[16]

In my readings I was unable discover an exhaustive list of our consciously or unconsciously inherited Calvinist values. Therefore I took note of scattered sources, gradually recognizing in these a self-evident set of values that have influenced my own world-view and behavior since childhood. To discover the original source, I turned to the abbreviated version of Calvin's *Institutes of the Christian Religion.*[17] This leads me to posit the following list of nuanced Calvinist virtues that lie behind and shape our Romand identity and customs:

Freedom and Individual Responsibility: The sense of freedom and individual responsibility that we in Romandy now take for granted originated in the Reformation, when Protestants—including the ministers—found themselves free to individually seek direct communion with God, and answerable to no other authority than God's alone. And, it was taught, people are free to seek God not in dogma or even at church, but to take individual responsibility for doing so by reading the Bible and striving to embody the Absolute in their day-to-day activities.

Purity and Perfection: Insofar as we now feel governed by the necessity to pursue perfection, we consciously or unconsciously embrace the Reformist virtue of moral purity in thought, word, and deed.

Work: Within our modern Romand work ethic lies the Reformist conviction that work is sacred and done for the glory of God rather than for personal merit. We remain convinced, at some level, that to be out of work is to live in exile from the community. We still frown on displays of idleness and extravagance, considering these to express contempt for work. Moreover we revere the sense of duty as such, placing this ahead of personal pleasure. At the same time, we retain the Reformist belief that prosperity results not from one's labor and other personal efforts; we attribute our prosperity instead to divine grace.

Education: Our modern valuing of education is rooted in the Reformist history that deemed the ability to read the Bible to be necessary for each and every individual. Indeed, according to Calvin, education and knowledge alone were capable of lifting us out of obscurantism and superstition—particularly Catholic superstition. Therefore he made schooling obligatory for all, and founded the Collège de Genève and the Academy, which later became the University of Geneva. Lausanne and Neuchâtel followed suit, founding universities of their own. It comes as little surprise that, in the course of history, a number of Protestant Romands developed new educational models, which have moved far beyond Swiss borders. We think, for instance, of Jean-Jacques Rousseau, Henri Pestalozzi, Valérie de Gaspérin, Jean Piaget, Edouard Claparède, and Jacques Dalcroze.

Social Justice: In Romandy today the sense of social justice is manifest in many ways, including equal access to education and health care for all citizens, and in the integration of our weakest members into the community. This notion of equality stems, on one hand, from the Reformist rejection of the Roman Catholic hierarchy for the conviction that we are all equal before God—and, on the other hand, from the Reformist encouragement to act according to individual conscience. Our recognition of social justice makes it our duty to share our earned wages with those less privileged than ourselves. When we behave with such conscience we are, consciously or unconsciously, in accord with the Reformed belief that prosperity results not from personal achievement, but from divine favor.

Austerity, Frugality, Modesty: In line with original Reformist belief we still hold the latter self-sacrificing modes to be virtues, while frowning upon those who indulge in luxury and ostentation. (Still today, partying spirits in Romandy are looked upon as frivolous and violating of Protestant virtue.)

Public Well-Being: The Reformist ideal of public well-being is discernable in our modern civic-mindedness and devotion to community service. Indeed this ideal motivates the careers of many of Romandy's politicians, who often campaign with reference to their Protestant affiliations; a number of them hold positions of responsibility in the Protestant Church before entering politics.

Tolerance: The *ideal* of tolerance that now prevails in Romandy is beautifully expressed in the words of Jean-Jacques Rousseau, the eighteenth century philosopher from Geneva:

> The Protestant faith is tolerant out of principle, it is essentially tolerant; it is as tolerant as it can be since the only dogma it does not tolerate is intolerance.[18]

Rousseau's writing, on one hand, reflects his own conversion from Catholicism. On the other hand, it contains the liberating spirit of the French Revolution, which led him to subversively campaign for freedom of religion for all faiths—not just for the Protestant and Catholic. Rousseau in this sense took part in a continuously evolving Protestantism. For example during the early seventeenth century, the reformed cantons in Romandy had already begun to tolerate, within limits, Catholicism and other Protestant denominations such as the Lutheran. However this "tolerance" had come under the proviso that the visible signs of such faiths remain abolished—for instance, the steeples of Catholic churches. Nevertheless the Reformed Church continued to disdain and disparage those they felt were on the wrong path—notably the Catholics, and the Protestant Anabaptists, Amish, and Mennonites, many of whom fled in the early eighteenth century, for example to Pennsylvania in North America. All the while, Reformist missionary activity undertook to convince others that the only true faith was in the Reformed Church.

In 1847 the Canton of Geneva granted freedom of religion for all faiths. In conjunction with this development a Jewish synagogue was soon built, as well as a variety of Christian churches, including Roman Catholic, Anglican, and Russian Orthodox. In today's Romandy, Reformist conversion tactics have disappeared, and religious tolerance has grown considerably. Remarkably, unlike the vast majority of Swiss, those in the three Protestant Romand cantons voted against the referendum on a ban on minarets in 2009. In Geneva the Protestants went so far as to publicly proclaim solidarity with the Muslim community.[19]

Introspection and Conscience The Romands' collective penchant for introspection and self-reflection stems from Calvin's own urging. His book, *Institutes,* begins with an avowal of the link between knowledge-of-God and self-knowledge. Calvin's example lies behind our seeking of self-knowledge today, when we strive to gain wider consciousness, for instance of our ignorance and vanity, and our spiritual poverty, weakness, and corruption.[20] This is the case even when we set out in search of truth via more personal routes, such as when undertaking Jungian analysis.

Numerous writers, from Jean-Jacques Rousseau to Jacques Chessex in the twentieth century, have granted a special place to introspection in their works. However none come close to Jean-Frédéric Amiel, whose diary of more than 16,000 pages was discovered when he died in 1881, and published in its entirety.[21] This erstwhile professor of philosophy at the Academy of Geneva lent his name to the "Amiel complex"—which designates those who strive for self-completion by introspection and journal-writing instead of living their lives!

Guilt: Our neglect to observe the foregoing ideals often evokes guilt and the feeling that we can never live up to standards, we can never be good enough. Guilt seems to be a burden shouldered by every member of the Reformed Church; we cannot aspire toward God, said Calvin, without first despising ourselves. These Protestants find salvation by the grace of God—but what about the secular among us? Etienne Barilier explains,

> [f]or the faithful overwhelmed by his sin, grace must intercede and overflow. But in a secularized society like ours, there is no longer a way out. What remains, is to delight in one's own self loathing![22]

The foregoing virtues—and my list is not exhaustive—have been with us since the sixteenth century, and remain as conscious or unconscious values and ideals. They characterize our Romand identity and behavior as well as the shadow that comes with it. In other words, when exaggerated or rigidly observed, Calvinistic virtues can transmogrify into their dark opposites. Indeed, to call someone a Calvinist today is not a compliment: it connotes a person who is narrow-minded, unforgiving, rigid, moralizing, stingy, inhibited, joyless.

Romand Protestantism: Contributions to Culture

We owe the current face of Swiss Romandy to a number of well-known citizens who, rooted in Protestantism, have also contributed to the cultural identity of Switzerland at large: the theologians, of course, and the previously mentioned educators, but also writers, philosophers, artists, and musicians who have been pioneers in their fields. Many of these descend from prominent Protestant families, especially in Neuchâtel and Geneva, and are still part of the intellectual, industrial, and commercial elite.

This is not the place to name all the outstanding or endearing personalities I discovered during my research. However, I am compelled to name two, who—in exemplary manner—helped to build our humanitarian culture characterized by virtues of compassion, charity, civic-mindedness, and neutrality: Valérie de Gasparin[23] and Henry Dunant,[24] both born to prominent Geneva families with roots in the Reformation. Before looking more closely at their contributions, let us consider the background of another historical influence: the nineteenth century Revival that originated in England and affected Protestantism throughout Europe.

Aspiring to awaken a dormant but "true faith," the Revival encouraged a diligent yet uncritical reading of the Bible—and it insisted on the necessity of active personal engagement. It thus inspired many personal initiatives marked by a blend of piety and social activism. A prime example is Valérie de Gasparin, a talented writer and musician, who devoted her life to this Revival movement. She authored many educational books and spent her fortune building schools, thermal baths at Yverdon for the poor, and the world's first secular nursing school, La Source, in Lausanne. She had already published newspaper articles denouncing the suffering of soldiers in the Crimean War when Henri Dunant requested her assistance in his own cause.

In 1859 Dunant was on business in Solferino (now in Italy) when one of the bloodiest battles in history took place, between France and Austria. Dunant thereupon became convinced of the need to create an organization that would care for all wounded soldiers, regardless of their allegiances. Upon his return to Switzerland he wrote *A Memory of Solferino*, which was widely distributed throughout Europe.[25] This little book in turn became the basis for the founding of the International Red Cross in 1863—and for his role as a founder, Dunant received the first Nobel Peace Prize in history, awarded in 1901.

Entering the Shadow: Jacques Chessex

We have already touched on aspects of the shadow that may lurk within the Protestant ideal: narrow-mindedness, unforgivingness, rigidity, moral self-righteousness, stinginess, inhibition, and joylessness. Among the preeminent modern Swiss Romand authors who proclaim their Protestantism and acknowledge its shadow is the previously mentioned Jacques Chessex. Internationally renowned in his lifetime, Chessex explored, among other things, the shadow cast by the Protestant virtues.[26] Chessex received several literary prizes, among them the *Prix Goncourt* in 1973. His final book, *Le dernier Crâne de M. Sade*,[27] translated roughly, *The Last Skull of M. Sade*, was published posthumously and received much publicity in 2010—as did his death in October 2009. As an introspective and extremely cultivated man, Chessex was well aware of his cultural legacy as a Swiss Romand—and he was well acquainted with his "Paris complex," that is, his persistent longing to be in Paris and to gain the recognition of Parisian intellectuals.

Both admired and controversial, Chessex leaves behind an important opus written in dense, lyrical, and poetic prose. Many readers are shocked by his shamelessly erotic images, some of which verge on being crude. I, too, was shocked, until discovering the remarkable inwardness of his style, and his ability to bring across with sparing words vivid images of nature, landscape, and baroque character. Like no other author, he evokes the atmosphere of Lausanne, the countryside of Canton Vaud, and the changing seasons.

Chessex lost his religious faith early in his life, yet he still claimed to be a Calvinist, underlining its somber and punitive sides. Shadow in the form of perverse eroticism and sordid tales seemed to fascinate him, and to belong to the whole in his writings as much as light and beauty. Reviewing the novels of the Vaudois author, C-F. Ramuz, Chessex remarked on his unconscious unveiling of the Protestant morale. For Ramuz's characters die tragically by the will of heaven—meaning that, as Chessex observed,

> the wages of sin is death. Ramuz, as a Calvinist, knows all too well, in his culture and in his bones, the hard theology of evil and its punishment and he uses it like a writer.[28]

Was Chessex revealing something of himself and his own novels when he wrote about Ramuz? As Chessex himself concedes, in his own works sin and death always go hand in hand:

> Indeed, Calvinistic violence, that absolute to separate sin from salvation, darkness and evil from the sacrifice of the pure, suited and still suits my basic temperament.[29]

Light seemed to have illuminated fully Chessix's late life, as he found serenity in his house in Ropraz, in the countryside not far from Lausanne. And yet in October 2009 at the age of seventy-five, he was holding a conference in a public library when a spectator admonished him, and he suddenly dropped dead. As if glimpsing his own end, Chessex had written earlier, "Calvin is abrupt. With Calvin comes the abyss, the vertigo, the call from the Almighty and the horror of the fall."[30]

Anne-Marie Jaton notes that Chessex's characters are intellectuals with awareness of the weight of words. "In this sense," she remarks, "they know that words can sometimes condemn one to death, and even kill."[31] Might Chessex's characters resolve the mystery of his death: a heart attack, brought on by the weight of killing words? God works in mysterious ways: As several journalists remarked, for a man who had devoted his life to literature, to die in a library is, in a sense, a beautiful way to go.

Conclusion

The question of Swiss Romand identity led me to study the history, lives, and works of authors from the three French-speaking Protestant cantons. My exploration made me more conscious of my own identity—as a French-speaking Protestant from Neuchâtel, with roots reaching into Romandy, and yet farther into Switzerland as a whole. It is, if nothing else, a highly complex identity, captured in its essence by Jacques Chessex:

> I call *Romand* he who is born on this side of the Jura, the Canton of Vaud for example, who knows that he originates from French culture, strongly influenced and enriched by history, tradition, and the feeling of belonging to one's country. A *Vaudois* is at the same time a son of Paris, a son of Calvin, and a son of the revolutionary Davel. Paris and France nourish and uplift him.

> He however perceives his origins in a hundred pressing ways—violent revolt against his provincial condition and an earthy respect for his cultural heritage, shyness and extreme pride through adulthood, a keen sense of being different, refusing to be swayed by fashion and appearances, innate religiosity, a sort of protestant romanticism, if you wish.[32]

Acknowledgments

For my work on this article I am indebted to the following Jungian events and colleagues:

The European Congress of the IAAP, Vilnius, Lithuania, June 25, 2009: Verena Kast, "The Cultural Unconscious and the Roots of Identity", unpublished lecture;

The Annual Assembly of the Swiss Society of Analytical Psychology (SGAP), Morges, Switzerland, May 9, 2009:

Rita Hurni, "La Culture de l'Autre comme Moyen d'Individuation", unpublished lecture;

Lucienne Marguerat, "A Cheval sur Deux Cultures, une Posture mal aimée mais bien Suisse", unpublished lecture, adapted and published as a chapter in this volume;

Kristina Schellinski, "Le Complexe Culturel et l'Identité du Citoyen du Monde déraciné", unpublished lecture.

NOTES

1. Joseph L. Henderson, *Cultural Attitudes in Psychological Perspectives* (Toronto: Inner City Books, 1984).

2. Thomas Singer and Samuel L. Kimbles, *The Cultural Complex: Contemporary Jungian Perspectives on Psyche and Society* (Rove & New York: Brunner-Routledge, 2004).

3. Joseph L. Henderson, *Shadow and Self: Selected Papers in Analytical Psychology* (Wilmette, Illinois: Chiron 1990), p. 103.

4. Konrad Lorenz, *On Aggression*, trans. Marjorie Kerr Wilson (London: Routledge, 2002), p. 75.

5. Denis de Rougemont, *La Suisse, ou l'Histoire d'un Peuple heureux* (Lausanne: L'Age d'Homme, 1989), p. 119, trans. Barbara Whitaker and Kristina Schellinski.

6. Among other Protestant Churches now established in Romandy as well as in the whole of Switzerland are the New Apostolic Church, the Evangelical Lutheran Church, the Methodist Church, and Jehova's Witnesses. Other faiths established here are Judaism, Islam, Eastern Orthodoxy, and the Anglo-Catholic Church (Anglican). Unfortunately my consideration of the influences of these other faiths would exceed my present limits.

7. Murray Stein, "Searching for the Soul & Jung in Zürich: A Psychological Essay," in *Psyche and the City: A Soul's Guide to the Modern Metropolis*, ed. Thomas Singer (New Orleans: Spring Journal Books, 2010), pp. 19-20.

8. Bernard Reymond, *Le Protestantisme en Suisse Romande. Portraits et Effets d'une Influence* (Genève: Labor et Fides, 1999), trans. Barbara Whitaker and Kristina Schellinski.

9. *Ibid.*

10. The accomplished sketch artist and citizen of Geneva, Rodolpfe Töpffer (1799–1846), was best known for his serial caricatures, which became known as the forerunners of the nineteenth century graphic novel as well as of the modern comic book. His work was introduced to the United States in 1842 with his work entitled *The Adventures of Mr. Obadiah Oldbuck*, which can viewed at http://leonardodesa.interdinamica.net/comics/lds/vb/VieuxBois01.asp?p=1 (accessed December, 2010).

11. Reymond, *Le Protestantisme en Suisse Romande*, p. 63.

12. Eds.' note: For Jungian perspectives on Zwingli, see for instance, *Who Was Zwingli? Spring: A Journal of Archetype and Culture*, Vol. 56 (1994) and Stein, "Searching for the Soul & Jung in Zürich", pp. 13-32.

13. Jean Calvin, *Institutes of the Christian Religion*, trans. Henry Beveridge, rev. ed. (Peabody, MA: Hendrickson Publishers, 2008).

14. See Yves Krumenacher, *Calvin au-delà des Légendes* (Montrouge: Bayard, 2009).

15. See for instance, Denis de Rougemont, *La Suisse, ou l'Histoire d'un Peuple heureux.*

16. See for example, *Un Homme nommé Calvin, l'Héritage de la Réforme, son Influence sur Genève, témoignages de Romands*, L'Hebdo hors série, spécial 500e anniversaire (2009): n. 22.

17. Jean Calvin, *L'Institution Chrétienne,* edition abrégée rédigée en français moderne par Henri Evrard (Lausanne: Presses bibliques universitaires, 2009), standard English translation of the unabridged title.

18. Jean-Jacques Rousseau, *Lettres Ecrites de la Montagne* (Lausanne: l'Age d'Homme, 2007), p. 87, trans. Barbara Whitaker and Kristina Schellinski. Eds.' note: See Jean-Jacques Rousseau, *Letter to Beaumont, Letters from the Mountain, and Related Writings*, ed. Christopher Kelly, trans. Christopher Kelly and Eve Grace (Hanover, NH: Dartmouth College Press, 2001).

19. Eds.' note: On the matter of religious freedom, the Swiss Federal Constitution limped somewhat behind some of the cantons themselves, and certainly behind Geneva. Indeed at the Federal level freedom of religion has been and continues to be an evolving process.

20. See Calvin, *Institutes of the Christian Religion.*

21. Jean-Fréderic Amiel, *Journal Intime,* éd. intégrale 1839-1881, 12 Volumes (Lausanne: L'Age d'Homme, 1994).

22. Etienne Barilier, "De Calvin à Castellion", in *L'Hebdo hors série,* spécial 500e anniversaire (2009), n. 22, p. 81, trans. Barbara Whitaker and Kristina Schellinski.

23. Gabriel Müzenberg, *Une Femme de Style, Valérie de Gasparin* (Lausanne: Edition Ouverture, 1994).

24. Serge Bimpage, *Moi Henry Dunant, j'ai rêvé le Monde: Mémoires Imaginaires du Fondateur de la Croix-Rouge* (Paris: Albin Michel, 2003).

25. Jean Henri Dunant, *A Memory of Soferino*, trans. The American National Red Cross, District of Columbia Chapter (Place unstated: The American National Red Cross, 1959).

26. Eds.' note: For his novels published in English, see Jacques Chessex, *A Jew Must Die,* trans. W. Donald Wilson (London: Bitter Lemon Press, 2010) and *The Vampire of Ropraz,* trans. W. Donald Wilson (London: Bitter Lemon Press, 2008).

27. Jacques Chessex, *Le dernier Crâne de M. Sade* (Paris: Grasset, 2010), English trans. by Barbara Whitaker and Kristina Schellinski.

28. Jacques Chessex, *Ecrits sur Ramuz* (Vevey: Editions de l'Aire, 2004), p. 44, trans. Barbara Whitaker and Kristina Schellinski.

29. *Ibid.* See also "Refuser l'Artifice, le Faux-Semblant, toute esbroufe", in *L'Hebdo, hors série,* spécial 500e anniversaire (2009): n. 22, p. 73, trans. Schellinski/Whitaker.

30. *Ibid.*, trans. Barbara Whitaker and Kristina Schellinski.

31. Anne-Marie Jaton, quoted in Roger Francillon, "Jacques Chessex et la tradition littéraire suisse romande", in *Jacques Chessex: Il y a moins de mort lorsqu'il y a plus d'art: Etudes recueillies par Gérard Froidevaux et Marius Michaud* (Lausanne: Bibliothèque des Arts, 2003), p. 42, trans. Barbara Whitaker and Kristina Schellinski.

32. Chessex, *Ecrits sur Ramuz*, p. 23 f., trans. Kristina Schellinski and Barbara Whitaker.

Brother Klaus of Flüe and the Prayer of the Heart: A Map of Individuation

FRANZ-XAVER JANS-SCHEIDEGGER

Translation by Edith Haidacher

Discovering Brother Klaus

Little did I suppose that I was to "encounter" Brother Klaus when I sought in 1996 to enter a monastery on Mount Athos in Greece. My hope in going there was to receive instruction in the eastern Orthodox tradition of hermetic prayer, the Hesychasm or the "prayer of the heart" (*Herzensgebet*).[2] The prayer of the heart

Franz-Xaver Jans-Scheidegger, dipl. theol., studied theology at the University of Lucerne and Zürich, and is known in Switzerland as a meditation teacher and theologian. He was born in 1943 in the Canton of Lucerne. He graduated from the C.G. Jung Institute Zürich in 1975, and is now a training analyst at the International School of Analytical Psychology Zürich. He is the current head of spiritual contemplation at the retreat center Via Cordis Haus, in Flüeli-Ranft, which is also the home of Brother Klaus. He has published books and articles in German dealing with the topics of mysticism, psychotherapy, contemplation, and the Zen tradition. With particular relevance for the subject at hand, he authored *Das Tor zur Rückseite des Herzens. Die grosse Rad-Vision des Nikolaus von Flüe als kontemplativer Weg*, which translates roughly to, *The Gate to the Back of the Heart: The Great Wheel Vision of Nicholas of Flüe as a Contemplative Path.*[1]

originated with the Desert Fathers at Mt. Sinai in the fourth century, and when the Turks invaded the region, the practice was transported to Mt. Athos. As the scholar Luc Benoist explains, "[t]he word Hesychasm, derived from a Greek word meaning quiet, denotes in fact a complex state of silence, solitude and peace."[3] That this complex state itself entails a state of unceasing devotion, and that it is rooted in the body, becomes apparent in the words of St. Simeon: ". . . prayer should be as uninterrupted as breathing and the beating of the heart."[4]

When I explained to the abbot that I had come to Mount Athos to learn this practice, he said to me,

> Go back to Switzerland! Why are you seeking instruction in the prayer of the heart here? You have a starets [a teacher of the Hesychasm] in Obwalden, namely Brother Klaus. From him you can learn the prayer of the heart! Take note, the holy Mount Athos is not only in Greece but also in the heart of Switzerland!

A little ashamed, I turned my enthusiasm for the Hesychasm from the holy Mount Athos to Brother Klaus's hermetic retreat in the Flüeli gorge. So, who is Brother Klaus, and what has he to do with the prayer of the heart?

Brother Klaus is the fifteenth century Swiss hermit, mystic, and patron Saint of Switzerland.[5] He was born as Nikolas of Flüe around 1417 to well-to-do and respected farmers in Flüeli-Ranft, located in the region of Obwalden. Obwalden itself is in the foothills of the Alps of central Switzerland, more specifically in the Great Melch Valley. The nearest city and main crossroad was and remains to be Lucerne, nearly twenty miles northeast of Flüeli-Ranft, as the crow flies. It was against this background that Nikolas abandoned his wife and ten children, his wealth, and his respected position in the community to become first a mendicant monk, and then a hermit living in a humble cell on the slope of the Flüeli gorge. With this change of life, Nikolas became known as Brother Klaus.

There followed for Brother Klaus many years of "looking into the dark mirror," as Jung writes.[6] This "looking" can be described as an element of Nikolas's unceasing devotion to the attainment of a hesychast-like peace. To this topic we shall presently return. Among the other legacies he leaves is that of the mystical visionary who is said to have subsisted miraculously for twenty years on nothing but the

Holy Sacrament. And despite his illiteracy, Nikolas was often sought for his wise counsel and skillful capacity as an intermediary in civil affairs—even long after he had taken up the life of hermit. His seventy years as a spiritual pilgrim and man of the peace ended in 1487, when he died alone in his cell. He is buried near Flüeli-Ranft. Brother Klaus was canonized in 1947 by Pope Pius XII.

Important Stages in Brother Klaus's Life

Brother Klaus's spiritual journey apparently began at a very early age indeed, for as he relayed to his longtime friend Haimo Amgrund, his first vision came *in utero*:

> Brother Klaus told him [Amgrund] that in the womb, before he had been born, he had seen a star in the sky that was shining through the whole world. Since living in the Ranft he always saw a star of the same kind in the sky so that he thought it was the same star.[7]

The pre-birth vision notwithstanding, his mother Emma, "a deeply religious woman," contributed to her son's spiritual development in other ways including introducing him in his youth to the circle of mystics, "The Friends of God."[8] As a young man Nikolas deepened his devotion to prayer, meditation, and fasting—and continued to receive unorthodox visions—while also helping to maintain his parents' estate in Flüeli-Ranft. In 1431 he became eligible to vote and to serve on the town council, and began to work variously as an alderman, magistrate, and military leader.

In 1447 he married Dorothea Wyss, settling with her in Flüeli-Ranft to continue a life of farming and community service. The two raised five daughters and five sons. In 1455 Nikolas began to receive spiritual guidance from Oswald Isner, the priest of the parish of Kerns (on the opposite side of the Flüeli gorge); Isner was to become his long-time confessor. His previously mentioned friend Heimo Amgrund, too, became a spiritual guide. Nikolas continued to be inspired as well by the Friends of God.

Military service was a duty required by Nikolas's position in a "family of landed farmers,"[9] and this he undertook, rising to the rank of captain. After leaving the military he became an active peace-maker and man of the law, serving for nine years as a judge in Obwalden. He declined the community's repeated requests that he become a councilman of Obwalden, asserting that, "One is safer below than on the heights."[10]

Around the age of forty-five Nikolas began to suffer from extreme melancholy, and to feel that family demands distracted him from a growing desire to devote himself to God.[11] On October 16th 1467, at the age of fifty, he "left everything and set off barefoot and bareheaded, dressed in a grey-brown tunic and armed only with a staff and a rosary."[12] Although Nikolas departed with his wife's consent, his was a highly unorthodox sacrifice of family ties, homestead, and even wealth—the onset, we might say, of his individuation process.

Walking from Obwalden toward the Friends of God in the French Alsace, Nikolas was gripped by an awful specter. It was his last vision, and sometimes called the "Liestal vision" after the place in which it occurred. As for the vision, his fifteenth century biographer Heinrich Wölflin relayed,

> [Nikolas] . . . had seen a piercing light resembling a human face. At the sight of it he feared that his heart would burst into little pieces. Overcome with terror, he instantly turned his face away and fell to the ground. And that was the reason why his face was now so terrible to others.[13]

The apparition of light was so shattering that it transformed Nikolas's physical countenance. He was altered to the effect that, "'All who came to him were filled with terror at the first glance.'"[14] According to Jung, this vision emerged from the collective unconscious, presenting Nikolas with a non-dogmatic, perhaps heretical, and nearly "fatal" experience of a Yaweh-like "divine wrath;" that is to say, it was an experience of an original "God-concept that contains the opposites in a still undivided state."[15]

Thus the Liestal vision was among the factors that hastened his return, or rather his flight home, after one year's absence. But here we might speak of a hidden telos, for with hindsight it appears that he was destined to set a spiritual example for the people of his own village—and also for all others who encounter his spirituality up to this day. It was now 1468, and he was fifty-one years old. Game-hunters stumbled upon him near his home in Flüeli, dwelling in a "shelter of boughs under a larch."[16] With the help of the local people, who were concerned that his shelter was inadequate, he built a small chapel on the slope of the gorge at Flüeli-Ranft, near his family home and a stone's throw from the Melch River. To the chapel they attached his abode, a tiny crude cell. Here he intensified his customary prayer and contemplation, and began his twenty-year fast. In 1469 the Suffragen Bishop Thomas of Constance arrived to bless the gorge chapel and test the truth of the claims about the hermit's miraculous fasting.

From 1471 onward, people of all ranks and walks of life began to seek Brother Klaus's guidance and prayer. In 1482 he parted with more of his family wealth to fund a vicarage for the chapel in the gorge. The appointed vicar in turn became Brother Klaus's personal chaplain.

Now, in his time the people of Obwalden were more withdrawn than they are today, and more critical of conspicuous persons and their admirers. In particular the communities scrutinized individuals like Brother Klaus, who pursued unorthodox goals or exhibited unorthodox behavior. In other words, the man Nikolas had earned enormous respect for being a rich farmer, a good husband and father, a brave warrior and truth-seeker, a banner-bearer and military captain, a municipal official and judge, an honest man and above all a man of piety. But Nikolas the man who abandoned his family and community, and who lived on as Brother Klaus the mystic visionary and hermit of the gorge was suspected of being either an insane idealist or a heretic.[17] As the news of Brother Klaus's miraculous fasting spread, people were increasingly curious to see him, hoping to obtain first-hand proof that he was not an imposter but a "living saint," as his followers called him.

More than eliciting simple scrutiny, the expression of extraordinary religious phenomena in Brother Klaus's time evoked the legitimate fear of the Inquisition. To avert such threat to their own "living saint," and to temper the swelling masses of visitors, the government of Obwalden stationed guards and a barrier around his abode in the gorge. And because the crowds travelled mainly through Lucerne—this being the nearest city and major crossroads—Lucerne's government cooperated by conducting security checks before issuing travel permits to the curious and the genuine pilgrims who were underway to the gorge.

During his early hermitage in the Flüeli gorge Brother Klaus remained disturbed by his Liestal vision. As Jung observes, the vision had constituted a

> fearful and highly perturbing [experience] that naturally needed a long labor of assimilation in order to fit into the total structure of the psyche and thus to restore the disturbed psychic balance.[18]

Brother Klaus spent many years contemplating his vision, in Jung's terms, seeking to "assimilate" and grasp its meaning. And although living the life of a hermit, nearly to the end of his days he remained in service to civil affairs. Indeed, Brother Klaus gained in renown as the man who saved the Old Swiss Confederacy when, in 1481, he averted civil war by his successful arbitration of a number of disputes among the ur-cantons.[19]

The "Book" that Taught Brother Klaus

Behind the biographical facts is an enormous arch—an arch of individuation, if you will—that spans Brother Klaus's spiritual life and development. The supporting pillars of this arch are condensed in the first two lines of Brother Klaus's well-known prayer:[20] "Oh my Lord and my God, take from me everything that distances me from you! Give me everything that brings me closer to you!" And the arch between the two columns is represented in third and last line: "Detach me from myself to give my all to you!"[21]

For Brother Klaus, the "you" addressed in this prayer is the reality to which one's whole being should be surrendered, namely, the divine and ineffable mystery of God. From the time he first left home, his life revolved completely around the question of how to be at one with the Divine. To this end, he found that, like a hesychast, one need constantly seek and immerse one's self in the peace that is "always in God."

How did Brother Klaus find his way from the terrifying Liestal vision to the experience of "the peace that is always in God"? Meditating upon the Liestal vision, he had an epiphany. This one—a vision of a simple mandala—he rendered as a drawing. In other words, as Jungians might do in a process of active imagination, in this drawing Brother Klaus gave concrete form to his Liestal vision, a shattering and ultimately ineffable experience. This drawing of a "'wheel with six spokes,'" framed by a square, he called the "'book'" from which he was "'learning and seeking the art of [the pilgrim's] doctrine.'"[22]

The *Pilgrim's Tract* (the title of Wöflin's fifteenth-century biography) relays Brother Klaus's description of his use of this "book" and how it brought him to apprehend the secret of the undivided deity. As he meditated upon the wheel image, he heard a voice, which asked,

> Do you see this image? This is the nature of the divine being. The center is the undivided deity in which all saints rejoice. The three tips that point to the inner circle are the three persons of God; they emanate from the one deity, encompassing heaven and the whole world, which are in their power. And as they go out from the divine power, so they also lead back into it, and are undivided in eternal power. This is the meaning of the image.[23]

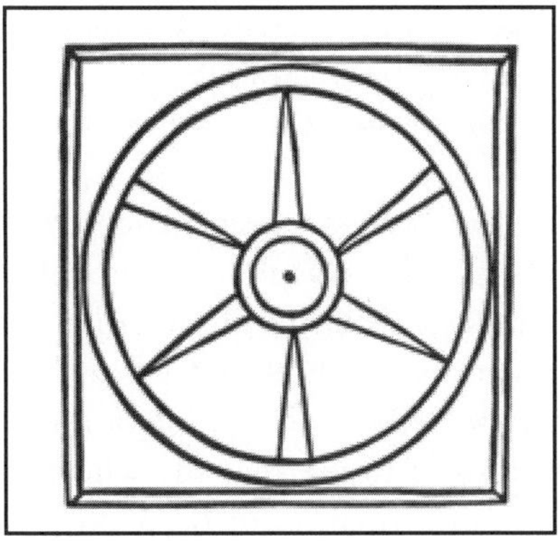

Figure 1: Artist Unknown, *Untitled*, Print by Peter Berger of Augsburg (ca. 1488), in Robert Durrer, *Bruder Klaus. Die ältesten Quellen über den seligen Niklaus von Flüe sein Leben und seinen Einfluss*, 2 vols.' (1917-1921(Sarnen: Regierungsrat des Kantons Obwalden, 1987), p. 363.[24]

Considering the mandala along with Brother Klaus's divinely apprehended explanation, we notice that the visionary image evokes new questions, inspires reflection, and can stimulate one's personal views on the continuity of creation. We can ask for example: What might the wheel reveal about the link between the visible creation in its abundance, in its unfoldings and infoldings—and the invisible and hence hidden, secret origin of life? What dynamism, what original source ceaselessly feeds the visible processes of our own transformation and development?

Answers to such questions begin to emerge as we observe that the spokes of Brother Klaus's wheel consist of two sets of three directionally opposed triangles, which together form a six-pointed star. His drawing as such expanded the orthodox Christian view of the Trinity, the three-fold one God, into a double trinity, an especially dynamic or energic one. The barely visible white dot at the image's center stands for the one God, and for this God as the unifying source from which the divine energy continuously emanates and returns. Moreover, Brother Klaus's wheel mandala adds to the deity the aspect of a quaternity, an archetypal symbol of equilibrium and wholeness. This is pictured most evidently in the image's outermost square frame. However at the same time, the quaternity is manifest as a hidden aspect or mystery that arises as the one dot in the image's center interacts with and joins the trinitarian three.

Remarkably, Brother Klaus's wheel mandala echoes his pre-natal vision of "a star in the sky that was shining through the whole world." Here we note how the experience of illumination pervaded his whole life. And yet, as the star of the wheel mandala appears to revitalize the original vision, it also represents his assimilation of the Liestal vision. We could go a step farther to say that the wheel mandala moreover presents a complete transformation of the God-image as a "piercing light," the "wrathful" and shattering One. For in the star, the source and perpetuation of all life is imagined as a manifold and soft luminosity that subtly circulates through and energizes all creation.

Taken as whole, Brother Klaus's wheel thus involves the onlooker in a contemplative *process*, that is in back-and-forth movement between the interior and exterior, by which one enters into the dynamism of "the source" itself. The movement subsides as one's gaze comes to rest on the dot at the center. Dynamically speaking then, this dot is the still point and the "one essence" in which Brother Klaus discovered the hesychast-like "peace [that] is always in God." In this all-encompassing presence of the divine—or one might say in such an experience of the Self, or of psychological wholeness—time and place play no role. Throughout all time and place, the ONE is just as perfectly present and luminous in the smallest particle as it is in the whole of creation.

In a comprehensive study of meditation mandalas, the scholar Heinrich Stirnimann says that the specifically *wheel* form of Brother

Klaus's mandala is unique and has appeared only in his story.[25] In other words, with the wheel mandala he formulated his experience in a symbol that uniquely joins elements of foregoing symbols. Take for example the six spokes of the wheel, which form the hexagonal star. The image as such is rooted in the Jewish Star of David, in which the unity of creation is symbolized by two interlocked triangles—one with the tip at the top, and the other one with the tip at the bottom. The circles formed by the concentric rings appearing in Brother Klaus's wheel appear elsewhere, for example, in the reflections of the fourteenth-century German mystic Heinrich Seuse, who used the image to convey to his spiritual daughter the mystery of God.[26]

Conclusion

The initiatory and transformational nature of Brother Klaus's pilgrimage, his individuation journey if you will, comes to light in what has been called a "mystagogic thread"[27] that runs through his life. That is to say, the visions manifested themselves at pivotal intervals of his religious quest, each time stimulating new insight into "what distanced him from and what brought him near" the divine mystery. To conclude, let us turn briefly to his "Fountain Vision" as one among many that guided his own journey. From this we might take guidance for our own personal work as well as for our work with others who seek transformation. The Fountain Vision, which is unfortunately too lengthy to reproduce here, begins with this image:

> There was a man who interrupted his sleep for God and for the sake of his suffering. And he thanked God for his suffering and his pain. And God showed mercy that he might find joy and delight therein. Then he lay down on his resting place.[28]

To follow Brother Klaus's example, we can realize our lives and relationships as being tantamount to a love story with God. At the same time, we recognize in our suffering our boundedness in the body and in the limits of time and space. In the limits of our corporeal being, we may gratefully comprehend the opportunity for a "caesura," that is for a pause in the ordinary rhythm of our lives. It is such pause that can open us to emotional change and to the experience of transcendent wholeness and peace. Said another way, it is this attitude and approach that invites the heart to open and to become warm. For those familiar with the symbolism of alchemy, I can briefly mention the correspondence of this stage with the transformational the stage of the *via purgativa* and more specifically, the *calcinatio* (the warming up of the substance to be transformed).[29]

The longing for the "one essence," or for the Self, or for psychological wholeness, is an experience that many of us strive for in a variety of ways, even today. For instance, self-discovery as a way of attaining inner truth and wholeness is offered as a "wellness goal" in many spas and leisure centers. The offering of spiritual instruction packaged with a range of recreational possibilities seems to guarantee well-booked courses and seminars. However, the path to discovering the source of one's humanity is more than a wellness experience (although it is conceivable that a wellness experience could ignite a spiritual journey).

A spiritual journey such as we have glimpsed in the life of Brother Klaus demands our discovery and on-going *rediscovery* of—to paraphrase his prayer—"everything that distances us from, and everything that brings us closer to the truth." It is an arduous path that characteristically involves suffering, sacrifice, clarification, and inner purification. Once undertaken this path ordinarily allows no compromise, no turning back. It can be quite a challenge to our "small ego." The journey as such bespeaks a Jungian individuation process, and in particular, the demand to integrate the shadow—an integration that leads to personal gratification and joy in the fruits of one's expanded horizons.

NOTES

1. Franz-Xaver Jans-Scheidegger, *Das Tor zur Rückseite des Herzens. Die grosse Rad-Vision des Nikolaus von Flüe als kontemplativer Weg*, 2nd ed. (Münsterschwarzbach: Vier-Türme-Verlag, 2002). See also for instance *Worte—geborgen aus Schwiegen: Wegweiser in die Kontemplation* (Munich: Kösel Verlag, Random House, 2002).

2. Emmanuel Jungclaussen, *Aufrichtige Erzählungen eines russischen Pilgers*, 16th ed. (Freiburg im Breisgau: Herder, 2008).

3. Luc Benoist, *The Esoteric Path: An Introduction to Hermetic Tradition*, trans. Robin Waterfeld, 2nd ed. (Hillsdale, NY: Sophia Perennis, 2003), p. 97.

4. *Ibid.*, pp. 97-98.

5. Alban Butler, *Butler's Lives of the Saints*, ed. David Hugh Farmer, new full edition (Kent, UK: Burns & Oates Ltd., 1999), pp. 212-216.

6. C.G. Jung, "Archetypes of the Collective Unconscious," *The Archetypes and the Collective Unconscious, The Collected Works of C.G. Jung*, eds. Sir Herbert Read, Michael Fordham, William McGuire, trans. R.F.C. Hull, 2nd ed., 5th printing (Princeton, NJ: Princeton University Press, 1977), vol. 9i, § 19. Future references to Jung's *Collected Works* [hereinafter "*CW*"] will be by volume number and paragraph number.

7. Roland Gröbli, *Die Sehnsucht nach dem "einig Wesen." Leben und Lehre des Bruder Klaus von Flüe* (Zürich: NZN-Buchverlag, 1990), p. 223, trans. Edith Haidacher.

8. Butler, *Butler's Lives*, p. 212.

9. *Ibid.*

10. *Ibid.*, p. 213.

11. Marie-Louise von Franz, *Archetypal Dimensions of the Psyche* (Boston: Shambhala Publications, 1999), p. 37.

12. Butler, *Butler's Lives*, p. 213.

13. Heinrich Wölflin cited in Jung, *CW* 11, § 478.

14. *Ibid.*

15. Jung, *CW* 9i, §§ 17-19.

16. Butler, *Butler's Lives*, p. 214.

17. Gröbli, *Die Sehnsucht*, p. 132.

18. Jung, *CW* 9i, § 17.

19. Jung notes that these "disputes [were] between the predominantly rural and the predominantly urban cantons . . . ." In *CW* 11, § 474, ff.3.

20. Eds.' note: Klaus's prayer is contained, among other places, in the Roman Catholic Catechism. See "Profession of Faith: IV, The Implications of Faith in One God," *The Catholic Catechism*, rev. ed., reprinted (London: Burns and Oates, 2006), p. 54, § 226 and ff. 50.

21. Heinrich Stirnimann, *Der Gottesgelehrte Niklaus von Flüe. Drei Studien* (Freiburg, Switzerland: Universitätsverlag, 1981), p. 71f.

22. Wölflin cited in Jung, *CW* 11, § 478.

23. Wölfin cited in Gröbli, *Die Sehnsucht*, p. 223, trans. Edith Haidacher.

24. Although the artist of this so-called "wheel picture" is officially designated "unknown," there is evidence to suggest that it was Brother Klaus himself.

25. Stirnimann, *Der Gottesgelehrte*, p. 273.

26. *Ibid.*, p. 271ff.

27. Gröbli, *Die Sehnsucht*, p. 238f.

28. Alban Stoeckli, *Die Visionen des seligen Bruder Klaus* (Einsiedeln: Benziger, 1933), p. 10ff, trans. Edith Haidacher.

29. Edward F. Edinger, *Der Weg der Seele. Der psychotherapeutische Prozess im Spiegel der Alchemie* (München: Kösel, 1990), p. 31ff. Eds.' Note: In English, see Edward F. Edinger, *Anatomy of the Psyche: Alchemical Symbolism in Psychotherapy*, 6th printing (Chicago: Open Court, 1994).

Giving a Hand to the Dead
Reflections on a Legend from Valais: "The Cold Hand"

MARIA ANNA BERNASCONI

Translation by Andrew Fellows

Introduction: The Place, the People, the Poor Souls

Valais is one of Switzerland's twenty-three cantons, a southern one, which lies in the center of the Alps. By the mid-nineteenth century the other Swiss had begun to regard the Valaisans as people of the backwoods. Even their Swiss German and

Maria Anna Bernasconi, lic. phil., was born and raised in Canton Zürich. She completed studies in psychology at the University of Zürich, and went on to graduate from the C.G. Jung Institute, Zürich, Küsnacht. She is a member of the Association of Graduate Analytical Psychologists (AGAP) and the Swiss Association for Analytical Psychology (SGAP). At the International School of Analytical Psychology Zürich (ISAPZURICH) she is a lecturer and training analyst. She is currently writing her doctoral thesis on the legends of the dead from Valais.

In the essay presented here, Maria enlarges on several themes she introduced earlier in "The Fountain of Memories Buried and Uncovered"[1] published in *Spring*'s *Symbolic Life 2009* issue. Whereas in "The Fountain of Memories" she was concerned generally with a revival of legend in this predominantly Roman Catholic region, here she delves more deeply into one of the very old legends of the "poor souls," the wandering souls of departed ancestors.

French dialects were perceived to be oddly archaic. As I wrote in my previous essay, this state of affairs was due largely to the fact that Valais consists essentially of a deep valley amidst high mountains:

> The valley runs from east to west with a slightly southern inclination until in the lower Valais near Martigny it makes a short bend to the north-west and opens out to the Lake Geneva. Aside from Mont Blanc, the highest mountains of the Alps are located in Valais, among them the world-famous Matterhorn. Originally Valais, which is the valley of the Rhone river, could only be reached through the narrow bend near Martigny. All the mountain passes into it are at a high level and hardly accessible. Until the beginning of the 19th century, Valais [kept] up quite well with the other mountain Cantons, but beginning in the age of railway traffic it fell more and more behind. . . . In the 19th and 20th centuries, traffic accelerated . . ., and [Valais was unable to] keep up . . . because its high mountains functioned as massive barriers in almost all directions.[2]

The people of Valais were not only held back from the developing world. As will become evident in our legend, "The Cold Hand," they lived as poor farmers under considerable hardship and risk due to the harsh terrain and extreme weather. At the same time the Roman Catholic Church was entrenched here, and protected by the mountains from the influences of the Protestant Reformation. This meant, among other things, that legends, superstitions, and Catholic beliefs, free of repression, were well preserved as vital and shared cultural phenomena.

All such conditions acted like the force of fate in binding the villagers together. In order to survive, for instance, they had little choice but to depend upon one another, often doing so by forming working cooperatives. As we shall see, "The Cold Hand" legend discussed below speaks in mythic language about the necessity of holding together as a community, and it is thus intimately linked to the culture from which it arises. But what interests me here especially is the central motif, that is, the necessity for the living to sustain links to the dead—in particular, to the "poor souls," the departed ancestors who are compelled to wander the earth. As explained in my previous essay,

> Partly this wandering [of souls] is a specific version of the Christian purgatory, partly the idea of this procession of the dead has developed from the Germanic idea of the army of the dead

> moving through the air at night with Wotan. The Valaisans in particular knew about these spirits of the dead, and in former times all children knew what to do if they met such a spirit or even a procession of dead.[3]

Before moving on to the legend, I wish to add that my interest in Valaisan legends of the dead began in my childhood with my father, who grew up in this region, who told me and my siblings the tales from there, and every summer took us back to his childhood home in this area. A flashback:

> It is 1961, I am about ten years old, and I'm sitting in our family apartment in the Zürich highlands, listening to the radio in the early evening. My father has tuned in to a broadcast from Radio Beromünster: *Legends in the [local Swiss-] German Dialect*, told by Karl Biffiger. Father has already told us many of these tales, which he knows by heart, but there are still some I've not yet heard. I hear them, too, every summer when we visit my grandmother at her house in Valais or when we go with her up to the alp to stay in her hut. But since I've gotten better at reading, I've also begun to read them myself.

Thus in childhood I became familiar with the Valaisan terrain and tales, long before I became intimately acquainted with the Grimm's fairytales. And as I learned already in childhood, the poor souls play a very large role in the lives of the Valaisans.

"The Cold Hand"

To my best knowledge Swiss legends of the dead are not collected in English.[4] Neither in German nor in any other of Switzerland's national languages do we possess a definitive compilation of these particular legends. However a number of collections have been assembled by pastors, teachers, and other educated individuals who were inspired by the Brothers Grimm in the nineteenth century.[5] These collections, put together at different times by different collectors, are by no means uniform. Rather, individual preferences more or less determine which legends are contained in each collection. The story of the "The Cold Hand" which is told below appears in the collection assembled by the folklorist Josef Guntern. The protagonist's name, "Nazhans," is a nickname that would translate literally to "Nathan John:"

> Nazhans once tended his neighbor's cattle in winter as a favor and spent the night in his hut. There was a knock on the wall, and before he knew it, the hut door and the inner door were unlocked. He only just had time to stretch out his right arm. It seemed to him as if another, ice-cold hand was pressed into his right hand, and then another and another, more than twenty, more than a hundred, and he was unable to defend himself or to discern anyone in the darkness. When at last the doors once again swung shut and he could withdraw his arm, his own hand had grown as cold as a glacier. The next morning he looked in vain for fresh tracks in the soft snow. Nazhans could not explain the phenomenon. Only this much was clear to him: "I will stay here no more."
>
> Back home, he said to the neighbor: "You could have told me that this house does not belong to you alone." "Yes, indeed, I share it many a night with the poor souls to whom I give my hand to warm their freezing hands at least for a few moments. You should not be grieved that the poor souls have initiated this charitable service with you, too. They will at some point give you a hand."
>
> A few years later Nazhans was making his way through deep, freshly fallen snow. As he reached the middle of a steep slope, the snow began to move slowly. To his horror, Nazhans saw a deep break in the overhanging snow high above. He was caught up in an avalanche, and the next moment hurtled over the terrible cliffs into the valley. Over and over again the heavy snow buried him, but a cold hand always pulled him out and put him back on top of the rolling avalanche. Uninjured, he rode on the broad back of the white monster down to the meadows above the village of Wiler.
>
> Only then did he remember the night in the cabin where his hand had grown cold as glacier, and his neighbor's words: "The poor souls will at some point give you a hand."[6]

Not only does this legend allude to the hard life in which neighbors were linked as if by fate to a system of mutual give-and-take. It portrays as well the real belief that this system of mutuality included a vital connection and active dialogue between the living and the dead. By way of another glimpse into my own childhood, let us imagine ourselves in the conditions that developed and sustained such belief:

Along with my parents and my two younger sisters, I have left Zürich to spend the summer in my grandmother's hut high up on an alp of Valais. As is the custom, my grandmother and the other farmers have moved from their valleys up to the alpine pastures, where they will spend the summer grazing their cattle and making cheese, and here they will stay until autumn begins. It is pouring rain, as it so often does in summer at this altitude of more than 6,562 feet (2000 meters). This weather is tedious, for as long as it continues, we children have little choice than to remain huddled together and crowded in the hut.

This hut, like the ones on the surrounding alps, is rather dark and very small, consisting of two stories. The ground floor is a stall, which shelters my grandmother's cows and goats. The upper floor is our living quarters. Half of this hut belongs to another farmer. Our living quarters, like his, consist of two small rooms. From the outside one enters directly into the kitchen. The kitchen has no windows, but it does have an open, wood-burning fireplace. Our wood supply is kept in a small outdoor shed. Because the alpine pastures lie above the tree line, we have to carry our wood from the forest below. The fireplace not only provides heat but is also our cooking place, equipped with a hanging cast iron kettle. We take our fresh water from a nearby fountain, which we also share with our neighbor. Mounted on the kitchen wall are a couple of boards that serve as shelves for our few plates, cooking utensils, and some provisions.

My mother will soon start making her minestrone, her soup with many vegetables and pasta, which she will garnish with grated cheese made here on the alp. I like her minestrone a bit better than the roasted flour soup that most of our neighbors make, though I understand that vegetables are hard to come by up here—and fruits are hardly to be found. The usual fare consists of dishes made with different grains, and then of course milk, butter, homemade cheese, and whey. With the minestrone we will have some of that good Valais sourdough rye, the bread that is baked only twice each year, in quantities to last six months. This bread is so hard that only my father can cut it, using a very sharp knife. It doesn't matter—the bread is good anyway. In fact with a generous slab of butter it is like a feast. It just requires careful chewing. And I hold each bite in my mouth awhile, to soften it with spittle. But I could never offer such

> food to my classmates down in Zürich, lest I become the laughing stock of the group.
>
> Adjoining the kitchen is our second room, where a bed takes up nearly the whole space. Our family of five sleeps in this bed, which has two levels. The lower level is a drawer that contains a mattress. At bedtime we pull out the drawer, and I sleep here with my sisters, while my parents sleep above. This room has one very small window, and the window has a narrow ledge that we use as a shelf. When we lean out the open window, we have a magnificent view of the valley below, and we can smell the animals that live in the stall directly beneath us. This is a perfect arrangement, because when the days and nights are chilled by rain, the animals' warmth warms us.

The time I spent on this alp with my family allowed me to vividly connect with the alpine life and hut of the legend. Indeed, in bygone times all alpine huts were built with this design. It made complete sense from the point of view of their purpose: During the summer and early fall, the farmers were fully occupied on the alps with their herds, milk, and cheese-making, so they had no time for leisure—and no need for leisure rooms. Their regular homes down in the valley weren't much different. They typically lived in two rooms that were only slightly larger, a design that took account of the long winter months that they would spend indoors. I should mention here that my father's family was no poorer than others inhabiting the upper valleys of Valais, and these families did not consider themselves to be poor. The sense of poverty was registered only in comparison with people living in Swiss cities, for instance in Zürich.

The Winter Setting

The story of Nazhans unfolds at the time of year when the vegetative forces of nature have withdrawn and sunk into hibernation. Snow is all around, signaling hostility to life, indeed death. From the human standpoint winter is a time of withdrawal and perhaps depression. Appearing in dreams, stories, and images, snow can symbolize the death of feelings towards others. Although the avalanche comes later in our story, it bears mentioning here because the threat was (and still is) real, and can be imagined into the set of dangers to which Nazhans and his real human counterparts were exposed, all the more so while living on the alp. Pictured in our legend as the "broad-backed white monster," avalanches in Switzerland today still can roar down the mountainsides with little warning, at worst to bury whole villages and leave tolls of death and material destruction, and immeasurable human helplessness. In earlier times witches or other evil spirits were blamed for such disaster. Valley inhabitants tried to ward off the dreaded forces with Christian and pagan rites, using exorcism, incantation, processions, and bell-ringing. Numerous votive pictures propped along alpine pathways still extol the saints who heroically rescued avalanche victims.[7]

While it signals death, a snowy landscape is also something fabulous and extraordinary. Snow transforms the landscape into something where miracles can happen at any time. Jung cites passages from an alchemical treatise in which snow is associated with Mercury, the great transmuter.[8] In her commentary on *Aurora Consurgens*, an alchemical treatise attributed to Thomas Aquinas, von Franz mentions the beauty of white snow as a reward for faith.[9] Yet according to the Church Fathers, it is a symbol of eternal damnation.[10]

Nazhans's "Agreement"

Nazhan's agreement to tend his neighbor's cattle in the winter bespeaks an actual custom that demanded neighborly support, and as well, the community's historical dependence on livestock farming (along with the cultivation of a few crops, including grapes for wine production). Although we might readily imagine the tightly bonded community, we need also imagine the remoteness and isolation of the alpine hut in which Nazhans abides the freezing winter night, having put out the fire and remaining all alone, save for the cattle he guards. Perhaps he hears the eerily whistling wind, crackling snow, tumbling rocks, and other less familiar, spookier sounds. The "knock on the wall," the swinging doors, "more than one hundred ice-cold hands": Such narrative elements symbolize the winter realities and threats, the dread of freezing to death, the haunted feeling, and the sense of the uncanny that pervaded the alpine culture and its legends. Under such circumstances, Nazhans is advised by his neighbor that he should be grateful, for he has received a visit from "the poor souls." Not only this, but these visitors came in "charitable service," and would "at some point give [him] a hand." Nazhans's neighbor thus reveals respect for the departed ancestors—and the conscious and collectively valued attitude that contributed to survival under harsh conditions.

Like most other people in the region, my father and grandmother held the steadfast belief that the poor souls were present, wandering alone or in groups, suffering the life of purgatory, and reaching out to the living. As they taught me, if one helps the poor souls, the poor souls respond in kind. The kinds of things people actually did to sustain this system of reciprocity between the living and the dead are depicted in other legends of this type. For instance in one, we are told of a woman who ritually left a little window slightly ajar in the winter to allow the spirits to enter and warm themselves. Another mentions a man who regularly put out a basin of water so the spirits could quench their thirst. The reciprocity of the system is also illustrated in a legend about a pious man who always prayed for the poor souls.[11] Although he was often tormented and threatened by the other villagers. One day, when he was caught in their attacks, the poor souls appeared, fighting on his behalf and driving away the cruel ones.

The point is that Nazhans is not grateful—much less does he recognize or willfully agree to help the poor souls. And so, when he reaches for the door, they force themselves and their "handshakes" upon him, indulging themselves in the warmth of his room and his bodily warmth. Growing "cold as a glacier," he is filled dread: "I will stay no more!" In a rational view Nazhans begins to assume the look of a man who is naïve and cowardly about winter on the alp. Within the specific cultural context of this story, however, he personifies as well unconsciousness with regard to the attitude of respect and things that need be ritually done in order to preserve this attitude.

Nazhans Survives

Approaching the end of our story, Nazhans finds himself on a steep slope when, to his utter surprise, an avalanche breaks loose. He can no longer stand up or hold on to anything. Everything is sliding, and when he is "hurtled over the terrible cliff into valley," the icy ground falls away from under him. This is the kind of situation that humans cannot handle alone, a time when ordinary mortals are completely helpless. Of a man like Nazhans who finds himself in such dire straights, we would be prone to say that he lacks an instinctual feel for the terrain and weather. But the Valaisans would add that he lacks connection with the ancestral spirits and their powers of warning. Or that such a man recognizes very well the fact that the poor souls exist, but fails to realize they have anything to do with him—much less does he expect help from them.

Still, although he is buried again and again by surges of snow, Nazhans survives, meeting a happy end after all: "[A] cold hand always pulled him out and put him back on top of the rolling avalanche. Uninjured, he rode on the broad back of the white monster down to the meadows above the village of Wiler." And, the story concludes, "Only then did he remember the night in the neighbor's cabin where his hand had grown "cold as a glacier" and his neighbor's words, "The poor souls will at some point give you a hand." Nazhans's harrowing adventure appears to instill in him, finally, a whole new respect.

But is it not remarkable that the poor souls rescue Nazhans despite his previous disregard for their existence? What message are we to take from this? Is it nothing more than superstition or archaic belief explaining a "narrow escape" that we might attribute to remarkable luck? It certainly counts for something that Nazhans himself is ready to give a hand to friends in need. The legend further implies that Nazhans's forced handshake in the hut constituted his *tacit* agreement to help the poor souls. In other words, in cases of miraculous survival, the system appears to extend benevolent containment for unconscious individuals. Most imminently, belief in the spirits as such stood as a constant reminder that one's survival and well-being depends on forces greater than one's own. This is the kind of recognition that keeps the ego in proper relationship to the psyche as whole. Nazhans's neighbor can be said to personify the collective conviction in this respect; compared with Nazhans, he seems to embody a kind of positive shadow, a complementary soul brother.

Symbolism of the Hand

Already in its title, "The Cold Hand," our legend seems to draw specifically on the archaic and rich symbolism of the hand itself, which appears in Paleolithic cave paintings from approximately 20,000 to 10,000 years ago in Europe, South America, and Australia.[12] The language of the hands is very expressive and is understood to some extent everywhere. Treaties are sealed with a handshake.[13] The handshake is a universally accepted and valued ritual greeting in the Western world. A handshake has many shades of meaning, but a basic element is a showing of mutual recognition and respect. In various Indo-European languages the expression "to give someone a hand" means to give help. Indeed, one of the main differences between our animal relatives and ourselves is our ability to make tools. For this we need hands with very fine motor control.

It was by our evolving to walk upright on two legs that our hands were freed for tool-making and other activities demanding complex manual skills. According to the neurologist Frank R. Wilson, the development of the human hand was an extremely important evolutionary step from pre-humans to modern humans.[14] The development of manual skills has significantly advanced the development of the brain. This is repeated for every human baby, as has been reported in Wilson.[15] We think, too, of the Roman Catholic and other traditions in which people are blessed or healed by the laying on of hands. In prayer the hands are raised or folded.

In *Symbols of Transformation* Jung emphasized the generative and creative aspects of the hand.[16] In the Neolithic era, hand representations continued, mainly of the Goddess.[17] Trade is conducted and power is exercised with the hands. Hands are therefore often symbols of power. This began with the hand of the great Goddess, and continued to the hand of Fatima, daughter of the Prophet Mohammed, and to the gestures of Kings who greet with a raised hand. Contact magic is practiced with the touch of the hand. The giving of hands often seals a marriage. In this context, there is little that gives us a stronger impression of bonding than the image of a gentle old couple going hand in hand along a path.

Margaret Mahler and her colleagues reported an interesting phenomenon in their observations of young children interacting with their mothers. When infants begin to move physically into unprotected space, they repeatedly return briefly to touch their mothers because the mother is still needed as a home base, a source from which to "refuel."[18] Did the spirits of the dead need the handshake to refuel, like the infant's touching the mother?

In sum it can be said that hands empower our ability to handle things and are therefore powerful tools. Symbolically speaking, we see here the overlapping of two large themes: on one side the meaning of the hand in the role of power—and on the other side, the meaning of the hand as a means of contact and connection with our fellow human beings.

What the Dead Say to Me

In earlier pages I mentioned my debt to my father and grandmother for my introduction to the life and legends of Valais. Well, times change, and I changed with them. Growing from adolescence to early adulthood, I began to distance myself from Valais, feeling that this very backward place had little to offer. At this stage in my life, the people of Valais and their legends seemed to me to be terribly moralistic. My own life was unfolding in urban Zürich and in the thoroughly modern twentieth century. What was I do to with my inheritance of a world that seemed stuck in the seventeenth century and dismissed by others while everybody else moved on? I saw no other solution than to free myself from it.

Many years later, however, there was a crucial change—when I was able to realize a long hoped for dream. In a nutshell: I entered training at the Jung Institute in Zürich, and in that context reencountered my past and the legends of Valais, especially the legends of the dead. This re-awakening grabbed me—or said otherwise, I was compelled by the poor souls to write my (unpublished) thesis, "What the Dead Tell Us." Ever since then, the influence of the Valais on me has continued. I have come to realize that through family history, the land, and the legends, the dead speak not only to me, but also to many different people, out of many different places and times.

The more lectures and workshops I've held on the topic, the more I've found myself in the role of an emissary for the cultural treasures from this region. The interest shown by others in the Valais, even by those from beyond Swiss borders, has given me great pleasure. I am also enormously pleased that my ancestors and their customs, having been so long ridiculed and even disparaged, are now receiving well-deserved attention. I am especially happy that the people of Valais, disregarding the outer world's denigrating view, have held unwaveringly to their traditions, tending them with respect, love and care.[19]

Following C.G. Jung we can say that with legends like "The Cold Hand" the Valaisans manifested a cultural system of belief, which in "establish[ing] a relationship to the unconscious," established also "a relationship to the collectivity of the dead; . . . the mythic land of the dead, the land of the ancestors."[20] Jung himself experienced in departed souls the "voices of the Unanswered, Unresolved and Unredeemed"[21] within in his own psyche and ancestral inheritance. Stressing the importance of connecting with the ancestors he reflected,

> The less we understand of what our fathers and forefathers sought, the less we understand ourselves, and thus we help with all our might to rob the individual of his roots and guiding instincts, so that he becomes a particle in the mass, ruled only by what Nietzsche called the spirit of gravity.[22]

I am convinced that it would do us all good to return to and explore the customs and traditions of our ancestors, for in this way we "come home," we become rooted in our origins. We need not venture far beyond our own borders, or look with envy upon things foreign. We need no longer deceive ourselves about or split off our own collective histories of suffering and shame. Obviously it would be of great value to have knowledge about the cultures in which our clients are rooted. And it can be important as well to experience the cultures of their ancestors, with whom our clients' own parents are more directly connected.

Helpfulness, solidarity, and sense of community should sustain "beyond the grave." By which I mean: A sense of community and the accompanying sense of responsibility to both past and future generations are urgently needed in our time. Moreover, the history of evolution has taught us that the human race has survived only because individuals have built up sophisticated social networks and cooperative systems.[23] This is no less true if we understand the spirits of the dead as intra-psychic phenomena, or as unredeemed or unfinished business. Something still haunts us as an autonomous complex that acts inwardly and outwardly to reconnect us with the fate that binds us together.

NOTES

1. Maria Anna Bernasconi, "The Fountain of Memories: Buried and Uncovered," *Symbolic Life 2009, Spring: A Journal of Archetype and Culture*, 2009, Vol. 82 (New Orleans: Spring Journal, 2009), pp. 153-170.

2. Bernasconi, "The Fountain of Memories," p. 157.

3. *Ibid.*, p. 159.

4. Eds.' note: For legends of Valais in general see, H.A. Guerber, "Legends of Vaud and Valais," in *Legends of Switzerland*, CIHM/ICMH Microfiche Series, Canadian Institute for Historical Microreproductions (1983) (Toronto: The Musson Book Company, 1900), at Open Library http://openlibrary.org/books/OL24344229M/Legends_of_Switzerland (acessed 11 August, 2011).

5. Alois Lütolf, *Sagen, Bräuche und Legenden aus den fünf Orten Luzern, Uri, Schwyz, Unterwalden und Zug* (New York: Verlag Hildesheim, 1976); Karl W. Glaettli, *Zürcher Sagen* (Zürich: Hans Rohr, 1970); Alfred Cérésole, *Légendes des Alpes Vaudoises* (Genève: Editions Slatkine, 1980); Walter Keller, *Am Kaminfeuer der Tessiner. Tessiner Sagen und Märchen aus dem Volke* (Bern: Feuz, 1960).

6. Abridged by the author after Josef Guntern, *Volkserzählungen aus dem OberValais, Sagen, Legenden, Märchen, Anekdoten aus dem deutschsprechenden Valais* (Basel: Krebs, 1979), p. 571. Translation by Andrew Fellows.

7. Hans Haid, *Mythos Lawine* (Innsbruck,Wien, Bozen: Studienverlag, 2007); see also Hanns Bächtold-Stäubli, vol. 5, p. 905 f.

8. C.G. Jung, *The Collected Works of C. G. Jung*, trans. R.F.C. Hull (Princeton, N.J.: Princeton University Press, 1969), vol. 13, § 263. Future references the Collected Works (hereinafter "*CW*") will be by volume number and paragraph number.

9. Marie-Louise von Franz, *Aurora Consurgens, A Document Attributed to Thomas Aquinas on the Problem of Opposites in Alchemy*, trans. R.F.C. Hull and A.S.B. Glover (Toronto: Inner City Books, 2000), p. 63, p. 145.

10. *Ibid.*, p. 234.

11. Hans Koch, "Die dankbaren Toten zu Baar," in *Zuger Sagen & Legenden* (Zug: Ballmer, 1974), p. 10 f.

12. G. Burenhult, *Die ersten Menschen* (Augsburg: Weltbild, 2000), pp. 18, 97, 112–113.

13. See J.C. Cooper, *An Illustrated Encyclopaedia of Traditional Symbols* (London: Thames & Hudson, 1978), p. 78 f. See also Hanns Bächtold-Stäubli (ed.), *Handwörterbuch des deutschen Aberglaubens* (Berlin: Walter de Gruyter, 1987), vol. 3, p. 1379, p. 1401.

14. Frank R. Wilson, *The Hand: How Its Use Shapes the Brain, Language and Human Culture* (New York: Pantheon Books, 1998).

15. *Ibid.*, p. 98f.

16. Jung, *CW* 5, § 266, § 271.

17. Marija Gimbutas, *The Language of the Goddess* (New York: Thames & Hudson, 1989), Hands and Feet of the Goddess, p. 305 ff., pictures: pp. 33, 164, 301.

18. Margareth Mahler, Fred Pine & Anni Bergman, *The Psychological Birth of the Human Infant* (London: Hutchinson, 1975), p. 69; see also p. 77, p. 90, p. 165, p. 187, p. 210.

19. I refer to respect and care such as that shown by the old man of the village of Saas Fe—who even in our present era of disbelief—cleared the paths every evening for the procession of the dead; reported by Katrin Riesterer and cited in Bernasconi, "The Fountain of Memories," p. 162.

20. C.G. Jung, *Memories, Dreams, Reflections*, ed. Aniela Jaffé, trans. Richard and Clara Winston, rev. ed. (New York: Vintage Books, 1989), p. 191.

21. *Ibid.*

22. *Ibid.*, p. 236.

23. See Richard Leakey and Roger Lewin, *Origins Reconsidered: In Search of What Makes Us Human* (New York: Doubleday, 1992).

Bound for the Eternal: The Religious Meaning of Folk Legends

GOTTHILF ISLER

Translation by Andrew Fellows

Scholars have been at loggerheads over the question of what does or doesn't constitute a legend for a long time. I am not going to join in this hair-splitting; I'd rather proceed in a more practical fashion.

Folk legends rightly belong to what people say, what they tell one another; they are the stories of the people. We tend to associate them with so-called "simple people," the people who live in small villages, in mountain villages, and on alpine pastures. We also imagine them as

Gotthilf Isler, Dr. phil., was born and raised in Zürich. He trained as a Jungian analyst at the C.G. Jung Institute in Zürich. At the University of Zürich he studied Folklore, European Folk Literature, and History of Religion. He is a founding member and past President of the Research and Training Centre for Depth Psychology according to C.G. Jung and Marie-Louise von Franz.

A version of this essay was originally published in German under the title, "Bezogenheit auf das 'Ewige,'" in Gotthilf Isler, *Lumen Naturae. Zum religiösen Sinn von Alpensagen. Vorträge und Aufsätze* (Küsnacht: Verlag für Jung'sche Psychologie, 2000), pp. 269-291.

belonging to earlier times when such stories used to be told—whereas today, people entertain themselves by listening to the radio, watching television, reading newspapers, and chatting about this and that.

However, not much is known about the old way of telling stories. The only thing we do know is that people got together more than today. In peasant areas people gathered mainly after work; in summer on a bench in front of the house, in winter in the warm *Lichtstube* or *Spinnstube* (spinning room). In our Swiss mountain villages there were four, five, or six such rooms where people came together in the evening to perform simple chores—until the beginning of the 20th century women used to bring their spinning wheels—and to sing, play cards, and smoke their pipes. When many people were together less heating was needed. Most of the time a single tallow candle had to suffice at any rate.

All the people of the village knew and were close to one another, close also in spirit, and gave one another spiritual comfort. Of course, there were enemies and deep hostilities—as in all villages; but if at all possible, the enemies sat in different houses.

This *z'Dorf gahn* (going to the village), as these gatherings were called in the mountain regions of Oberwallis and Berner Oberland, could become a passion.[1] The children usually slept at home, though the youngest were often brought along to these gatherings in the cradle by their parents. A house in Grächen (in the Swiss Canton of Wallis) is said to have had a floor that never dried out all winter because so many people came and went, mostly to play cards.[2] In Betten, another village in Wallis, the men allegedly "played cards so much during the winter that their women had no wood left for cooking and heating, because the men couldn't be budged from the game to gather wood in the forest." In the village of Eisten people talked about a man who came a long way down from his alp to one of the evening sessions. "He stayed all night to chat[3] and play. In the morning he said: 'Looks like I have to nip back up to feed the cattle'," but it was a two hour walk to get there.[4]

In most places people didn't actually gather specifically to tell or listen to stories. Most of the time the chat was about everyday things, just as it is for us today—people talked about current affairs, complained about illness, disaster, and death. People liked stories about fistfights and strong men, hunting and military service, about how so-and-so did well in marriage, or why Vreneli is such a poor thing for having gotten involved with Hansli.[5]

But sometimes somebody would bring up a particular topic, perhaps a supernatural experience or an account of one by someone else, or maybe just a single word—and the audience was under the spell of mythical happenings, and one story led to the next. In his collection of legends from the Haslital (in Berner Oberland), Melchior Sooder gave a good description of such evening gatherings. He remembered, among other things, that:

> One winter evening we had gone to the village. Below the *Bachefellenen* a tawny owl cried out from the rose-apple tree. All work stopped. There was complete silence. There was fear and anxiety on every face. Only the ticking of the wall clock and the cry of the bird could be heard. "Who is it crying for?" When the cries could no longer be heard, the women told how the owl announced deaths here and there, or how one had been heard in the wall of the *Totechlefelli* [or the *Totenuhr*, the knocking of the woodworms] and that a relative would die soon afterwards. "Hey," a woman tried to calm the others down, "how could that possibly be? The owls are just attracted by the light." But for the rest of the evening the conversation revolved around the uncanny bird that announces death.[6]

You see—here we encounter a different dimension. Here we are in the realm of legends. When legends are told, we are moved in a particular way, perhaps gripped, terrified, or sometimes inspired. Here the "other side" is present, the living spirit. We are accustomed to think that the spirit is something we have to create, towards which we must strive. We tend to forget that there is such a thing as a "holy" or "unholy" demonic spirit that "bloweth where it listeth,"[7] that is autonomous and spontaneous and takes hold of us without having to be created first. One doesn't even have to believe in it, because its effect is proof enough of its reality.

The experience of this autonomous spirit is probably the origin and basis of all legends. Such an experience is often a ghostly apparition or vision. In his book about a village in the Canton of St. Gallen, Amden, which sits high above Lake Walenstadt, Paul Huger tells of a woman who had exceptional visions all her life. This woman's dead husband also appeared to her:

> A few weeks after his death I had fallen into a light slumber after midnight. Suddenly I heard him coming up the stairs behind the house. I immediately recognized him by his footsteps. I awoke and thought: "It's been so hard that he's been gone for such a long time." It was only then I remembered that he was dead. He opened the front door, walked through the hall, opened the kitchen door and approached the bedroom door, just as he always did. Then he came in. I lay there with my face turned away and waited for him to do something. I was overcome by great joy. He pulled the wool blanket down over my shoulders. After a while I felt cold. I pulled it back and looked around. There was nobody there, but still I felt a great joy.

The woman was "completely certain," Hugger added, "that the man came in order to show her his release from purgatory. It is a widespread belief among the people that the souls of the dead are permitted to convey this message to the living."[8]

He also reports an encounter with an old woman who had lost her husband a few weeks before. When he enquired about her well-being, he received the following answer:

> "Well, I've been longing for my husband." And then her face suddenly lit up with great joy: "He appeared to me. On the third day. Before he died I had told him: Come and tell me then what it is like in eternity." She had gone to bed at seven. "At ten there was a sudden rushing noise and then he came." As for how he looked then: "He was totally white and looked content. But he didn't say anything. Yes, we were very much in love."[9]

Science has no definitive explanation for such experiences. There are no sound criteria that establish whether there are ghosts or not. As modern people, we have to live with this uncertainty. But we do know that such phenomena are experienced, and that they are often among the most important things in the lives of those who experience them. From reports of such experiences in good legend collections we can see that such occurrences, together with those which foretell death, are remembered for decades and clearly stay with certain individuals for a lifetime.[10] If we really want to understand people, we should not dismiss things that are important to them.

These two experiences related above are consistent with the Christian belief in the "*arme Seelen*," which in German always refers to the "poor souls of the departed." The immortality of every individual's soul forms the center of the Christian message. However, what—at least in recent times—can only be heard from the pulpit is proven beyond all doubt by such experiences to be one's very own personal truth.[11] News of the well-being of their deceased husbands was experienced by both widows, and beyond that the certainty that life does not end with death and that it will continue in the world beyond. The widows' certainty of life in the beyond corresponds with a view the church arrived at in the Middle Ages, according to which our earthly existence is a relatively minor prelude to the immeasurable duration of eternal life. "We are not in this world to have heaven down here, but in order to earn it!" a seventy-year-old hill-farmer woman told me twenty-five years ago on an alpine pasture in Canton Wallis. This is a medieval attitude in its unadulterated form.[12]

This view of the world gives too much emphasis to the hereafter for our sensibilities, but it enabled these people to live. They had the advantage of being able to live in a cosmos that was ordered down to the last detail. Medieval man lived trusting in a benign father in heaven who holds his fate securely in his hand from birth until death and beyond. He knew that "no sparrow falls without the Father's will," as it says in Matthew 10:29.[13] This knowledge, the loss of which we are these days growing more and more painfully aware of, made it possible to bear the dark sides of life too: the dirt, the often extreme poverty, the hunger, the helplessness in the face of pain, illness, death, and even human injustice. It was a knowledge that, despite all, life is meaningful. This is probably the essence of all religions: that the material reality of life is compensated by the reality of the spirit which is not only beyond doubt but must also be constantly considered.[14] Just as in the Christian faith, this knowledge was also kept alive in folk legends. These stories were not just about supernatural experiences. When such tales were passed on from generation to generation, they changed and became more like myths and fairy tales. The storyteller's imagination began to get involved. If a ghost was only heard in the original version, how it looked might subsequently be added, and even later what it said and did and how the person was drawn into relationship with it. In Erschmatt in Canton Wallis an 80-year-old peasant laborer told me in spite of his skeptical attitude towards legends:

> In the fall three hunters stayed overnight at the *Bachalpe*. Just as they were going to sleep, all at once the door opened and they heard noises as if alpine dairywomen had begun to work and as if they were making cheese. They got up and wanted to help them. When they came down there was nobody there, not even embers in the fire. Nothing happened to them.—This story was told by Fritz Meichtry who was there himself. He was one who was not easily frightened; otherwise he wouldn't have gotten up to have a look![15]

That story has already been passed on, but the storyteller still knew the witness; the legend is probably very close to the actual experience. Later on, such a legend might look like this, as reported by the author Johann N. Ritter von Alpenburg:

> On an alpine pasture near the so-called "*ebenen Ferner*," [a glacier] the *Imsterkaser* [a mountain hut] was haunted by the ghost of an alpine dairywoman after the summer season. Once a hunter stayed there overnight. Soon the female ghost came through the door in her dairywoman's outfit and cooked some gruel, took it while it was still hot to the hunter's bunk, and whispered softly: eat. But the hunter was a coward; he didn't dare to say a word, much less to help himself. The dairy woman was sad and left, sighing deeply. To this day the hunter regrets his cowardice, because he thinks that if he had been more courageous he could have redeemed the woman, and perhaps in doing so have even made his own fortune.[16]

Here the motif of the offered ghostly food has been added. If the hunter had been brave and accepted the gruel, he could have redeemed the poor soul. In these legends the offered gruel is always associated with guilt: in most cases the ghost in its former life had committed the crime of wasting or contaminating milk. It had committed a sin against the gifts of nature. Therefore it must atone for this now. The gruel is often unappetizing and made of ash. Eating it would mean sharing in the guilt of the repentant person. Rejecting it may cost your life.

At the Lamark alpine pasture in the Tyrolian valley, *Zillertal*, a herdsman rejected the gruel offered to him by a little man.

> "If I'm hungry I'll cook something myself!" he retorted with some irritation. The little man was seized by a boundless rage, grabbed the feckless herdsman and threw him right over the roof of the

> hut so that he lay dead on the ground. From the next day on, the herdsman's ghost worked, and nobody noticed anything.[17]

But on a different alpine pasture in the *Zillertal,* called the *Loschbodenalpe,* a brave girl summoned up the courage to taste the horrible gruel of ash and water that a repentant hunchbacked *Almputz* [an alpine ghost] had prepared for her.

> And, oh, what a miracle! The disgusting dish tasted delightful, surpassing even the best *Melchermus* [a gruel made by a dairy man]. The girl ate up a whole pan of the gruel in one go. When she finally put down her spoon and looked up, the *Almputz* was gone. In its place stood a lively young lad [. . .].[18]

With her deed the girl had brought about the redemption of the ghost.

Legends have a happy or an unhappy ending depending on the behavior of the "hero" or "heroine." It all depends on the attitude of the human being, so too in legends of a very different type—for example, in treasure legends. Some of you might know the beautiful story of the Brunnenburg (a castle in Italy's Southern Tyrol), in which a herder girl followed a little golden snake into a crack in the ground and found a cave full of treasures from which she was allowed to take as much as she could carry.[19] In other versions it is often a dog that shows the way to the treasure. Most people are afraid to follow and therefore, of course, never find the treasure. However, in Valendas (in Canton Graubünden), an old woman followed a little snow-white poodle that led her to an overturned water trough where, not far below the ground, she found a buried vessel filled with gold pieces and gems. "From one hour to the next she became a rich woman."[20]

Sometimes both types of behavior, positive and negative, are shown in the same legend, as in a wonderful story from the *Glödnitztal,* a valley in eastern Austria, which Oskar Moser heard from an old woman by the name of Apollonia Kreuter.

> Near the *Prosenstein* [a rock face] a woodsman followed a woman in white through a door in a rock wall into a cave, where a little coal-black dog was sitting on a chest. The woodsman was allowed to take more and more money, but each time he had to take the key from the mouth of the dog, carefully take the dog down from the chest and then put it back when he was done. He quit

> his job, did nothing but drink, and paid for the other barflies. "I have heaps of money!" he would say. . . .

I'll just quote the end:

> And then they get drunk over and over again, and keep running out of money. He must have gone to get money many times; oh my God, a chest full of cash can't be carted off that fast. Now he's about to go there again, and he's drunk, punch drunk! So he walked in the door, knocked the dog off the chest and said: "You heartless beast, must you sit on the chest every time!" He took the key, unlocked the chest, took the money, but didn't put the dog back in its place, he didn't put it back. That was the last time, after that he didn't find anything.—The chest with the money is still there, but nobody can find it anymore.[21]

If many legends are compared, one finds that most, as in this example, seem to contain every possible behavior towards entities from the world beyond. Broadly speaking, in Grimm's fairytale "Mother Holle" the "positive" and "negative" types of behavior are embodied in the stepdaughter and daughter respectively, often called *Goldmarie* and *Pechmarie*, i.e., "Gold Mary" and "Tar Mary."[22] Where legends and folktales were still alive in the community, people knew how to relate to the beings from beyond: to the poor departed souls, as we have seen, to the guardian animals and other creatures of nature, then the witches, the devil, and finally—or first and foremost, if you wish—to God and the saints. In legends there lived a very differentiated knowledge about the otherworld and its powers; a knowledge of how to behave so that these powers brought luck and blessings and didn't destroy one.

The beings from beyond simply embody in images, in the mind's eye, the living, autonomous spirit I mentioned by way of introduction. In the case of ghost apparitions and genuine parapsychological events, our scientific conscience forbids any certainty: are these apparitions really of the deceased? We must leave this question open. However, with elaborated legends we can't take the entities from the other side literally. We are too enlightened, too rational to believe that a poor soul wanted to force a hunter to eat ash gruel, or that a storm was unleashed by a malicious witch, or that a snake fed on breadcrumbs and milk really gave a little crown as a gift to bring us wealth and happiness for our whole life, or that there really are three old men who live in a mountain in order to help us and the fatherland in difficult times.

These legends had an effect, they were taken seriously, or else they wouldn't have been passed on. We can safely assume that most people believed they were true. But *we* need to understand all these entities and powers *symbolically*: they are expressions of an inner, psychic truth, not a truth of consciousness, the ego, but those parts of the soul of which we are unconscious and yet we share with all humankind.

Thanks to Carl Gustav Jung we know that there is an autonomous collective unconscious which must be understood as the precondition and primal realm of all conscious activity. When the contents of the unconscious become visible in visions, fantasies, and dreams, they appear as psychic images. It seems that the soul generally expresses that which we cannot know in images because we can't look directly into the unconscious. These images can be ordered according to certain types, which led Jung to the assumption that there are ordering factors in the unconscious which he initially called primal images, and later on, archetypes. When archetypes are experienced, they have a numinous effect, i.e., demonic or divine. It is a wonder to me that all the fantastic things that people have told of are real and potent—not in an external sense, but as an inner fact, an inner truth. Psychology has discovered that there are powers which act exactly like demons or God or gods: just as pitiless and terrible, but also just as helping and healing.[23] We don't know for sure where the "place" of these powers is, whether they are external or internal. In all likelihood that which used to be experienced as external—in the form of certain creatures, for example, or fairies or witches—or the Devil—is nowadays mostly experienced internally in dreams or fantasies. Where we experience such creatures externally, we now speak of projections and presume that it is in fact an inner phenomenon which is experienced externally. This notion of "nothing but projection" is a difficult chapter in Jungian psychology, and many puzzles about the connection between the internal and the external world remain. If someone has a vision, they are convinced that it is an external truth. Just try proving to someone who saw a UFO that it is really an internal fact!

However, there are certainly psychic factors which "arrange" the images of our fantasies and dreams, i.e., they order them according to inner necessity. We don't just dream this or that by chance. Dreams are very often enigmatic and difficult to understand, but when we do succeed in understanding them we find that they have a meaningful connection with our life. Most of the time they present a certain contrast to the ego's view of itself or its immediate environment or life and the world in general. It is as if the unconscious wanted to tell us through our dreams: See, you should look at this or that differently or more carefully. It is not what you think!

In my youth, for example, I was rationalistic, idealistic, and "enlightened" and thought I would have nothing more to do with Christianity, that it was more or less finished with and dead. When I was in my early twenties, I had a very impressive dream in which I was holding a silver crucifix, which was as long as my hand was wide—and it suddenly came to life. This did not lead me to become a church-goer, but from then on I knew that in no way was Christianity over and done with for me, that Christ lives in a mysterious way. He manifestly embodies a psychic truth. In this way, a dream can correct an erroneous attitude of ego consciousness which is not appropriate for the standpoint of the soul.

In the same way, folk legends corrected, compensated for the people's conscious attitudes. Throughout the creation or recollection of these stories, unknown psychic factors were at work, presumed ultimately to be the archetypes of the collective unconscious, which have always made the contents of the unconscious in so-called mythical images so plausible for people.[24] We may assume that, during those evening gatherings or other occasions, especially when the subject came round to the supernatural, that one story called up another, one idea the next. We don't make ideas, they happen to us. Surely they were the archetypal contents of the unconscious that were "constellated," and that were appropriate to compensate for the particular conscious attitude. As we know, these ideas and notions are important for the psychic balance of individuals or communities.

I assume that the living spirit of the unconscious played a part in these conversations. So-called popular belief was not a religious system, nor something like a scaled-down dogma—the legends didn't need an ecclesiastic institution in order to stay alive, nor did they have one. Popular belief kept on reconstituting itself through the eternal presence of the unconscious in these notions whenever legends were told. It is not unlike a round of joke-telling. One idea follows the next, the sparks of the living spirit fly, and overwhelming fun brings tears to our eyes, melting down all hardening of the ego. It shows us how life could be quite different.

The spirit that lives in the images of legends comes from the same spontaneity, but has a different character. Most of the time it is darker and eerier, but also in some way "holier." In contrast with the transience of a joke, which is no sooner heard than forgotten, legends often contain an aspect of the "eternal." This aspect seems also to belong to the archetypes. They, the builders of our dreams and spontaneous ideas, are the psychically archaic and primal in man and probably in animals too. We don't know at what stage of evolution the archetypes appeared because we have no direct knowledge of the capacity for imagination in animals. They probably appeared together with life itself and acted as structuring factors in evolution.[25] When one stirs an archetype, one touches the archaic, that which has always been. This is why archetypes convey a feeling of the "eternal" and the divine.

Naturally there are archetypal situations in everyday life. The birth of a child is such a situation for its parents; the newborn brings up feelings of the greatest happiness and love. Or, if you were once head over heels in love—if you allow yourself to remember it—maybe then you had the feeling you had already known this person "for ages"(as Goethe with the woman from Stein). Being in love is an archetypal, an "eternal" situation: Time and again, for as long as there have been people, love has awakened the same feelings of a connectedness that transcends time or is eternal.

When people told these legends, when they took them seriously and were able to live with these archetypal ideas, they were relating to the archaic, the heritage of mankind, that which is (relatively) eternal. It was a connection with the inner ancestors, a relationship, so to say, with "childhood" and the timeless aspect of the human soul. The religious historian Mircea Eliade spoke of *illud tempus* (the sacred time of origins), which is invariably given a new lease on life in myth: the recollection of the magic morning of the beginning, when all was new and good, and the cosmos was in order. For example, when we remember Christmas, the Christian myth, the birth of Christ, we are present at the new beginning, at the birth of *lux moderna,* the new light of the world.

In legends things are anything but all good, quite the contrary. Much that is eerie and dark lives in them. And yet, the telling of legends is healing, because they correspond with what has always been man's spiritual life. However, it is precisely from the archaic that the newest of all paradoxically arises: the collective unconscious is simultaneously the source of all new creation, the maternal basis of all growth of consciousness. If one examines a large number of legends very carefully, and pays attention more to what changes than to what stays the same, the old established, traditional motifs of legend appear in endlessly new combinations to compensate for conscious attitudes, just as in dreams.

When I told you my dream of the crucifix that came to life, I left something out. The dream had an uncanny aspect: the previously rigid Christ, made of solid silver, suddenly bent one arm up and the other down, so that the two arms formed an "S." I was terribly afraid, and upon awaking thought: "This means 'snake' or 'Satan'!" This Christ was not the traditional Savior, but apparently contained both aspects, Christ and His antagonist. This ambivalent Christ is the living symbol of our time! I had this dream almost forty years ago, and as you can imagine it hasn't made my life any easier.[26]

But it is in precisely this way that folk legends compensate for the standpoint of Christian consciousness. The church speaks of a loving God, the God of love, and we strive for the good and shun evil. In contrast, in legends the divine is often terrible, even demonic, but unavoidable and, so to speak, "necessary for salvation." It was thought for a long time that pagan and pre-Christian elements lived on in them. In the time before psychology—roughly before 1900—it was acceptable to see legends this way. But psychologically speaking, they contain much more the other-than-Christian, the not-yet-redeemed, that wants to belong to an extended idea of God for the future. Legends were not "made" by anyone, but are much more something that is found. Like dreams, they are an expression of psychic facts, of psychic reality. A religion is not somebody's brainchild, but has much more to do with the driving force of the human soul, born from the hearts of the many.

To again allude to compensation: That which is high, pure, and "holy" in Christianity, is mostly low, dirty, and ostracized in legends. The hero of the legend is he who is able to deal in the proper way with the "other" side, with what remains unredeemed, and he usually stands *extra ecclesiam*, outside of the church. The treasure in legends often appears during church holy days, for example on Good Friday in the Canton of Uri, or it may be found only during Christmas mass when all the pious sit in church. Even if a poor peasant may only picture a pile of gold and silver coins when he hears the word treasure, it is no ordinary gold, but a highest good. The treasure has more to do with the divine in man, with the meaning of life, than with worldly riches. It resembles the gold of the alchemists, which for some represented the image of God in man. But this highest good is guarded by the devil or a stinking goat, or by a snake, or even a dog. Whoever wants to take the treasure must be able to deal correctly with the devil or this animal. The animals symbolize our own animal soul, our unconscious animal and instinctive nature, a realm that Christianity has neglected. In many legends, the treasure-guarding virgin must be kissed in her form as a snake to be redeemed—then the redeemer gets the treasure, and his family becomes rich and happy for seven or nine generations. If he does not dare to kiss the snake, he brings misfortune to as many generations. So he brings misfortune not because he fails to be "noble, helpful and good" (Goethe), but because he doesn't dare to confront the snake, because he fails when faced with the problem of animal nature or evil. It is never the point of these legends to abandon or to disregard Christianity and the very important moral differentiation that Christianity has brought us. Rather, it seems to me that the legends demand a Christian attitude in its deepest sense, with which we may accept the neglected psychic or godly realms that have been overlooked in the Christian concept of redemption. On this topic Jung wrote:

> Only on the basis of such an attitude, which renounces none of the Christian values won in the course of Christian development, but which, on the contrary, tries with Christian charity and forbearance to accept even the humblest things in one's own nature, will a higher level of consciousness and culture become possible.[27]

Compensation through folk legends touches upon three major themes: the recognition and redemption of the feminine archetype, the feminine divinity, and with that, a religious attitude towards nature in the broadest sense—the soul, too, is part of nature—and finally even a religious consideration of evil. Whereas the church deprived the individual of a good deal of responsibility and has a hard time abandoning the image of a shepherd guarding his flock, legends emphasize the unique value of the individual; everything depends on the personal deeds of the individual, on his courage and integrity. However, in the church as in legends, it is all about the relationship with transcendental powers, the relationship with that which is infinitely larger and more important than the ego with its limited aims.

Jung wrote in his memoirs:

> The decisive question for man is: Is he related to something infinite or not? That is the telling question of his life. Only if we know that the thing which truly matters is the infinite can we avoid fixing our interest . . . upon all kinds of goals which are not of real importance . . . . The more a man lays stress on false possessions, and the less sensitivity he has for what is essential, the less satisfying is his life. He feels limited because he has limited aims . . . . If we understand and feel here in this life we already have a link with the infinite, desires and attitudes change. In the final analysis, we count for something only because of the essential we embody, and if we do not embody that, life is wasted.[28]

The real message of the church is this orientation toward the infinite and the eternal, and people were able to connect with these dimensions as long as they remained secure in the maternalistic church. Legends did exactly the same thing—less comforting, less sublime, put perhaps in a more lively and down-to-earth way. When this relationship with the living spirit is lost, life has very little meaning left. A little while ago, a distant neighbor recovered from a severe illness. She proudly announced: "We used to donate a bell to the church when our good health returned. But that was really stupid! This time I've had my kitchen renovated!" Can you see how small her life is?

I don't know how this woman is doing now. However, in the legends God gives a direct answer to egotism and arrogance, as in this story of a woman from Uri:

> A woman who was afflicted with a disfiguring disease was cured of it at Einsiedeln. As a token of her gratitude she gave to the Mother of God her *chrallis Halsbätti* (precious rosary) or, as others would have it, her gold necklace. Back at home everybody wanted to know, as one can imagine, how she was redeemed from her malady: "Don't ask me," she sneered once under this

> interrogation, "*wemmä der Wagä salbet, sä gahd'r*" ("if you grease the cart, it runs"). In a trice the jewelry was back around her neck, and so was the disease back in her body.[29]

You can say: Well, that's just old hat—*Vox Romae, vox Dei* (the voice of the church is the voice of God)! But it's not about the church, it's about God and the religious attitude. It is one of Jung's fundamental insights that man's soul becomes sick if he thinks he can rule his life with the will of his ego alone. A lack of meaning in life is behind neuroses and several physical ailments. For Jung the goal of the therapeutic process was: "transformation—not one that is predetermined, but rather an indeterminable change, the only criterion of which is the disappearance of egohood."[30] It is the same experience of which Paul said: "I live; yet not I, but Christ liveth in me."[31]

When necessary, legends unmistakably criticize the church and its clergy, for example in a story from the Austrian state of Carinthia:

> In the village of Maria-Wörth the great woman's day was celebrated. Boats came from every direction and brought devotees from near and far who wanted to take part in the procession. Only a poor *Halterbub* [herder boy] over in the village of Pritschitz had to stay home and tend the cows since he had neither shoes nor clothes to participate in the festivities. He stood sadly in the pasture, and looked in the direction of Maria-Wörth. He watched the procession and heard the prayers of the crowd which sounded to him like "*Platschiken-Platschaken*" [the sound of splashing water]. He felt a great longing to come close to the Mother of God too. He hurried down to the lake, folded his hands in earnest devotion and, imitating the sounds of the prayers drifting across the water, he stepped out and walked across the lake. In Maria-Wörth the priest and the faithful saw the child come across the water. They rushed down to the shore to see the miracle from up close. There they heard to their astonishment how the child said, "*Platschiken-Platschaken*" with earnest devotion. "Child," the priest said, "what are you saying? That's no prayer." And he taught him the words of a prayer. "Now, my child, turn back and recite the prayer you have learned from me." Obediently, the youngster went back onto the water and recited this prayer. A moment later, he disappeared under the waves.[32]

Here is a clear contrast of naive, genuine religiosity and mere traditional faith. The boy lost his life because he allowed others to persuade him.

In the Lechtal valley, in the Austrian state of Tyrol, there was a similar case in which a woman defended herself against a cleric:

> In Madaun there lived a grandmother who was so old that she could no longer manage the three-hour walk to the Elbigen Alp parish church on Sundays and holy days. But the priest wouldn't tolerate any exceptions and demanded that the old woman attend church like the rest of his flock. On the next Sunday the old woman set out and prayed ceaselessly until she reached Elbigen Alp. There the priest confronted her and asked how many "Our Fathers" she had prayed on her way there. The old woman said: "Three." The priest considered that too few. The old woman said: "Gosh, it's hot today", and hung her umbrella in the air where it stayed quite still. This convinced the priest of her devotion, and from that day on he always trusted what she said.[33]

There is a variant in which the old woman protested:

> All things have a point, and the important point here is how and where and when one prays; at my age, in our valley, what with the difficult path and the wild weather, three "Our Fathers" are worth more than a whole valley full of praying people somewhere else.[34]

The legend is reminiscent of that about the "saintly man" who can hang his hat or coat on a ray of sunlight. For him, the personal experience of a divine spirit has become a "supporting reality." In his case he was excused from having to come to mass because he was judged by the priest to be holier than himself. It is clear that the old woman, much like the "saintly man," is a model of internalized religiosity.

To conclude: Those for whom the external images have gotten lost, for whom they grow mute, are forced by inner necessity to search in the depths of their souls for what they can no longer find in the outside world. We can find it if we pay attention to our dreams in a religious way. Only what we experience ourselves can really support us. But it is no easy task to walk this path that leads inside and, paradoxically, it cannot be walked without becoming enmeshed in guilt. Jung writes: "This path to the primordial religious experience is the right one, but how many can recognize it? It is like a still small voice, and it sounds from afar. It is ambiguous, questionable, dark, presaging danger and hazardous adventure: a razor-edged path, to be trodden for God's sake only, without assurance and without sanction."[35]

Without sanction, without support, and yet with a religious attitude. A man from Eisten in Canton Wallis was reproached for waiting for treasure to appear in a remote farmyard on Christmas Eve. It wasn't right, he was told, to spend Christmas Eve there, he should be praying! But he defended himself: "I am certain that no man prayed more that Christmas Eve than I did. I was there for long enough . . . ." And he went on to describe how he had watched the long procession of lights of the churchgoers from the villages and hamlets as they went to midnight mass and back home during that long night.[36]—"No man prayed more than I did!" I can sympathize with him—and moreover he couldn't get the treasure.

Legends are so important because they are psychically true and because they concern all of us. We cannot revisit them by throwing our enlightenment overboard and becoming superstitious again. We can't go back to the Middle Ages. However, we can try to understand legends again. In his essay "The Stages of Life," Jung wrote, "Apart from the mere intellect,

> . . . there is a thinking in primordial images, in symbols which are older than the historical man, which are inborn in him from the earliest times, and which, eternally living, outlasting all generations, still make up the groundwork of the human psyche. It is only possible to live the fullest life when we are in harmony with these symbols; wisdom is a return to them. It is a question neither of belief nor of knowledge, but of the agreement of our thinking with the primordial images of the unconscious.[37]

These primal images of the soul live on in legends. They do not show us a perfect world, but what true religion is, and they show us what it means to be oriented towards the infinite and to be rooted in it. In our troubled times we are in need of this as never before.

NOTES

1. *Schweizerisches Idiotikon. Wörterbuch der schweizerdeutschen Sprache* (Frauenfeld: Huber, 1881ff). Band 13, p. 1481 and p. 1502.

2. Josef Guntern, *Volkserzählungen aus dem Oberwallis. Sagen, Legenden, Märchen, Anekdoten aus dem deutschsprachigen Wallis,* Schriften der Schweizerischen Gesellschaft für Volkskunde, vol. 62 (Basel: Krebs, 1978), no. 445.

3. *Schweizerisches Idiotikon.* Band 2, p. 1448: "hängeren-verhängern" means "to lose time chatting."

4. Guntern, *Volkserzählungen*, no. 444.

5. Eds.' note: "Vreneli" and "Hansli" are the endearing and/or diminutive forms of the typical names, Verena and Hans. The way they are used here would be equivalent to the English, "every Tom, Dick and Harry," which can refer as well to a woman doing something that every person ordinarily does.

6. Melchior Sooder, *Zelleni us em Haslital. Märchen, Sagen und Schwänke der Hasler aus mündlicher Überlieferung* (Basel: Schweizerische Gesellschaft für Volkskunde, 1943), p. 12, partly told in dialect (reprint Hans Dauwalder, Meiringen: Brügger 1984), 20f.

7.1 John 3:8, *The Holy Bible*, King James Version. All further references to the King James Version will be by author, book, and verse.

8. Paul Hugger, *Amden. Eine volkskundliche Monographie* (Basel: Schriften der Schweizerischen Gesellschaft für Volkskunde, vol. 41, 1961), p. 220.

9. *Ibid.* (partly told in dialect).

10. Arnold Büchli, *Mythologische Landeskunde von Graubünden. Ein Bergvolk erzählt. Das Gebiet vom Badus bis zum Calanda,* vol. 2, 3rd enlarg. edition (Disentis: Desertina, 1989), p. 514f.

11. Christine Détraz and Philippe Grand, *Ces histories que meurent. Contes et légendes du Valais* (Sierre, Lausanne: Editions Monographic, 1982), p. 35.

12. Gotthilf Isler, *Die Sennenpuppe. Eine Untersuchung über die religiöse Funktion einiger Alpensagen,* vol. 52 of the *Schriften der Schweizerischen Gesellschaft für Volkskunde*, 2nd edition (Basel: Krebs, 1992), p. 36.

13. *The Holy Bible.*

14. C.G. Jung, "The Psychological Foundations of Belief in Spirits," in *Structure and Dynamics of the Psyche, The Collected Works of C.G. Jung,* eds. Sir Herbert Read, Michael Fordham, Gerhard Adler, William McGuire, trans. R.F.C. Hull (Princeton, N.J.: Princeton University

Press, 1966), vol. 8, § 572. All future references to Jung's *Collected Works* [hereinafter *CW*] will be by volume number and paragraph number.

15. Isler, *Die Sennenpuppe*, p. 80.

16. Johann N. Ritter von Alpenburg, *Mythen und Sagen Tirols* (Zürich: Meyer und Zeller, 1857), p. 181 (Niederwalluf bei Wiesbaden, 1971).

17. Erich Hupfauf, *Zillertaler Reimkunst und andere Beiträge zur Zillertaler Volkskunde*, Schlern-Schriften no. 209 (1960), p. 97.

18. Erich Hupfauf, *Sagen, Brauchtum und Mundart im Zillertal.* Schlern-Schriften no. 148 (1956), p. 90. On the topic of eating ghost food see Isler, *Die Sennenpuppe*, pp. 205-213.

19. Ignaz Vinzenz Zingerle, *Sagen aus Tirol* (Innsbruck: Wagner, 1891), p. 566.

20. Büchli, *Mythologische Landeskunde von Graubünden*, p. 660.

21. Oskar Moser, *Die Sagen und Schwänke der Apollonia Kreuter* (Klagenfurt: Heyn, 1974), p. 50. I am grateful to Professor Moser for his kind help in translating this from the dialect.

22. Eds.' note: See for instance, Jakob & Wilhelm Grimm, "Mother Holle," *The Complete Grimm's Fairy Tales*, 2nd ed. (London: Routledge & Kegan Paul, 2002), No. 24.

23. See Marie-Louise von Franz, *Projection and Re-Collection in Jungian Psychology: Reflections of the Soul*, 8th edition (La Salle, London: Open Court, 1997), chapters 5-7.

24. On the following subject matter, see Isler, *Die Sennenpuppe*, pp. 247-251.

25. Hansueli F. Etter, "Evolution und Tiefenpsychologie—eine Synthese, "*Archives suisse d'anthropologie générale* 46, no. 1 (1982): 17-31.

26. On the topic of a dream about a horned head of Christ, see Gotthilf Isler, "Von der Notwendigkeit mit dem Bösen umzugehen," *Jungiana*, vol. 3, Reihe A (1991), p. 100.

27. Jung, *CW* 13, § 71.

28. C.G. Jung, *Memories, Dreams, Reflections*, ed. Aniela Jaffé, trans. Richard and Clara Winston (New York: Vintage Books, 1989), p. 325.

29. Josef Müller, *Sagen, Schwänke, Legenden aus Uri*, ed. Daniela Walker (Altdorf: Historischer Verein Uri, 1987), p. 230.

30. Jung, *CW* 11, § 904.

31. Galatians 2:20.

32. Georg Graber, *Sagen und Märchen aus Kärnten* (Graz: Leykam Verlag, 1935), p. 292.

33. Zingerle, *Sagen aus Tirol,* p. 853.

34. Johann N. Ritter von Alpenburg, *Deutsche Alpensagen* (Vienna: Braumüller, 1861), p. 160.

35. Jung, *CW* 9i, § 399.

36. Guntern, *Volkserzählungen aus dem Oberwallis (Stalden),* p. 1858.

37. Jung, *CW* 9i, § 794.

The Swiss *Betruf* as Magical Ring

Josef Marty

Translation by Andrew Fellows

Introduction

In this essay I will examine from a psychological perspective the Swiss *Betruf*—the alpine herder's "prayer call"[1] or chant. This is the old tradition of a ritually sung litany that, likening the Gregorian chant in tonality, asks for God's protection and blessing for alpine pastures.[2] The custom is known throughout the European Alps, and remains entrenched today especially in Catholic regions of the Swiss Alps, notably in central and eastern Switzerland as well as in the Romansh areas of Graubunden.[3] I have spent many years listening to prayer calls while hiking in the Alps—and yet, it was the opportunity to write for this issue of *Spring* that presented me with the chance to make a study of my long-standing interest in the phenomenon. To

Josef Marty, lic. phil., studied psychology, religion, philosophy, and theology at the University of Zürich and the Theological Faculty of Chur. Since earning his diploma at the C.G. Jung Institute in Zürich he has maintained a private practice in Lucerne. He is President of the Swiss Society for Analytical Psychology (SGAP), and a member of the Association of Graduate Analytical Psychologists (AGAP). His professional areas of interest include the comparative study of religions, ethnology, and active imagination. Being moreover an alphorn player, he is directly involved with one type of music that has traditionally functioned to guard and bless Switzerland's alpine pastures.

buttress its Jungian context, my study is largely indebted to the Swiss physician and ethnologist Eduard Renner (1891-1952).[4] As the first to write about the custom in our time, Renner views the *Betruf* as a manifestation of the archaic "apotropiac ring,"[5] that is, as one among the rituals and symbols that once served to magically invoke the good and ward off the evil. Unfortunately Renner's seminal work was never translated to English.

When the day's work is done, after the cows have been gathered, milked, and fed, and twilight descends, the lone Swiss alpine herder ritually climbs up to a point on his alp, his high mountain pasture.[6] Here he chants his *Betruf*, strengthening the reach of his voice by calling through a large wooden milk funnel ("*eine Folle*") or through his cupped hands, and slowly turning to cast his song in the four directions of the compass. He thus prays for shelter and protection for all humans, animals, and all that belong on the alp, believing that his invoked protection extends as far as his voice can be heard—even into the valleys below. During the summer months from June to September, when the cows have been herded from the valleys to graze on the high alpine pastures, this scene can be witnessed on many alps in Switzerland. The daily evening *Betruf* is for many alpine herders an essential ritual that determines the weal and woe of the alp and all living beings on it.

History

As should gradually become clear, the origins of the *Betruf* extend back to archaic times. The first known written record of the *Betruf* in Switzerland dates to the year 1411, and pertains to the practice in the Alpstein, a mountain range near Appenzell.[7] In a different document, dated 1565, Rennwart Cysat, the chronicler of the city of Lucerne, reported that nearby alpine herders were singing to ask gracious God and his Mother, the Queen of Heaven, to ward off all evil specters, to bestow happiness, and to prevent accidents.[8] Cysat also reported that neglecting to perform the *Betruf* could be harmful, and could result in particular in the kidnapping of one's whole herd of cattle.

Today the *Betruf* is chanted using a number of different psalm-like texts, many of which begin with the words, "Lobet, oh lobet." Etymologically speaking, "lobet" stems from the Celtic word for cow, "lopa."[9] In some Swiss German dialects "Lobe," or the diminutive "Lobeli," still *is* the word for "cow." Thus, to call their cows home for milking the alpine herders chant, "Chum Lobeli, chum, chum"—"Come dear cows, come, come."[10] The etymology points to the Celts as one of the groups that settled pre-Christian Switzerland, and to the reasonable conjecture that the *Betruf* has a basis in animal magic.

Elements of pre-Christian ritual magic must have been detectable in the *Betruf*, otherwise its performance would not have met with the suspicion of early Christian magistrates. For instance, in 1609 the Lucerne Council banned the *Betruf* because they were convinced it was a pagan cow-blessing and they wanted to put an end to this idolatrous and superstitious activity.[11] Subsequently Catholic priests began to reformulate various *Betruf* texts to eliminate their "pagan" elements. Thus, for example, "Lobe" (cow) was rewritten to create a Christian text: "loben, Gott loben"—"praise, praise God."

Function

A deeper look into the function of the *Betruf* provides access to the world view of the Swiss alpine dwellers, revealing especially their close relationship to the mountains, which are at one and the same time containing and threatening: On one hand, the mountains offer a place to live and work—and on the other hand, due to their wild nature, they threaten to destroy property and lives. In the world emerging from this paradoxical situation, humans live as a part of nature, which is constantly changing and ultimately untamable. It is self-evident that anything acquired—be it family, house, or alp and herd—deteriorates if not given sufficient attention and kept in order. In this view, the people themselves are the guarantors that nature does no harm. If nature nevertheless gains the upper hand, the people realize that, being a part of nature themselves, they cannot stand fast against her greater powers. The people know that they cannot control nature, but must engage carefully with her ever-threatening chaotic changes.

In the alpine dwellers' experience of nature's superior force Edward Renner recognizes "the experience of the numen: Numen, the great dread of the unknown, impersonal and incomprehensible! But numen also means the call and will of the overpowering."[12] In other words, humanity is in the grip of the unfathomable, and must be vigilant at all times against it so as not to be overwhelmed. Under this influence, Renner observes that the mountain people of Uri developed a world view characterized by three cornerstones: "the it," "the ring," and the "heinous deed,"[13] or the sacrilege.

Renner's "it," in German, the "*Es*,"[14] is not to be confused with the Freudian "Es" or "Id," that is, the unconscious as the repository of infantile instincts and drives and the source of neurosis. Rather, the "it" here is an archaic notion held by alpine dwellers to articulate their experience of nature as a force that is uncanny, mysterious, incomprehensible, and dominating. Renner emphasizes that the "it" is no "abstract thought but a *form of experience*, in itself highly alive and active. It explains every event, even the inexplicable."[15] When the mountain people say, "'It rains,'" or "'It snows,'" Marie-Louise von Franz explains,

> this has the implication that the "it" rains, or the "it" sends snow. Or, the "it" sends avalanches, or the "it" sends a mountain crashing down on your hut. We, too say "It rains," "It snows," but for us there is no such implication. . . .[16]

Conceived to be neither good nor evil, but merely "indifferent," the "it" can break through into the ordered world at any moment, and then not only individuals experience the disaster, but the entire community may as well. Belief in the "it" thus demands of the alpine dwellers a respectful attitude toward nature as well as awareness of the need for protection against nature's dangerous forces.

With the "ring"[17] Renner refers to a specific type of protection: the invisible circle that circumscribes the alp in particular but also the surrounding vicinity, to safeguard the herd and all else within. The herdsman invokes the ring with his solemn chanting of the *Betruf* litany and his adherence to other ritual rules—for example, his daily performance at twilight, his exorcizing attitude, and his projection of song in the four directions of the compass. A *Betruf* litany that we shall presently view invokes the ring by word and moreover attributes it with very high value by describing it as "golden."

"The heinous deed"—the sacrilege—is the willful or reckless violation of certain rules, which stands to disturb or even destroy the protective ring. Thus to commit sacrilege is to court disaster, for it opens the gates to the uncanny "it," which can penetrate into the human realm with devastating consequences. Von Franz illustrates with a story from the Canton of Uri, which also demonstrates the ability of the "it" to "speak" to humans: A herder and his boy were high on an alp with their herd. One evening, when the two were outside,

> [they] suddenly . . . heard a voice high up on the mountain slopes saying, "Shall I let it down?" The herder replied, "No, you can keep it, you can hold it." The boy was very frightened. The next evening the same thing happened. The voice said, "Shall I let it down?" and the man said, without respect . . . "Oh, you can hold it." The next evening the boy was so frightened that he decided to run away. Just as he finished packing up . . . the voice said, "I can't hold it any longer!" And the boy ran off. At that very moment, the whole mountain slid down and buried the cattle, the herder, everything. The boy escaped just in time to tell of it.[18]

The sacrilege in this case was the herder's careless neglect of the basic rule that he belongs to nature, and that when nature creates in him an uncanny feeling, his proper response need be one of respect—such as the boy demonstrated when he reacted with fear and ran away.

The notions of the "it," the ring, and the sacrilege instill in the alpine herder an alertness to everything that could jeopardize the balance between his homestead and nature, which surrounds and contains him. The herdsman's chanting of the *Betruf* is the great ritual gesture through which he defines the territory from which harm should be excluded and through which he pursues two further aims. One is to ask for the blessing of the heavenly powers for the alp and all that lives on it. The other is to banish all that is harmful and threatens the alp, cattle, and humans. Among the threats are the storms, rock-falls, and fires sent by the "it," by life-giving but also life-consuming nature. Moreover, there are dwarves and other earth spirits who may harm or steal the cows—and also ghosts that not only scare people but frighten the cattle and cause their milk to dry up.

The Christian reshaping of the pagan *Betruf* has hardly obscured its magical character. While God's blessing is sought in the Christian sense, and the devout feel protected in this way, it remains that magical acts—such as chanting—convey a sense of security. As I mentioned earlier, many different textual variants are chanted under the auspice of the *Betruf*. Let us briefly look at a text from Urnerboden, Switzerland's largest alpine pasture, located in Canton Uri. In this particular Swiss German dialect, "lobä"—a variation on "lobe," the old word for "cow"—

has acquired the meaning of the Christian imperative to "praise" God, or to "honor and glorify" him:

Alle Herzä lobä, alle Schritt und Tritt, i Gottes Name lobä!!
Hier auf dieser Alp ischt a goldener Ring, da isch diä liäb Müättergottes mit ihrem härzallerliäbschte Chind Jesus.
Ave Maria! Ave Maria!
Jesus! Jesus Chrischt! güätigschter Herr Jesus Chrischt, behüäte und bewahre alles, was auf dieser Alp ischt und dazugehert!
Es walte Gott und der heilige Michael, dem empfählet is miär mit Líb und Seel,
es walte Gott und der heilige Wändelin,
es walte Gott und der heilige Sankt Antoni, der söll is ds' Veh behüätä und bewahre,
es walte Gott und der heilige Johannes,
es walte Gott und der heilige Jakobus,
es walte Gott und heilige Alois,
es walte Gott und die liäb Sankt Agatha, diä söll is behüätä und bewahre vor em zítlichä und ewegä Fír,
es walte Gott und diä liäb Müätter Gottes,
alle Heiligä und üserwählte Gottes alli,
es walte Gott und diä hochheilig Drífaltigkeit:
Gott dr Vater, Gott dr Sohn und Gott dr heilige Geischt!
Behüät is Gott vor Hagel und Blitzschlag, vor Pescht, Hunger und Chriäg, bewahre unser Gott!
Gelobt sei Herr Jesus Chrischt!:
Es walte Gott und das hochheilige Kriz, Amen!
Léschet Fír und Liächt, dass is Gott und Mariä wohl behüät![19]

All hearts praise, every step of the way, in God's name praise!!
Here on this alp is a golden ring, here is the dear Mother of God with her most beloved child Jesus.
Ave Maria! Ave Maria!
Jesus! Jesus Christ! Kindest Lord Jesus Christ, protect and preserve all that is on this alp and belongs to it!
let God and Holy Michael reign, receive my body and soul,
let God and Holy Wendelin reign,
let God and Holy Saint Anthony reign, to protect and preserve us and our cattle,
let God and Holy John reign,
let God and Holy Jacob reign,
let God and Holy Alois reign,

> let God and dear Saint Agatha reign, may they may protect
> and preserve us from the temporal and eternal fire,
> let God and the dear Mother of God reign,
> all the saints and all those chosen by God,
> let God and the Holy Trinity reign:
> God the Father, God the Son and God the Holy Spirit!
> God protect us from hail and lightning, from plague, famine
> and war, our God spare us!
> Blessed be the Lord Jesus Christ!
> Let God and the sacred cross reign, Amen!
> Put out the fire and light, so God and Mary may well guard us!

This litany is typical of the kind that the herdsman must chant each day in the customary solemn manner and on behalf of his whole community. Like others, it reveals some of the rituals and rules to which all must adhere in order for the *Betruf* to achieve its protective effect: The text begins with a somewhat mysterious invocation, "All hearts praise, every step of the way, in God's name praise." This opening implies that, on the alp, every thought and deed must always be an act of praise. The chant would thus emphasize that the *Betruf's* effectiveness depends as well on everyone's daily work and the spirit in which it is carried out. Indeed, seemingly minor events such as the spilling of milk and the preferential treatment of a favorite cow may be regarded with suspicion and held as heinous deeds or sacrilegious acts that can disturb the ring and even unleash evil.

The litany soon invokes the key element, the "golden ring," and subsequently summons into it the presence of the Madonna and Christ Child, the patron saints, and the Holy Trinity. As each of their very specific powers become part of the ring, we are again reminded of pre-Christian figures and magical incantation: The Madonna and Christ Child could stand for and invoke the life-giving powers of Mother Nature herself. St. Michael is invoked to protect against lightning and tempest. St. Wendelin, the patron saint of the alpine herders, guards against the loss of the herd. St. Anthony is the patron saint of farmers and their livestock. According to legend, he used the sign of the cross to expel demons that beset him in animal form, including pigs. St. Anthony is not only the guardian of livestock, but also the one who banishes the temptations of the flesh. John the Baptist also protects livestock, and wards off diseases of the mind that can afflict people in the solitude of the alp and make them depressed. St. James is the patron saint of the good harvest and good weather. St. Alois, the patron saint of chastity, also protects against disease. St. Agatha protects against fire.

The litany concludes with the enjoinder, "put out the fire and light so God and Mary may well guard us." Remarkably this appeal comes after the "Amen" that we might ordinarily expect to conclude a hymn or prayer. It thus emphasizes two duties that each and every member of the community must fulfill *after* the *Betruf* has been sung: The implicit one is to live in accordance with nature's diurnal rhythms. And yet before surrender to the night and sleep there is more to be done: all fires must be doused, lest neglect of this last daily task lead to destructive blazes and firestorms.

As becomes apparent again, in such enjoinders as "put out the fire and light," the herdsman's performance of the *Betruf* alone is not enough to create the ring of protection around the alp. When all is said and done, it is the people themselves who need insure that no mishap occurs. And this they do in their painstaking observance of rules that are built into the sung *Betruf* and its surrounding norms, rituals, and legends. Each individual thus contributes in concrete ways to maintain the ring, that is, to maintain order—and this is done not only for one's own sake, but to safeguard the community as whole. Let us consider this collective obligation in the light of Renner's statement: "[T]he great apotropaic gestures are vested in the presence of human beings and their seizing from the world [that which they need in order to live]."[20] From this standpoint it comes as little surprise that protection may be obtained even *without* the actual performance of the *Betruf.* In other words, Renner allows us to conclude that the magic that wards off chaotic reality inheres ultimately in the community's attainment of a devout and watchful attitude, and as well, in their adherence to clear rules that serve to avert disaster.

In reminder of the individual responsibility and the importance of attitude, a legend recounts,

> An alpine herder neglected the whole summer long to chant his *Betruf.* But in other ways he was careful, and did attend to the ring. At the season's end, on his last day on the alp, he saw that

> the summer had been good. Then he remembered to chant his *Betruf* in thanks. After that the "it" appeared and wreaked havoc with uncanny force.[21]

And so we see that even a well-intended *Betruf*—if chanted without regard for the daily practice—can amount to a heinous deed and the loss of the protective ring.

Psychology of the *Betruf*

The magical ring of the *Betruf* as discussed thus far recalls the archetypal mandala, with the effects, origin, and purpose noted by Jung as follows:

> Age-old magical effects lie hidden in [the mandala], for it is derived from the "protective circle" or "charmed circle," whose magic has been preserved in countless folk customs. It has the obvious purpose of drawing a . . . magical furrow around the center, the temple or *temenos* (sacred precinct), . . . in order to prevent an "outflowing" or to guard by apotropaic means against distracting influences from outside.[22]

It could well be said that the chanted *Betruf* takes its place among the "countless folk customs" (like ring dances, incidentally) that preserve "age-old magical effects" and give rise to the drawn mandala: By incantation the *Betruf* casts a protective ring around a *temenos*, the alp, to guard against calamities sent by the "it"—such as the devastating downpour of rain, avalanches that sweep away everything in their path, and also to ward off the ghosts that threaten to kidnap the herd. Among the various *Betruf* texts is one describing a ditch that surrounds an alp to protect three boys within, who are said to be the three persons of the Holy Trinity.[23] Corresponding directly with the "magical furrow" mentioned by Jung, the text imagines the ring of the *Betruf* as an actual ditch that demarcates a center, distinguishing that which is within from that which is outside, to hinder the ingress of overwhelming threat.

While the *Betruf* aims to protect against the hazards of *physical* nature, in its emphasis on "proper attitude," it also concerns psyche's *inner* nature, the perils that lurk within, and the consequent need for psychological protection and differentiation. For as Jung so often emphasizes,

> [the unconscious] only awaits the moment when the partition falls so as to overwhelm conscious life with destruction. . . . Man has been aware of this danger to the psyche since the earliest times, even in the most primitive stages of culture. It was to arm himself against this threat and to heal the damage done that he developed religious and magical practices.[24]

The alpine-dwellers' awareness "of this danger to the psyche" is implicit in the ritual *Betruf* as such, and takes many forms within this context. In this light the "it" translates to an image of the collective unconscious as a chaotic, uncanny, and ultimately untamable *psycho-spiritual* reality—the force of which can appear at any time and leave one just as unprotected as does natural disaster. The dread of the "it" could project the dread of mental storms, avalanches, and fires—or said otherwise, the fear of catastrophic flooding by the unconscious. Threatening dwarves, earth spirits, and ghosts may be grasped as symbolic images of the human temptation to do harm or even to do evil. The ritual of the *Betruf* in this sense would serve to exorcize inner demons.

Just as a community of people must wrest an ordered outer life from the chaos and dangers of nature, so too, must an ordered *inner* life be wrought from the bedlam and perils of the unconscious. And just as the *Betruf* places a protective ring around the outer order that has been so hard-won from nature, so does it seek to protect the inner order so painfully gained from unconsciousness. From a depth psychological perspective, the overall effect of the *Betruf*, with its collective rituals, rules, and symbols is to develop and maintain what could be called a "ring of consciousness," which—to follow Jung—encircles the Self, "the innermost personality, . . . to prevent [its] 'outflowing,'"[25] and to ward off the "overwhelm[ing]" force of the "destruc[tive]" unconscious."[26]

Conclusion

With the notion of the "it," which encompasses the undifferentiated totality of things—time, place, man, and beast—the Swiss alpine dwellers recognize themselves to be at one with nature and at the same time beset by her chaotic and ever-changing force. The "it" is woven into a larger world view by which the *Betruf* aims—like other old rituals—to influence and alter in the community's favor nature's potential to wrest away and destroy all that has been built up. The apotropaic ring created by the chanted *Betruf* insures that life on the alp is not at nature's mercy—provided that the community members protect the ring itself by their avoidance of sacrilege. This they do by carefully observing ritual rules, the observance of which, it may now be said, keeps them ever mindful of nature and the unconscious—*and constantly in constructive dialogue* with these two ultimately untamable forces.

NOTES

1. Translation by Thomas Jay Garbaty, "The Betruf in the Swiss Alps," *The Journal of American Folklore*, Vol. 73, No. 287, Jan.–Mar., 1960, p. 60. My explanation: "*Betruf*" is pronounced roughly, bēt|ruf. It a Swiss German word, which varies in the spelling according to the dialect, and combines "*beten*" (to pray) and "*rufen*" (to call).

2. In contemporary research the *Betruf* is the subject of folkloric and ethnomusicological investigation. In addition to Garbaty (above) see for instance: Brigitte Bachmann-Geiser, "Der Betruf in den Schweizer Alpen," *Histoire des Alpes—Storia delle Alpi—Geschichte der Alpen*, ed. Association Internationale pour L'Histoire des Alpes, no. 11; Alpine Kulturen (Zürich: Chronos, 2006), pp. 27-36.

3. Tonisep Wyss-Meier, *Der Betruf im deutschsprachigen und rätoromanischen Raum: Sammlung von Text und Erläuterungen* (Appenzell: Verlag Druckerei Appenzeller Volksfreund, 2007), p. 16.

4. Eduard Renner, *Goldener Ring über Uri*, 2nd edition (Neuchâtel: Mühlrad-Verlag H.R. Müller, 1954.

5. Renner, *Goldener Ring über Uri*, p. 213 ff. "The apotropaic ring" is translated from "*der bannende Ring.*"

6. Today, women too attend the herds on the alps and even chant the *Betruf*. However, the work traditionally belonged to men, and the customs around the work developed historically in relationship to their role. Therefore when referring here to the alpine herder I will use the masculine form.

7. Wyss-Meier, *Der Betruf im deutschsprachigen und rätoromanischen Raum*, p. 16.

8. Renwart Cysat, *Collectanea chronica und denkwürdige Sachen pro chronica Lucernensi et Helvetiae*, no. 1, part 2 (Luzern: Diebold Schilling Verlag, 1969), p. 686.

9. Search key "cow:" "laogh m. *calf*; W. llo, Br. leue: phps. from *lapego-, Alb. lopa (*làpà) *cow*," in George Calder, *A Gaelic Grammar*, digitized by the National Library of Scotland, scan date, 20081106172421 (Glasgow: Alex. MacLaren, circa 1923), § 128, p. 183. Author's italics. At Internet Archive, http://www.archive.org/details/gaelicgrammarcon00cald (accessed 4 August, 2011).

10. Eds.' note: See Max Peter Baumann, "Kuhreihen," *Historical Dictionary of Switzerland* (Bern: The Historical Dictionary of Switzerland, August 18, 2010, ©1998-2008), at http://www.hls-dhs-dss.ch/textes/d/D11889.php (accessed July 14, 2011): [our translation] Related to the *Betruf* is the chanted "*Kuhreihen*," literally, "cow rows," which refers to the line-up of cows for milking. As a type of folksong the *Kuhreihen* dates at least to 1545. Textual variants typically contain the word "Lobe" or "Lobeli" for "cow." In the late seventeenth century this music was reported to have been the cause for devastating homesickness ("*delirium melancholicum*") in Swiss living abroad. So much was this the case for Swiss mercenary soldiers that it led to desertions and eventually to a ban on the music, the violation of which was punishable by death. The *Kuhreihen* are now traditionally sung during the annual procession that leads the cows from the valleys for grazing in the high alps; they are also sung ritually on some alps at dusk and dawn to seek protection for the herd. For more on the sung *Kuhreihen* from a Jungian perspective, see John Hill, *At Home in the World: Sounds and Symmetries of Belonging* (New Orleans, Louisiana: Spring Journal Books, 2010).

11. Max-Peter Baumann, "Der Betruf in der Innerschweiz" (Ethnomusikologie/Volksmusik, Otto-Friedrich Universität Bamberg, January 19, 1999), Section 2, at http://www.maxpeterbaumann.de/Ritual-Betruf.htm (accessed July 12, 2011).

12. Eduard Renner, *Goldener Ring*, p. 62. (This and all subsequent translations of quoted text by Andrew Fellows.)

13. *Ibid.*, p. 245 ff.; "the heinous deed" is translated from "*der Frevel.*"

14. *Ibid.*, p. 193 ff.

15. Renner, *Goldener Ring*, p. 194, my emphasis.

16. Marie-Louise von Franz, *Archetypal Patterns in Fairy Tales* (Toronto: Inner City Books, 1997), p. 59.

17. Renner, *Goldener Ring*, p. 213 ff.

18. Von Franz, *Archetypal Patterns*, p. 59.

19. "Betruf vom Urnerboden" [traditional], in Vera Rüttimann "Der Ruf der Bergbauern," *Kirchenbote: Wochenzeitung für das Bistum Osnabruck*, Nummer 29, 22. Juli 2007, at http://www.kirchenbote.de/downloads/dm_2007/22_07.osnabrueck_03.pdf (accessed July 12, 2100).

20. Paraphrase from Renner, *Goldener Ring*, p. 227. "The great apopotraic gestures" is translated from "*die grosse Banngesten.*"

21. C.G. Jung, "Commentary on 'The Secret of the Golden Flower'" in *Alchemical Studies, The Collected Works of C. G. Jung*, eds. Sir Herbert Read, Michael Fordham, Gerhard Adler, William McGuire, trans. R. F.C. Hull (Princeton, N.J.: Princeton University Press, 1991), vol. 13, § 36. Future reference to Jung's *Collected Works* [hereinafter "*CW*"] will be by volume number and paragraph number.

22. Bachmann-Geiser, "Der Betruf in den Schweizer Alpen," p. 32.

23. Jung, *CW* 11, § 531.

24. Jung, *CW* 13, § 36.

25. Jung, *CW* 11, § 531.

Alles wird gut, 47° 9' / 8° 32' 69 Video Stills on Canvas

DOROTHEA RUST

Translation by Stacy Wirth

Eds.' Note: The enigmatic title of this contribution will be translated and explained in the pages to come. Important to mention here is that this essay is Dorothea Rust's response to Stacy Wirth's questions about a performance that led to her exhibition of sixty-nine video stills on canvas.[1]

Dorothea Rust, M.A.S., is a dancer, artist, and licensed practitioner of the Alexander Technique. Born in 1955 in Zug, a small canton occupying a plateau in central Switzerland, she grew up in intimate contact with the region's rural landscape. Remaining as much of an influence as her years of dance training in New York is the extensive time she spent growing up with her farmer relatives—especially the summers with them, tending cattle on their high alp. She now holds a degree in the visual arts and a Master of Advanced Studies in Culture and Gender Studies, both from the *Zürcher Hochschule der Künste* (ZHdK). As a freelance teacher, she works in cooperation with artists from other fields as well as with lay people, and has been artist-in-residence in a number of universities. Her body of work includes dance and performance art, installations, pictures, and video. Here she reflects more than twenty years of engagement, with an expressed debt to the Judson Church group of the 1960's, and as well, to collaborations with a number of contemporary New York artists such as the choreographer Deborah Gladstein and the musician Malcolm Goldstein. She has presented in solo and jointly with other artists throughout Switzerland, in North and South America, and in India. Her work has been awarded by the Cantons of Zug, Zürich, and most recently Basel.

This work was originally commissioned for and exhibited by the Cantonal Hospital of Zug.[2]

THE LOWEST COMMON DENOMINATOR

My performances and artistic interventions are part of an ongoing process: I am continuously drawn in by the immediate, physical presence of bodies, objects, ideas, spaces, terms, names—and this, in many different situations—whether they arise in the outdoors, in abandoned buildings, galleries, museums, theaters, or other public places.

Physicality is, so to speak, the lowest common denominator that we humans share with other living beings, living things, and inanimate objects. Every single body and every object has its own weight. Each particular shape and each particular uprightness or bearing expresses a particular way of handling the force of gravity. Each way of handling gravity in turn contains its own inventiveness and play—and also its own hazards. A sense of vulnerability and the risk of injuring or losing the body resonate somewhere within us, always.

Among the elements included in my performances, there is always this physicality. And there is always my interaction with the specific place, such as a city bridge or a riverbank. Within such places, my spontaneous bodily movement congeals into patterns, in which I perceive tasks that demand my fulfillment and eventually my understanding. My carrying out of tasks always involves everyday movement, dancerly gestures, and my use of natural materials (such as branches and stones) and found objects (such as buckets, chairs, table legs). Sometimes I use voice. I may bring language into play, for instance using terms and names that I find in newspapers and on the internet. Because I always engage with the elements of chance and improvisation, the outcomes remain open-ended—or, as Jungians might say, I am open to the influence of synchronicity. This could mean, for instance, that I respond to people who happen to pass through my space at any given time.

Finally, with this admixture of elements, my performances often evoke a sense of archaic, symbolic ritual that reaches beyond ordinary perceptions of time, space, and meaning.[3]

A Particular Point of Departure

"*Alles wird gut*" translates in English to, "everything's gonna be alright." This re-assuring idea belongs not only to the title of the essay you are now reading. It is as well the message I received in nearly thirty languages—from German to Serbo-Croatish to Urdu—when a certain hospital staff agreed to formulate for me their strongest common wish, and to express this wish in their native languages. This particular staff is employed in a hospital in the green industrial outskirts of the city of Zug, and this particular hospital is new.[4] The glass and steel structure arises from the earth as a glistening symbol of high-tech medicine, on first glance seeming to starkly oppose the encircling sky, fields, and meadows. Yet like a great mirror, the building reflects and thus incorporates surrounding nature into its own façade. And its enormous windows, viewed from inside, are like wide gateways to the outdoors. As I wandered the sun-drenched corridors a particular set of windows led my gaze and imagination to a grassy green hill arising at the compass point, 47° 9' / 8° 32'.

Thus, these people, this place, and the wishes they hold formed a particular point of departure for my work. They have lived on in the title of my resulting picture exhibition, and now, too, in the title of this essay. The idea for my exhibition began to emerge when I was invited by the curator Susann Wintsch to participate in a project that, over three years' time, would make of the new hospital the site of a series of artistic events. Her goal was to "… positively and poetically influence everyday life in the hospital."[5] From the outset she was especially attracted by the extensive and large windows, which are,

> … a central element of the hospital's architecture. In opening the view to the outdoors they form a bridge that spans one reality to another. For, those who gaze out the windows allow their thoughts to wander—they stream out to the fields, over the hilltops, enter new spaces and times.[6]

Accordingly, Susann Wintsch invited me along with several other artists to "physically enter and explore the landscapes" framed by these windows, and to "leave [our] footprints" in this turf.[7] We were encouraged to photograph, film, and so forth, with the only requirement being to bring our results back to the hospital's interior. Our results would in turn "… create other 'windows' that afford a poetic gaze, both to the inside and the outside."[8]

A Going Out . . .

So it is that on a beautiful day in April, I went to my chosen grassy knoll at compass point 47° 9' / 8° 32', to perform and film seven tasks that had congealed out of my foregoing explorations in that landscape. As it emerged, my tasks here dealt very specifically with our precarious relationship to gravity, an elemental force that besets all living things everyday, and that we realize in the motions of our bodies and relationship to material objects. What were those tasks, inspired by this landscape and some found objects I'd brought along with me? Retold now as if relaying a dream:

Using an old wooden ladder I climb up a cherry tree in full blossom on the hilltop. From the crown of the tree I toss into the sky slips of white paper bearing the message in thirty languages, "everything's gonna be alright."

An old steel-wheeled side-table rolls over the hills, hobbles through fields and meadows—transporting stones, and apples with it, too.

The messages fluttering down from the sky to the earth—are they to dig up—or to bury? Will everything be alright? Who knows? Who decides?

I whirl a heavy stone tethered to end of a rope, and dance wild circles in a meadow with a garland of apples around my neck and shoulders.

Lying on a wooden dolly, I take off, navigating a hilly country road toward the village of Allenwinden—a strenuous going-forward as my only propulsion is the force of my own paddling against the unyielding ground.

With the help of a pitchfork I levy myself up to cross the road.

My precisely juxtaposed movement fragments are about this basic force—gravity—which both obstructs and gives cause for joy in our every (self-)uplifting, our every going forward, our every shifting, every transporting. My movement is about the outbreak of spring as expressed in the rupture of each blossom from the tree. It is about nature, and things of nature that cling to our bodies. It is about the felt paradox of our largeness and smallness—the paradox of our strength, levity, and confidence, lived with the on-going background resonance of struggle and a portion of helplessness.

. . . AND A COMING IN

Playing further with the foregoing ideas, I withdrew to my studio to distill three hours of filmed performance footage into video stills. I then had the video stills printed as a series of sixty-nine pictures on canvas. My somewhat unconventional printing of video stills on canvas (rather than on photo paper) was to reiterate the motif of the high-tech juxtaposed with the elemental, with canvas as such lending the images a painterly look and sensuous tactile quality. The canvasses form several sub-series, with the sets of pictures ranging in size from the quite large to the rather miniature—that is, from about 100 x 55 inches to 5 x 3 inches.[9] These sets I hung throughout the hospital on five floors, on walls adjacent to the monumental glass windows. Thus nature, re-envisioned to include images of the human dilemma, is brought within the hospital's interior. And the windows come to play as an interface that invites nature and re-envisioned nature to gaze upon one another.

Between the trajectories of these two gazes emerges yet another interactive and indeed poetic performance that takes place in the day-to-day human realm. Now the players are the visitors, patients, and staff, who discover and re-discover the canvasses as they go about their hospital routines: ascending the stairs, descending the stairs, turning to look out, turning to look in, stepping back, drawing near, leaning, sinking, arising, puzzling, imagining, whispering, chortling. They are as if one body, filling the hospital corridors with contrapuntal rhythms, rivulets, and streams of motion—synchronous with nature out there and with the flow of the images lining the interior walls. And as if all together humming, "*Alles wird gut*—everything's gonna be alright."

On reflection it seems rather self-evident that, in its evocation of elemental nature and human vulnerability, my performance outdoors ritually embodied a counterpart to the high-tech, glistening glass hospital. Less expected and perhaps more compelling is something I haven't yet mentioned. That is, the sense of archaic ritual *healing*, which developed first during my outdoor performance—and that arises now in the on-going "performance" within the corridors of this architectonic icon of advanced medicine. And this points to the idea that modern medicine may still be bound to religion and connected with our belief in the meaning and healing power of images.

NOTES

1. The images in this article, selected from the complete series entitled, *Alles wird gut 47° 9' / 8° 32: 69 Videostills auf Leinwand*, are reproduced by permission of the artist © Dorothea Rust, 2010.

2. *Alles wird gut 47° 9' / 8° 32: 69 Videostills auf Leinwand* was originally curated by Susann Wintsch and exhibited in the framework of her concept that made the Cantonal Hospital of Zug (*Kantonsspital Zug*) the site of a series of events contributed by a number of artists over the duration of three years. The series was commissioned by the Department of Education and Culture of Canton Zug, the Division of Culture. Rust's sixty-nine images were displayed in the Cantonal Hospital of Zug from 20 August, 2009 to 10 January, 2010 and thereafter in the corridors of the Cantonal School of Menzingen, Zug (*Kantonsschule Menzingen, Zug*).

3. Eds.' note: In a review of her recent site-specific performance amidst antique stone ruins in the Swiss village of Baden, Dorothea Rust is said to be, "a wildcat slinking down from a high mountain, a lizard

slithering with caution over a wall, a snake encircling a bench with calculation—or perhaps something entirely other." (Daniela Poschmann, "Dorothea Rest legte einen Flüsterbogen über der Ruine Steine," Aargauer Zeitung, June 24, 2011 at http://www.aargauerzeitung.ch/aargau/baden/dorothea-rust-legte-einen-fluesterbogen-ueber-der-ruine-stein-110289656 [accessed Oct. 18, 2011], trans. Stacy Wirth).

4. The Cantonal Hospital of Zug is located in the village of Baar, near the canton's capital city of Zug. The building was designed by *Zürcher Architekturbüro Burckhardt + Partner* and completed in 2008. For glimpses of the architecture see, www.burckhardtpartner.ch/de/projekte/projektliste/Kantonsspital und Pflegezentrum Zug Wettbewerb 1. Rang/ancProject_photos; and http://www.gurimur.ch/gurimur/ref_spitaeler_de_fr_en_it.htm (both accessed Oct. 222, 2011).

5. *Vom Fuss der Mauern in den Horizont* (*From the Foot of the Wall to the Horizon*). Contact Person, Prisca Passigati, unpublished internal memo on Susann Wintsch's curatorial concept for the Cantonal Hospital of Zug (Zug, Direktion für Bildung und Kultur, Amt für Kultur, Kanton Zug: undated), no page numbers, trans. Stacy Wirth.

6. *Ibid.*

7. *Ibid.*

8. *Ibid.*

9. The actual image sizes: 98.4 x 55.1 in; 66.9 x 37.4 in; 37.4 x 20.9 in; 98. x 5.9 in; 5.5 x 3.1 in (250 x 140 cm; 170 x 95 cm; 95 x 53 cm; 25 x 15 cm; 14 x 8 cm).

Eranos: A Place, an Encounter, a Story

CHRISTA ROBINSON

Translation by Stacy Wirth

Eds.' Note: An issue of *Spring* on Swiss Culture would not be complete without an article about Eranos, located in Ascona, in the Ticino region of Switzerland bordering Italy. This special gathering place is where C.G. Jung and other luminaries, at the invitation of Olga Fröbe-Kapteyn, met for many years to present their latest ideas and share them with their colleagues. *Spring* is delighted to have Christa Robinson, a former president of the Eranos Foundation, offer her insights about Eranos with us.

Christa Robinson was born in Zürich in 1940. Her grandfather and both of her parents, all physicians, were the family doctors of the Jung family in Küsnacht. Christa has a background in the arts, receiving a diploma from the School of Fine Arts and Crafts in Zürich (*Kunstgewerbeschule*) and an M.A. from the Hochschule for Applied Psychology in Zürich. A member of the Swiss Society for Analytical Psychology, she is currently a faculty member and supervisor at the International School of Analytical Psychology Zürich (ISAPZURICH), where she was formerly the Director of Studies. She conducts her private analytical practice in Zürich and Ticino, and lives with her husband in Ticino.

A person of many interests, including architecture, Christa constructed with her own hands a small wooden house in *Weisstannental*, a forgotten valley in the

Swiss mountains, where she lived for several years while continuing her analytical and supervisory work in Zürich. And, beginning in 2003, Christa rebuilt a school in western Mongolia for 600 nomad children, a project which has become an important reference point for the very poor part of this country.

Christa's publications and presentations include: "Treatment of Chronic Psychosis" (a joint presentation with Tony Frey) at the 1976 International Association for Analytical Psychology (IAAP) Congress in Rome, and later published in the *Journal of Analytical Psychology*; "The Red Velvet Curtain or: How Prospective Psychotherapists Might Imagine their Work and How It Really Is", GORGO (a German journal of archetypal psychology), pp. 81-84, Volume 11, 1986; "King Olaf and the Hen: Harsh Lights on a Failure", GORGO, pp. 73-77, volume 13, 1987; "Hearing a Similar Voice: An "Enterview" with Christa Robinson", in Robert S. Henderson, *Living with Jung: "Enterviews" with Jungian Analysts, Vol. 3* (New Orleans, LA: Spring Journal Books, 2009); "Images of Archetypal Forces: An "Enterview" with Christa Robinson about the *I Ching*," Robert S. Henderson, *Jung Journal: Culture and Psyche*, Vol. 4, No. 2, Spring 2010.

Christa's first visit to Eranos was on May 1, 1976, and it proved to be a decisive one. From that time onward, she participated in and helped with all the annual Eranos conferences. Additionally, she travelled to Eranos on a monthly basis to assist Rudolf Ritsema, the president of the Eranos Foundation, with his Chinese-German translation of the *I Ching*. In 1990, when Ristsema decided to dedicate himself fully to the translation of the *I Ching* into Europe's four main languages, Christa accepted his invitation to assume the management of all practical matters of the Eranos Conferences, including the administration of the Eranos Foundation, fundraising, and building maintenance. This entailed weekly commutes to Eranos from Zürich where she maintained her analytic practice.

When Ritsema suffered a bout of ill health in 1994, Christa—again at Ritsema's invitation—took on the role of president of the Eranos Foundation, though Ritsema still retained his powers of decision. Christa served in this capacity until 2001 when she stepped down as Foundation president.

Christa's article looks at Eranos through the lens of the Greek goddess Hestia, particularly considering the manner in which Olga Fröbe-Kapteyn created and maintained the Eranos Conferences, and also exploring the many images and associations to Hestia that arose at Eranos before and during Christa's time there.

> Without exception, time leaves us all with great responsibilities. But perhaps most burdened are those entrusted to guard the values of spirit and ensure that these irreplaceable goods remain preserved for future generations. It is no mere coincidence that Eranos sprang up in [Switzerland], a country in which four different cultures and languages stand under the law with equal rights. This international foursome, united under [the symbol of] the Swiss cross, offered solid grounds for the scholarly work that emerged at Eranos.
>
> — *Olga Fröbe-Kapteyn, founder of the Eranos Conferences*[1]

It's Sunday morning. I'm sitting in the train, on my way from Zürich to Ticino for what seems to be the thousandth time.[2] It's raining. The window panes are dirty. Children are laughing. It's an Italian train. Southward, ho! Life bustles here, as it does often. I'll transfer in Bellinzona, the station so familiar—in snow, in heat, in gushing rain, with blocked toilets, its beautiful restaurant, high stuccoed ceilings, closed now for years.

I'll reach Locarno soon. My bus ride from Locarno to Moscia will last a mere twenty-six minutes. Moscia, a small neighborhood close to the village of Ascona, is nestled on the shore of Lake Maggiore. From the Moscia bus stop it will be a few steps to the gates of Eranos—thoroughly rusted by 1976. And I'll experience the feeling of coming home.

Eranos may be best known as the name of the annual summer conferences that, over nearly seven decades, assembled many of the world's leading scholars, including C.G. Jung. The founder of the Eranos Conferences, Olga Fröbe-Kapteyn, virtually disappears in the history. To this matter I shall return.

Eranos is a place, a swath of terrain that once consisted of a steep, rocky mountain slope sweeping from the shore of Lake Maggiore up toward Monte Verità, the "Mountain of Truth." In this story, Monte Verità takes its place as the site of an anarchist colony that formed in 1900 with the aim of casting off bourgeois society and an industrializing civilization. The settlers vowed to re-discover humanity's "harmony with nature," to be found in "the unity of body, soul, intellect," and in "psychical and intellectual potentiality, unknown or repressed."[3]

An early nineteenth-century photograph shows two people from Monte Verità standing in the lakeside vineyard they had created in Moscia, at the spot that was to become known as Eranos. Of this craggy terrain they had made cultivatable land, and planted grapes to produce wine. The whole undertaking required special knowledge and intensive physical labor. I have sometimes wondered, why didn't they simply plant potatoes to fill the many mouths at Monte Verità?! In the background of the scene one sees the three-hundred-year-old Casa Gabriella, which housed the wine press. Back then the second-story floor of Casa Gabriella slanted toward the lake at an angle of some fifteen degrees, making it easy for the workers to slosh away the remnants of their wine production with buckets of water. In 1920 Olga Fröbe-Kapteyn took up residence in Casa Gabriella. She is said to have been undisturbed by the slanted floor.

How did Olga Fröbe-Kapteyn come to settle in this rugged, secluded place, supplied with only the most basic necessities? What forces propelled the joining of this woman and this land as two entities that would seem so unlikely to become intertwined in a common destiny?

The concrete facts about Olga are more or less known. She was born in London in 1881, the daughter of a philosophical anarchist mother and a Dutch businessman. In 1890 the Kapteyn family moved to Switzerland. From 1906 to 1909 Olga attended the Zürich Academy of Arts and Crafts (*Kunstgewerbeschule*). She then occasionally worked as a circus artist with a preference for horseback riding. In her later life she burned the evidence of her wild years. A photograph taken when Olga was in her sixties suggests her intention to preserve the self-image she maintained at Eranos—a solemn, word-spare woman who wore a wig and was renowned for her "no." Yet behind Olga's measured restraint we discern a person possessed not only of unbending will, but also of great vitality.

But once again I have digressed from the beginning, taking a non-linear course that is in itself characteristic of Eranos. After all, Eranos crystallized into a famed center thanks only to a weaving together of seemingly disconnected threads of geography, science, and the arts. The lectures from the Eranos Conferences, collected in the seventy-volume *Eranos Jahrbücher* (*Eranos Yearbooks*), are held today by many libraries worldwide.[4] These *Jahrbücher* document the small but essential contribution of the Eranos Conferences to the tradition of the humanities and natural sciences in the twentieth century. Like the photograph of the elderly Olga Fröbe-Kapteyn, the *Jahrbücher* remain one of the few outward and visible signs of Eranos's existence—saying precious little, however, about its coming-to-being, its inner life, and its decline.

Olga Kapteyn said yes to life in 1909 when she married Iwan Fröbe, a Croatian musician and conductor of Austrian descent, and settled with him in Berlin. Tragically, however, Iwan was killed in a plane crash in 1915—a World War I army flight test—just around the time their twin daughters were born. One of the two, Ingeborg, was mentally disabled and placed in a home for the handicapped in Germany.[5] Bettina, the other daughter, apparently extraverted and cheerful by nature, was, however, aversive to her mother.[6]

In 1920 Olga moved to Moscia to take up residence in the old Casa Gabriella. At the same time, she began studies in Theosophy and meditation, and entered Alice A. Bailey's very idealistic, esoteric movement and Arcane School.[7] In 1930-31 Olga organized on Bailey's behalf a "summer academy" that took place at her Moscia property. It was during these years that Olga befriended Ludwig Derleth, the German occultist and philosopher whose major ouvre and vast work of fiction was *Der Fränkische Koran* —" '*The Koran of the Franks*' [i.e., of the western peoples]."[8] She was also introduced to other prominent scholars of the time.

The early 1930's saw Olga approaching the age of fifty. By this time she had already considerably transformed her Moscia property. Of the craggy lakeside slope and vineyard she had fashioned a garden replete with a lotus pond and goldfish. To Casa Gabriella she had added a second building, Casa Eranos, which housed a conference hall and one simple apartment. Shortly afterward she built Casa Shanti, consisting of two simple apartments. To save money, Olga rented Casa Shanti to the German Emma von Pellet, who in turn shared the abode with an American, Alwine von Keller.

Both Emma von Pellet and Alwine von Keller had undergone analysis with C.G. Jung, and are otherwise no insignificant figures in this story. Emma von Pellett was the daughter of the Master of Ceremonies to Emperor Frederick William Victor Albert of Prussia.

Being a rather masculine type, she did not reflect the feminine ideal of her social class. She loved sports and fast cars (and was the first woman to drive a Maserati in Switzerland!). Her true identity seems to have been crushed as she underwent the courtly education that was compulsory for young people of her social stature; entailing adherence to a rigid code of manners, it had the effect of putting a straightjacket on her individual personality. Jung terminated analysis with Emma after only a few sessions, considering her to be a hopeless case. Since Emma could be nasty and biting, she played the watchdog for Alwine, whose sunny nature attracted throngs of visitors of many kinds—to the annoyance of Olga and sometimes to Alwine's own exasperation. Emma and Alwine can be said to have embodied two extremes of Olga's personality. Thus we can imagine the complex constellation of energies from which the Eranos vision was to develop.

In the early 1930's Olga also became acquainted with the German philosopher Hermann Graf Keyserling and his "School of Wisdom," which he had founded in 1920, to "foster intercultural understanding . . . [and] cultural renewal based on critical awareness of the growing mechanization and intellectualism in European culture."[9] It was through the School of Wisdom that Olga was introduced to C.G. Jung; here, too she got to know Richard Wilhelm, the theologist, sinologist, and translator of the *I Ching*, and the religious scholar Rudolf Otto. From Richard Wilhelm she gained a life-long interest in the *I Ching* and the work emerging from it. From Rudolf Otto she inherited, among other things, the name "Eranos." This he had taken to symbolize a feast of the mind and spirit, drawing on the Greek "eranos," meaning a banquet in which guests shared with each other contributions of song, dance, poetry, and discussion. In fact "Eranos" was to have been the name given to one of Otto's own projects, which he was unable to realize due to ill health. Not only did Otto hand over the name "Eranos" to Olga, he also gave her a list of potential lecturers for the Eranos Conferences which she had begun to envision. These conferences would focus on relations between East and West and explore them from many disciplines. Neither Wilhelm nor Otto survived to witness the flowering of this new project of Olga's called Eranos, yet both of them had planted the seeds for it in the grounds of time.

When Olga contacted C.G. Jung about beginning the Eranos Conferences, he agreed to lend his support under two conditions. One was that Olga cease her affiliation with Alice Bailey and the Arcane School. (Olga's automatic drawings, done under Bailey's influence, were described by Jung as "works of the devil.")[10] Jung's second condition was that he would have nothing to do with the organization of the conferences and that his own lectures must be included with those of other scholars representing the largest possible variety of disciplines. Thus Olga organized the first and subsequent Eranos Conferences. This she did intuitively, following the motto, "non-organization is the highest level of organization," and allowing plans to take concrete shape in due time.

In August of 1933, an ominous time for Europe, a light was sparked when Olga announced the first Eranos conference. It lasted one week, was open to the general public, and delved into the topic *Yoga und Meditation im Osten und Westen* (*Yoga and Meditation in East and West*). A glance at the contents of the first *Jahrbuch* (Eranos Yearbook) brings across a sense of the contributions and scholarship that struck the note for the future. In translation from the German, the following provides the list of speakers at the first Eranos conference and the topics on which they presented:[11]

- Prof. Dr. Heinrich Zimmer, University of Heidelberg: *On the Meaning of Tantra-Yoga*
- Mrs. Rhys Davids, President of the Pali Text Society, University of London: *Religious Exercises in India and the Religious Man*
- Dr. Erwin Rouselle, Director of the China Institute at the University of Frankfurt am Main: *Guidance of the Soul in Living Taoism*
- Dr. C.G. Jung, Zürich: *On the Empiricism of the Individuation Process*
- Dr. G.R. Heyer, Munich: *The Sense and Meaning of Oriental Wisdom for the Western Guidance of the Soul*
- Prof. Dr. Friedrich Heiler, University of Marburg: *The Contemplation of Christian Mysticism*
- Prof. Ernsto Buonaiuti, University of Rome: *Meditation and Contemplation in the Roman Catholic Church*

This first Eranos conference blossomed into decades of annual summer events with high caliber interdisciplinary lectures that sought to promote in-depth intercultural understanding of relations between East and West. During the conferences, which lasted for several days, the presenting scholars stayed for the entire event at Eranos on Olga's estate, immersing themselves at her round table in intimate exchange and debate, and sharing meals. For many the place would become a lighthouse, offering against the growing gloom of the time a steady beam of hope that, here, the fire of a free and open spirit was kept alive.

During the 1930's Olga traveled frequently to Berlin to arrange exit visas for her lecturers so that they could travel from Germany to Switzerland for the conferences. This made her, in the eyes of the Gestapo and the Americans, a person to be viewed with suspicion. Consequently her path was often obstructed. However, despite these trials, her estate continued to transform. Olga built a harbor for Jung's boat and others'. She added a lakeside bathing area for her guests, and garden niches with granite tables and benches to encourage discussion, meditation, and rest. Soon Olga would come to be called "esteemed mother," "Great Mother."

During the lonely winter months Olga tended the fire of the Eranos vision. It was a very specific vision that opposed the dominant spirit of the time, for it steadily imagined a place that fostered free thought, and spiritual and intellectual encounter. An archetypal energy had seized her and made her its own—to let go only with her dying breath.

My own impression is that the archetype behind the woman Olga Fröbe-Kapteyn was less the Great Mother than that of the Greek virgin goddess Hestia—or, to put it slightly differently, Olga Fröbe-Kapteyn's nature was essentially a Hestian one.[12] The goddess—described paradoxically as the first-born and last-born of Kronos und Rhea—appears only rarely in Greek myth, possibly because her nature did not lend itself well to story-telling: In ancient Greek "hestia" means "hearth," or "fireside." And indeed Hestia was revered as the goddess of hearth and home—and as the deity who created and bequeathed to humanity the art of house-building. Perhaps singularly among the Olympians Hestia was held to be a serene deity, the inward one, the one who is constant, and the one who is shy and is yet also the asylum-giver. She declined activity in the outer world, but she was intimately related to humankind. As the light first burned in the hearth, so was Hestia the beginning and end of all things—she was both the point of origin and destination.

While Hestia was rarely the subject of myth or art, the centrality and magnitude of her veneration in ancient Greece is evident in the prevalence of shrines honoring her. Consisting primarily of a hearth and ritually tended sacred flame, these were found in the innermost sanctums of most temples, at the centers of many cities and public buildings, and most importantly at the center of every home. The goddess shared in all sacrifices offered to other deities—and ritual observance demanded that sacrifices be offered to Hestia first before they were offered to any other god.[13] All meals were preceded and concluded with sacrifices to Hestia. In the home Hestia's hearth was the place of communal cooking, dining, and story-telling, and thus formed the focus and gathering place of domestic life. Held to be the manifestation of Hestia herself, the hearth made of the home also a sacred place and focus of spiritual life.

Widely and ever present as the hearth, Hestia was symbolized as such, that is architectonically, and not in anthropomorphic form. Accordingly, her main shrine at Delphi was rather simply adorned with hearth fires rather than with statues. Hestia as goddess without a body—Hestia as "no-body"—represents an essence that is unseen but potently felt, namely, the eternal flame of life.[14] But just as importantly, as both physical object and symbolic image—Hestia as hearthfire offers a protected place for gathering, developing inward focus and illumination, and providing soul with nurture and containment:

> [W]ithout Hestia, there can be no focusing on the image, for there is no psychic house to give protective walls, to differentiate what is in here and what is out there, no joyous feast, no celebrations of life, no food for the soul.[15]

Hestia in this sense reminds me very much of Olga Fröbe-Kapteyn, who built the houses in Moscia and created Eranos as a place of encounter. She selected each year's theme and which lecturers would be invited to present; she established the daily protocols, the schedule, the dinners, and even the dress code. Yet, she as a person tended to vanish behind the vision of Eranos. Just as the hearth is the immovable center and gathering place of the home, Olga, with Eranos, stood as a central and centering force that drew people together, illuminating their stories, debates, and quarrels. For many Eranos was a place that united psyche and the world. Adolf Portmann, a frequent lecturer at

Eranos and a professor of zoology in Basel,[16] for instance, noted that the yearly Eranos conference held each summer constituted the end and the beginning of the year for him.

At any rate, the banquets at Olga's round table occasioned lively discussion and debate. Anecdote relays that neighbors complained about Jung's bellowing laughter persisting late into the night; others are said to have expressed astonishment about a prominent Zürich analyst who, out of sheer enthusiasm, jumped stark naked into Lake Maggiore.

The Eranos Conferences continued through the most trying war years—despite rationing, despite closed borders, and despite the shortage of funds flowing in from abroad. Seemingly the conference topics had little to do with the events of the outer world. Yet, as Adolf Portmann put it:

> Eranos is never content to play the role of a seismograph that measures already occurring subterranean quakes. Our conferences try again and again, in [this] time of greatest threat, to participate in a transformation of values.[17]

Olga's selection of lecturers was guided by her intuitive perception of their ability to "combine imaginative and creative thinking with stringent scientific discipline."[18] It was a call to sustain the tension of opposites, to discover the possibility of midpoints between extremes—between Mythos and Logos, between the heights and the depths. Some called it "inspired science."[19] This principle remained in force at Eranos. The scholars challenged themselves to bridge two equally one-sided worlds: the rational and sometimes sterile—and the irrational and emotional, prone to fall under the sway of sectarianism and authoritarian regimes. In the oppositional tension lay the potential for the discovery of a "third" factor—the *tertium non datur*—namely, the personal solution and answer to existential conflict.

The garden and buildings at Eranos were modestly equipped and adorned to discourage distraction from the spiritual work, and apart from travel expenses, no remuneration was offered to the lecturers. Olga understood Eranos to be a place outside of time, an image in the background that was felt and gave rise to different fantasies. The lecturers and audiences began to formulate psychological transferences onto Eranos, likening it to Avalon, King Arthur's Round Table, or Shambala.

Other visitors departed after only a day's stay, feeling this was not the place for them—"and all of this rain—unendurable!"

The transferential imagery witnessed Eranos, the place, constellating in individuals the fantasy of a center—in Jung's sense of a supraordinate symbol and personal goal of individuation. This kind of center is different, in my opinion, from the Hestian idea of a place or *topos* that contains an individuation process and brings it into awareness—the container being an a priori condition of the process. In my view it is important to make this distinction. And I wonder if or how these kinds of transferential fantasies might have contributed to what seemed to me to be a gradual shifting of the meaning of the Eranos Conferences from which the focus on the archetypal gave way to more of a focus on the personal.

Up through the 1950's the Eranos Conferences flourished, repeatedly yielding ground-breaking thought in the various disciplines represented. Due to ill health Jung held his last Eranos lecture in 1951. Thanks to Jung's affiliation with the place, however, Olga received bounteous encouragement and financial support from individuals and groups in the United States. Among them were the philanthropists Mary and Paul Mellon; William McGuire, the co-editor of Jung's *Collected Works*; and the Bollingen Foundation, the American publisher of Jung's works.

But then shadows began to emerge. Admitting Hestia's inevitable dark side, we again find spatial imagery that characterizes the pathologies latent in her nature and perhaps also mirror what had begun to manifest in the Eranos project itself: "off-base," "off-center," "spaced out."[20] The soul gone astray is a soul that has lost its center and ground.

Olga grew weak and began to occupy herself with the question of who would carry on her work. Her chosen successor, by contractual agreement, was the Swiss Walter Robert Corti, her close friend and a highly cultured medical doctor.[21] Corti was immediately confronted with the diminishing strength of containment at Eranos. With Olga's illness, the hearth had already cracked, and materialistic interests crept in. Because of financial pressures, attempts were made to assess the potential value of the property making up Olga's estate where the Eranos Conferences took place. Luxury apartments were considered, built in terrace fashion on the mountain slope. In Olga's bedroom, where she lay dying, further possibilities were discussed as to how the property could be made more marketable. It was suggested that Olga's room could be improved with an enlargement of the small windows in it. Yet Olga had intentionally kept the windows small because she cherished the atmosphere of seclusion and the darkness, which she enhanced by always keeping drawn the dark green velvet curtains. Another proposed idea was to eliminate direct access to the second floor by removing the spiral staircase leading up to it, a staircase which Olga had added and fashioned in Art Deco style.[22]

Eventually, due to contractual differences, Olga forfeited to Corti the piece of the Eranos property that lay on the upper mountainside. Corti then sold his share and with the profit made from the sale established in 1962 "The Academy Guild" (*Bauhütte der Akademie*), a think tank which, inspired by Plato, devoted itself to ethics research and particularly to the cause for peace. My mother was president of the board, and my memories of the foundation's activity are many. But Jung's prediction that this project would end as a stillbirth held true.[23]

Olga died at the age of eighty-one in 1962. She had asked Adolf Portmann and Rudolf Ritsema to take over Eranos upon her death and create an Eranos Foundation. Her sudden death demanded new leadership immediately. Portmann and Ritsema (along with his wife Catherine) rose to the call to assume the Eranos offices of president and on-site director, respectively. At this juncture another Hestian aspect began to emerge, one containing a medical fantasy: In German the word for "hearth" or "hearth fire," namely "*Herd*," also can mean the "seat of an illness." That is, illness as such is imagined as a place of soul and trial by fire with an uncertain outcome.

Although the Ritsemas and Portmann devoted themselves to Eranos without reserve, the loss of a centering force seemed to grow more palpable. Significant patronage was lost. The Bollingen Foundation, for example, became inactive in 1965 and was largely subsumed by the Andrew W. Mellon Foundation. As a result the Eranos Estate and conferences relied increasingly on donations. By 1976—when I began commuting from Zürich to assist with Rudolf Ritsema's German translation of the *I Ching*—the shortage of funds could already be felt in many places.

Eranos underwent further changes as well. The still high-caliber lectures became increasingly intellectual. Breaks and meals at Olga's old round table appeared to be less frequently devoted to discussion of conference topics. For some participants, a tendency grew to market the event and to exploit it for personal gain. "If you publish my book I will organize your presentation at an important conference elsewhere, e.g., in Japan." By this time, to present a lecture at Eranos held a reward of enviable status, and sometimes even a salary increase at home. Yet Olga herself had attracted distinguished scholars to Eranos with little more that the offer of room, board, and rich conversation. As the desire for prestige gained ground, her founding values began, it seemed to me, to slip into the background. The traditional celebrations began to be held off-site. Apart from the usual closing concerts, still held on the Eranos properties, the parties took place increasingly at private Ascona houses. Other previously valued conventions gradually dissolved, such as the strict dress code and the courtesy of all presenting scholars to attend all lectures—regardless of the language. Small things? To be sure, but no less pointing to Hestian pathology: the "off-base" became celebrated.

Observing these disquieting changes, in 1987 Rudolf Ritsema announced his intention to refocus the Eranos Conferences: while continuing the convention of morning lectures on a variety of topics from year to year, the afternoons would be devoted exclusively to work with the *I Ching*. Also, to regain the intimate, experiential character of the earlier conferences, he indicated his interest in holding three to four smaller conferences per year instead of the traditional one held over the course of several days each summer. Thus the conference of 1988, entitled "*Gleichklang oder Gleichzeitigkeit*/Concordance or Coincidence", was the last conference conducted in the tradition initiated so many years earlier by Olga.[24]

To better understand this shift, we can follow Kirksey on her "final etymological excursion" to reconsider Hestia as "focus." A focus is also "the center of activity or area of greatest energy, of a storm, volcanic eruption, etc., also a center or hot bed of intrigue, sedition....[Thus we see that] the center is not [only and not always] a place of harmony or integration.[25]

The search for a new focus at Eranos led Rudolf Ritsema to return to the beginning, to re-attempt the synthesis of East and West that had engendered the conference's original intellectual and spiritual zenith. He justified well the shift, appealing to Olga Fröbe-Kapetyn's original aim to explore relations between East and West. He also consulted the *I Ching* and referred to his work with Olga in this direction that dated back as far as 1944. But unfortunately his attempted changes unintentionally let loose storms of fury and betrayal.

Biting, one-sided commentary on the Eranos Conferences flowed without reserve. Proponents of the political left in Switzerland were major denouncers. They maintained, for instance, that the event was esoteric and abusive of the human yearning for healing. A respected Swiss news journal devoted a special edition to C.G. Jung, including an article on Eranos, in which it was described as "a strange bastard [arising from the parentage of] science, culture and life help."[26]

It was in 1990 that I began to work for the Eranos Foundation on a volunteer basis, agreeing to organize the conferences, the fund raising, and the management of the property which was in dire need of repairs. During this time, while residing in Olga's apartment in Casa Gabriella, I developed the impression that certain archetypal Hestian energies were coming to dominate in personal realms, and consequently had begun to take the form of pathology. Such a central shift containing pathology, reflects a need for re-adjusted focus.

Sometimes, Hestia's psychic storms demand that we remove ourselves from center stage to allow other characters to enter. We must move in relationship to the pathological image to adjust to its "focus," so that the image gains central importance. This adjustment of focusing in itself amounts to the movement of soul. It is no journey to the underworld with Hermes, nor a Dionysian frenzy, nor a Panic-stricken flight. It is a way of "finding place" for one's illnesses and wounds.

In a last gargantuan effort that endured ten years Rudolf Ritsema translated the *I Ching* from Chinese into the four main European languages, incorporating as his interpretive basis the analytical and archetypal body of thought of C.G. Jung and James Hillman.[27] Thus we have Ritsema to thank for four very precise verbatim translations that offer for the understanding of the Western mind the wisdom of this great book.

In the meanwhile problems at Eranos arose. Sometimes shifts in archetypal energy accompanied by personal identification result in inflation. Instead of burning within the hearth, Hestia's fire appeared to burn in people instead—in outbursts of rage and in broken relationships. Here it bears mentioning that the Greek name for our goddess "Heschara" also can mean "burnt place," and gives rise to the English word "scar." For me, this is what Eranos came to reflect, and I among others felt a scarring. So, in June 2001 I laid the key to my apartment on the kitchen table—"my" apartment, which had been Olga Fröbe-Kapteyn's. It was a departure with no words of goodbye.

After such an experience of scarring, says Barbara Kirskey, to obtain focus and a new attitude towards life requires adjustment—and to undertake such adjustment is part of the psychological activity of Hestian focusing. We are involved in adjusting when we seek "a center as a place of illumination" and energy. As part of the archetype of the journey home to the hearth", to seek focus is to experience "Hestia, builder of the house, so that the soul may dream in peace."[28]

Hestia manifested herself in this place, Eranos, to become an encounter, a story, a history. Her fire will alight again, perhaps in a new place.

NOTES

1. Olga Fröbe-Kapteyn, "Vorwort," *Eranos Jahrbuch 1944 (Band XI): Die Mysterien,* Hrsg. Olga Fröbe-Kaptyen (Zürich: Rhein-Verlag, 1945). Trans. Stacy Wirth. Unless mentioned otherwise, all subsequent translations from German to English are by Stacy Wirth.

2. Eds.' note: Ticino (in German: Tessin) is a Swiss canton that borders on Italy and retains Italian as its official language. See the contribution in this issue of *Spring* by Elena Krinke, "Between Ticino and Northern Switzerland Stand Not Only the Alps."

3. Mara Folini, *Monte Verità: Ascona's Mountain of Truth*, Guides to Swiss Monuments SHSA, Series 63, Nos. 628/629, trans. Werner Bier and Kathrin Gurtner (Bern: Society for the History of Swiss Art, 2000). Eds.' note: Monte Verità grew to become a vibrant cultural center, attracting the likes of the psychologist Otto Gross; the dancers Rudolf Laban, Mary Wigman, and Isadora Duncan; the writer Hermann Hesse; the artists Jean Arp and Paul Klee; the anthroposophist and school founder Rudolf Steiner; and for a short stay on his way to Eranos, C.G. Jung. Today Monte Verità is open to tourists, and it is the site of academic conferences sponsored by the science and technology department of the University of Zurich (ETH).

4. From 1933 to 1961 the *Eranos Jahrbücher* were edited by Olga Fröbe-Kapteyn, bound in ecru linen, and published by Rhein-Verlag in Zurich. Upon Olga's death in 1962, Rudolf Ritsema took over the editorship, beginning with Volume 28. Although Olga was unable to realize her dream of publishing the complete twenty volumes in English, selected papers were published in six volumes, Joseph Campbell, ed., *Papers from the Eranos Yearbooks*, trans. Ralph Manheim, Bollingen Series, (Princeton, NJ: Princeton University Press).

5. Later the Nazis relegated Ingeborg to the category of the "worthless" and "dispensed" with her. Thus on her last visit to her daughter Olga found nothing but an empty house.

6. To her life's end Olga rejected Bettina—even disinheriting her in favor of the Eranos Foundation. This injustice was corrected after Olga's death, when three individuals paid Bettina her due inheritance with funds freed by the mortgages they took out on two buildings on the Eranos property. These three were Adolf Portmann, Rudolf Ritsema, and James Hillman, who was a frequent lecturer at Eranos. While the wrong was righted, Olga's act of disinheritance may reveal an imbalance in the relationship of Logos and Eros at Eranos—an imbalance that had become evident long before she created her last will and testimony.

7. Alice A. Bailey, born in Britain, moved to the United States in 1907. She established the Arcane School in 1923. In her words,

> Mr. Richard Prater, an old associate of W. Q. Judge and a pupil of H. P. Blavatsky . . . turned his entire Secret Doctrine class over to me. Among the papers which he gave me was one in which H.P.B. expressed her wish that the esoteric section should be called the Arcane School. . . . . It is a school wherein true, occult obedience is developed. . . . [Individuals] are taught . . . prompt obedience to the dictates of their own soul. Alice A. Bailey, "From the Unfinished Autobiography of Alice A. Bailey," at *Lucis Trust*, http://www.lucistrust.org/en/arcane_school/introduction/extracts_on_the_arcane_school, accessed June 22, 2011.

8. Ludwig Derleth, *Der Fränkishe Koran: Das Werk* (1932), Hrsg. Christine Derleth, Dominik Jost (Gladenbach, Hessen: Verlag Hinder Deelmann, 1971). See also, Raymond Furness, *Zarathustra's Children: A Study of a Lost Generation of German Writers* (Rochester, NY: Camden House, 2000), pp. 127-128. Having taken some forty years to

complete, *The Frankish Koran* illuminated Derleth's vision of a purified and militant Catholicism, in a narrative that included elements of the Near East, the Holy Land and the Crusades.

9. "The 'School of Wisdom'," at *Institute der Praxis für Philosophie*, http://www.ipph-darmstadt.de/index2.php?content1=weisheit_uk (accessed June 22, 2011).

10. Rudolf Ritsema, personal conversation with Christa Robinson.

11. Olga Fröbe-Kapteyn, "Inhalt," *Eranos Jahrbuch 1933 (Band I), Yoga und Meditation im Osten und Westen*, Hrsg. Olga Fröbe-Kapteyn (Zurich: Rhein-Verlag, 1934).

12. For my discussion of Hestia throughout I am grateful to Barbara Kirksey, "Hestia: A Background of Psychological Focusing," in *Facing the Gods* (Irving, TX: Spring Publications, 1980).

13. Plato, "Cratylus," *The Collected Dialogues of Plato, Including the Letters*, trans. Lane Cooper, F.M. Cornford, W.K.C. Guthrie, *et. al.*, eds. Edith Hamilton and Huntington Cairns (New York: Pantheon Books, 1961), p. 438.

14. *Ibid.* Plato observed the goddess's name was interchangeable with another word which means the "essence." Thus he reasoned that "the essence of things be called....[Hestia]"—and it "was natural" that sacrifices were offered first to Hestia, i.e., to the "essence."

15. Kirksey, "Hestia," p. 106.

16. Adolf Portmann (1897-1982) was born in Basel, Switzerland, studied zoology at the University of Basel and worked later in Geneva, Munich, Paris, and Berlin, but mainly in marine biology laboratories in France (Banyuls-sur-Mer, Roscoff, Villefranche-sur-Mer) and Helgoland. In 1931 he became professor of zoology in Basel. His main research areas covered marine biology and comparative morphology of vertebrates. His work was often interdisciplinary comprising sociological and philosophical aspects of life of animals and humans.

17. Adolf Portmann, "Eranos and Its Meaning," in *Über Eranos*, Adolf Portmann, Henri Corbin, Rudolf Ritsema, Hrsg. (Self-published booklet, 1978), pp. 2-3.

18. Hans Thomas Hakl, *Der verborgene Geist von Eranos: unbekannte Begegnungen von Wissenschaft und Esoterik: eine alternative Geistesgeschichte des 20. Jahrhunderts* (Frankfurt: Verlag neue Wissenschaft, 2001), p. 377. Eds.' note: A translated version of this work should be available in March, 2012: Hans Thomas Hakl, *An*

Alternative Intellectual History of the Twentieth Century (Sheffield, London: Equinox Publishing Limited, 2011). See http://www.equinoxpub.com/equinox/books/showbook.asp?bkid=170 (accessed June 27, 2011).

19. Hakl, *Der verborgene Geist.*

20. Kirksey, "Hestia," p. 111.

21. For details, see Walter Robert Corti, "Der Mensch als Organ Gottes," *Eranos Jahrbuch 1959, The Renewal of Man (Band XXVIII)*, Hrsg. Olga Fröbe-Kapteyn (Zürich: Rhein-Verlag, 1960), pp. 377-405.

22. Rudolf Ritsema, in personal conversation with Christa Robinson.

23. Corti's difficulty to establish a physical domicile for The Academy Guild contributed to the collapse of this project in his time. However, previously, in 1944, Corti had founded a project that survives still with worldwide renown: the Pestalozzi Children's Village, established originally for the care and protection of war-damaged children. See Ernst Menet, *Walther Robert Corti* (© 2009, Akademie für ethische Forschung, Zürich at http://www.wrcorti.ch/index.html, accessed June 27, 2011).

24. See *Eranos Jahrbuch / Eranos Yearbook 1988, Gleichklang oder Gleichzeitigkeit / Concordance or Coincidence (Band 57)*, Hrsg. Rudolf Ritsema (Ascona/Frankfurt am Main: Eranos Foundation/Insel Verlag, 1990). Contributors: Rudolf Ritsema, Ulrich Mann, Jean Brun, David L. Miller, Gilbert Durand, Herbert Pietschmann, Michel Hulin, William J. Peterson, Wolfgang Giegerich, Hayao Kawai.

25. Kirksey, "Hestia," p. 111.

26. Hans Heinz Holz, "Die Eranos-Jünger," *DU*: *Carl Gustav Jung. Person, Psyche und Paradox*, 652.8/1995 (Zurich: TA Media, 1995), pp. 92-93.

27. In the English translation: *The Original I Ching: The Pure and Complete Texts with Concordance*, trans. Rudolf Ritsema and Shantena Augusto Sabbadini (London: Watkins, 2007).

28. Kirksey, "Hestia," p. 111.

The Foundation of the Works of C.G. Jung

ULRICH HOERNI

A New Foundation—Why? or "For What Purpose?"

On April 16, 2007, representatives of the former Community of the Heirs of C.G. Jung (hereafter, the Heirs)[1] established the Foundation of the Works of C.G. Jung[2] (hereafter, the Foundation) with its legal domicile in Zürich . (The Heirs transferred to this new Foundation Jung's author's rights, publishing contracts, the *Red Book*,[3] the *Black Books*,[4] other archival material, the books of Jung's private library, and some funds. The Foundation board of three to nine members may include both descendants of C.G. Jung and external persons. The Foundation has non-profit status, i.e., its disposable means must be invested in projects that comply with the founding purpose. As a legal entity, the Community of the Heirs of

Ulrich Hoerni was born in Zürich in 1941. Having earned a degree in architecture at the Swiss Federal Institute of Technology Zürich (ETH) in 1967, he went on to work until 1994 as an architect in Denmark and Switzerland. In 1981 he joined the Executive Committee of the Community of Heirs of C.G. Jung, and served as its manager from 1997-2007 and as its chair from 2004—2007. From 1994-2007 he was the delegated manager of archival and editorial matters, and in this function was involved in the planning of new publications, among others, *The Red Book*. Since 2007, he has been a member of the board and manager of the Foundation of the Works of C.G. Jung, Zürich (*Stiftung der Werke von C.G. Jung, Zürich*).

C.G. Jung was disbanded in 2008. Since a large number of Jung foundations already exist all over the world, the reader may wonder why an additional Foundation of the Works of C.G. Jung should be necessary. In the statutes governing its incorporation its aims are drawn up as follows:

• Conservation and advancement of accessibility of the literary estates left by C.G. Jung and Emma Jung-Rauschenbach including visual artistic works

• Administration of the intellectual property of these estates

• Advancement of scholarly correct publications of the works by C.G. Jung and Emma Jung

• Advancement of studies concerning their lives and works

Without going into the details of the statutes, one of the Foundation's main objectives is the furthering of publications. For this purpose, the Foundation cooperates with archives, scholars, editors, publishers, and the like. Such an objective implies the existence of unpublished works by Jung—possibly even in substantial quantities. Given that Jung's *Collected Works* (hereafter, CW)[5] have been available for decades, this implication that there are still large amounts of Jung's works that have not yet been published may be difficult to fathom. For those looking into the matter more closely, it has indeed for quite some time given rise to assumptions, speculations, rumors, questions, criticism, and controversies. To regain rational grounds for discussion—and with this, to explain the purpose of the new Foundation—it may be most sensible to undertake an overview of the present state of Jung's publications.

The Collected Works of C.G. Jung

Since 1902 Jung published with various publishing houses. In 1947 he signed a contract with the Bollingen Foundation and Pantheon Books New York, and Kegan Paul, Trench, Trubner & Co. Ltd. London, for a project that was initially designated, "The New Edition," and then the "Collected Works;" an appendix outlined the planned contents:

Part I: (titles of 9 well-known works by Jung)
Psychology of the Unconscious

> Psychological Types
> Contributions to Analytical Psychology
> Modern Man in Search of a Soul
> Psychology and Alchemy
> Collected Papers on Analytical Psychology
> Two Papers on Analytical Psychology
> Studies in Word Association
> Psychology and Religion
>
> Part II: All other existing works of the author (whether published in book or serial form or as an article or lecture in any publication or unpublished), which the publishers may from time to time designate for inclusion in the New Edition.[6]

An Editorial Committee consisting of C.G. Jung, Herbert Read, and John D. Barrett ran the project; an Executive Subcommittee consisting of Read, Michael Fordham, and Gerhard Adler was responsible for deciding upon the selection of the material to be included and the editing details. There was, however, a certain hierarchy: given a difference of opinion within the Executive Subcommittee, "Read's decision should be binding on the other two members;"[7] all decisions made by the Subcommittee were then subject to the approval of the Editorial Committee, whose decisions, in turn, were subject to the approval of the Bollingen Foundation.

Jung's contract with the Bollingen Foundation and Kegan Paul also outlined the scale of the project: "It is contemplated that the New Edition may consist of several volumes, and that the preparation of the New Edition may require a number of years."[8] Despite a certain vagueness and some contradictions, the consequences of these clauses meant the following:

- the New Edition was planned as an unspecified selection from a corpus of works;
- the contract stipulated a process rather than a clearly defined project;
- the decision-making authority was with the publishers (i.e., neither Jung nor the editors had final powers of decision).

It is noteworthy that Jung signed such a contract. For, until this time, he had attached utmost importance to his own personal dealings with all details related to his publications. Now he handed over, to a large extent, the responsibility for his life's work to other people. As would become clear, he preferred to invest his energies in new projects rather than in the distribution of his previous works. For although he had grown old and had already looked death in the eye, there was still much of the pioneer and researcher in him.

Thus the editors set to work. A detailed concept was, it seems, developed step by step. An outline from 1953 presented only little new information—while CW Volume 1 of 1957 stated more precisely what the CW as a whole was to contain:

• Jung's previously published scholarly works, based on manuscripts written by himself. And such works were to appear in their latest versions (since Jung had the tendency to revise his writings again and again).

• The texts were to be arranged partly thematically, partly chronologically.

• This collection of texts—at that time called "complete"—would amount to seventeen volumes, the contents of each now specified. An additional volume was planned to contain various shorter texts, a general index and a bibliography. It seems that the publishers considered the number of seventeen volumes the upper limit, presumably for commercial reasons. It also became evident—explicitly or implicitly—what the CW would not contain:

• text variants
• clinical material
• correspondences
• notes made by third parties of Jung's talks, lectures, seminars, and interviews
• fragments, drafts, concepts, research material
• autobiographical and private material
• visual artistic material

The editing project was a challenge for all parties involved. Jung and his manuscripts were in Küsnacht; the Bollingen Foundation was in New York; the editors were in London; the translator was first in southern Switzerland, then in Mallorca. Europe was still suffering from the destructions of war, and modern means of communication like fax or email did not exist. Jung had his secretary, but no further staff to work on the CW. Nor was there a catalogue of his publications and manuscripts. It was William McGuire, the executive editor of the Bollingen Series who co-ordinated this network. After the concept of the seventeen volumes had been established, Bollingen Foundation and the publishers expressed their wish to expand the program. Thus, in 1957 Jung agreed in principle to the CW's inclusion of some of his seminars, that is, notes from them that had been taken by third parties. These, however, were not to be put on a par with his manuscripts, since Jung lacked the time to proof them for errors. The specific seminars for publication were not selected until 1965.

In 1957 Jung further consented to the CW's inclusion of his correspondence. For this project he appointed a special editorial group consisting of his daughter, Marianne Niehus-Jung, and Aniela Jaffé. Dr. Gerhard Adler functioned as contact person to the CW. Furthermore, Jung imposed the following restriction: "An important matter will be to eliminate letters which for private, family or similar reasons should be withheld from publication."[9] Since only one volume of correspondence was planned, the editors were forced to make a selection.

Another project, outside the scope of the CW, was undertaken in 1957: Jung authorized Aniela Jaffé and Pantheon Books to use—according to their best judgment—his private material, i.e., notes of talks with him[10] as well as excerpts of autobiographical notes made by him[11] for publication. Since the character of these writings was not scholarly, they were by no means to be included in the CW.[12] It was thus that the book *Memories, Dreams, Reflections* came into being, again representing a selection from extensive material.[13]

In other words, four publication projects were underway: CW, seminars, correspondence, and autobiographical material. Beginning in 1955, to these projects was added the publication of the CW in German, which Jung called "Gesamtausgabe" ("complete edition;" hereafter abbreviated to GW for the published title, *Gesammelte Werke*).[14] This was based on the concept developed by the Bollingen Foundation in 1953 for the Anglo-American edition. For the German language edition, Jung established a separate Editorial Committee consisting of Marianne Niehus-Jung, Lena Hurwitz-Eisner, and Dr. Franz Riklin—who was at the time the head of the C.G. Jung Institute

Zürich. In 1960, in case of his inability to continue working, Jung appointed his son-in-law Walther Niehus-Jung as his representative for negotiations with editors and publishers. Unfortunately, Jung did not live to see the completion of these projects. He died in 1961. As to the manuscripts, he had ordered his "hand-written estate," with certain exceptions, to go to the Swiss Federal Institute of Technology (hereafter, ETH).

Now, the concept for the seventeen volumes of the CW was called into question with the rediscovery of a number of unpublished manuscripts. In 1964 the Editorial Committee finally settled the question of which contents should go into each volume. A renewed selection led to an arrangement including the present-day Volume 18, *The Symbolic Life*, as well as the additional Volume 19 and Volume 20, entitled respectively, *General Bibliography* and *General Index*. In 1973 a selection of letters was published,[15] and the publication of the CW followed in 1979. Publication of the selected seminars ensued from 1984–1996.[16] All in all, the completion of the agreed-upon projects—a total of about thirty volumes—took almost fifty years. Concerning the yet unused material there were no obligations, plans, or instructions. Part of it was left to rest for quite a while. Since 1980 manuscripts have been handed over to the newly established Jung Archive at the ETH.

After Jung's death in 1961 the Heirs assumed ownership of Jung's author's rights and became the contracting party for publishers. Likewise the Heirs took over the editing and funding of the German language GW. However, by 1969 all the editors of the GW had died. They were succeeded by Dr. Elisabeth Rüf and Lilly Jung-Merker. In 1981 the Community of the Heirs of C.G. Jung constituted an Executive Committee of descendants of the second generation. The completion of the GW took until 1994. In the meantime the growing number of Jung descendants demanded a new and more adequate form of organization for the literary estates. This led to the establishment of the new Foundation in 2007.

The four initial projects (CW, seminars, correspondence, autobiographical) were never expanded. There were, however, from 1970 onward, new publications, which had been negotiated with the Heirs, for example correspondences (Freud-Jung, Pauli-Jung, Jung-White),[17] the *Zofingia Lectures*,[18] interviews, audio-recordings, and visual artistic works. The Heirs also made available material and copyrights for many other books, exhibitions, films, etc. Gradually, all unpublished items came again into focus, bringing to light the importance to the history of psychology Jung's text variants, drafts, fragments, concepts, and the like. In 1992 the Heirs began to go through the accessible archive material, and to consider new publications. In 1998, they decided generally to go forward. However, by this point in time, they lacked an organization that could oversee extensive editorial projects, for the old structures provided by the Bollingen Foundation no longer existed. With their sight set on new publications, the Heirs entered into a co-operation agreement with the Philemon Foundation in 2004.

To sum up, it can be said:

- The initial publication programs, which had been arranged with Jung, were carried out. The original editorial organization no longer exists.
- Jung's published works are, with regard to concept, a selection. The unpublished material is still shelved at the ETH and in various other archives.
- Within the bounds of possibility, the publication of further works is foreseen.
- New editorial structures have been established; the Foundation of the Works of C.G. Jung is among them.

Due to matters of copyright, the Foundation is involved in all Jung publications. On the one hand, there are follow-up publications related to the CW: translations, anthologies, digitalization; on the other hand, there is material that had remained either unselected or unavailable for inclusion in the CW. Specific tasks of the Foundation—besides its supervisory function—are the localization, procurement, identification, and release of archive material intended for publication. Thereby the authenticity of each text needs to be clarified. A delicate matter inheres in those notes and scripts that were written by third parties, but never formally authorized by Jung for publication. In addition, texts and even single quotations need to be checked for sensitive data. The Foundation also supplies information about Jung's work and person.

On the whole the Foundation serves as an interface between archive, editing, and publication. The actual contracts are handled on the Foundation's behalf by a literary agency in Zürich .[19] This holds for both the works of C.G. Jung and the less extensive works of Emma Jung-Rauschenbach. Further tasks arise in connection with Jung's private library in Küsnacht. For clarity's sake, it may be said what the Foundation does not aim to do: interpret Jung's works; comment on secondary literature; train analysts. Nor is it a public archive or a publishing house.

The Foundation's aim is to publish scholarly editions of original texts presented with contextual information. These might be published in co-operation with others or by the Foundation itself. There is much material awaiting publication, but the focus will be rather on quality than quantity.

Projects

The first publication following the Foundation's establishment was the long-awaited *Red Book*,[20] edited by Sonu Shamdasani, a joint venture of the Foundation of the Works of C.G. Jung and the Philemon Foundation. The two Foundations further collaborated in the conception of the *Red Book* exhibitions in New York, Los Angeles, and Zürich.

In 2011—fifty years after Jung's death—a volume edited by Ann Lammers was published, namely the correspondence between C.G. Jung and Dr. James Kirsch, an interesting documentation of the time period between 1930 und 1960.[21] The Foundation of the Works of C.G. Jung is further in the process of realizing its plans for the digitalization, restoration, and conservation of historical books shelved in Jung's private library in Küsnacht. The Philemon Foundation itself is working on several new publications, and developing ideas for further projects. All of these new undertakings will document the development of Analytical Psychology and add new facets to many existing works, even if they will hardly be as spectacular as the *Red Book*.

NOTES

1. The entity's legal name in German is *Erbengemeinschaft C.G. Jung.*

2. The new Foundation's legal name in German is *Stiftung der Werke von C.G. Jung, Zürich.*

3. C.G. Jung, *The Red Book: Liber Novus*, ed. Sonu Shamdasani, trans. Mark Kyburz, John Peck, Sonu Shamdasani, Philemon Series in arrangement with the Foundation of the Works of C.G. Jung, Zürich (New York: W.W. Norton & Company, 2009).

4. The *Black Books* are unpublished and document Jung's early experimentation with active imagination; they have been displayed recently along the *Red Book.* The *Black Books* contain material that Jung later incorporated in the *Red Book.*

5. *The Collected Works of C.G. Jung*, trans. R.F.C. Hull, eds. Sir Herbert Read, Michael Fordham, Gerhard Adler, trans. R.F.C. Hull, executive ed. William McGuire, Bollingen Series XX (Princeton, NJ: Princeton University Press; and London: Routledge and Kegan Paul, Ltd.), 20 Volumes. (Future references to Jung's *Collected Works* will not be credited in these endnotes.)

6. Appendix to the Agreement of 25 August, 1948, C.G. Jung and the Bollingen Foundation.

7. Agreement of 24 March, 1947, Bollingen Foundation and Kegan Paul Trench Trubner.

8. Agreement of 25 August, 1948, C.G. Jung and the Bollingen Foundation.

9. Letter of 29 January, 1958, C.G. Jung to the Bollingen Foundation, John D. Barrett.

10. Letter of 21 October, 1957, C.G. Jung to Aniela Jaffé.

11. *Ibid.*

12. *Ibid.*

13. C.G. Jung, *Memories, Dreams, Reflections*, recorded and edited by Aniela Jaffé, trans. Richard Winston and Clare Winston. Translation originally published by Pantheon, Random House, 1963, rev. ed. (New York: Vintage Books, 1961/1989).

14. C.G. Jung, *Gesammelte Werke von C.G. Jung in 20 Bänden* (Düsseldorf: Walter-Verlag).

15. *C.G. Jung Letters*, Volume 1: 1906–1950 and Volume 2: 1951–1961, eds. Gerhard Adler and Anelia Jaffé, trans. R.F.C. Hull, Bollingen Series XCV (Princeton, NJ: Princeton University Press, 1973).

16. See for instance the list of seminars in C.G. Jung, "Seminar Notes," CW 19, pp. 195-202.

17. Jung, *The Freud/Jung Letters*, trans. and ed. William McGuire, Ralph Manheim and William McGuire, Bollingen Series XCIV (Princeton, NJ: Princeton University Press, 1974); *Atom and Archetype: The Pauli/Jung Letters 1932-1958*, ed. C.A. Meier, trans. David Roscoe, Introduction by Beverley Zabriskie (Princeton, NJ: Princeton University Press, 2001); *The Jung-White Letters*, eds. Ann Conrad Lammers and Adrian Cunningham, consult. ed. Murray Stein, Philemon Series (London: Routledge, 2007).

18. *The Zofingia Lectures, Supplementary Volume A To The Collected Works of C.G. Jung,* ed. William McGuire, trans. Jan Van Heurck, Introduction by Marie-Louise von Franz, Bollingen Series XX (Princeton, NJ: Princeton University Press, 1983).

19. Paul & Peter Fritz AG, Literary Agency, Jupiterstrasse 1, CH-8032 Zürich.

20. Jung, *Red Book.*

21. *The Jung-Kirsch Letters: The Correspondence of C.G. Jung and James Kirsch*, edited Ann Conrad Lammers, trans. Ursul Egli and Ann Conrad Lammers (London and New York: Routledge, 2011).

Celebrating the 75th Anniversary of Jung's Bailey Island Lectures

This year marks the 75th anniversary of Jung's Bailey Island lectures in which he explored the dreams of a young scientist, now known to us as the physicist Wolfgang Pauli. Jung came to Bailey Island, Maine, at the invitation of Drs. Beatrice Hinkle, Esther Harding, Kristine Mann, and Eleanor Bertine. The latter three of these dynamic women had private practices in New York City and summered on Bailey Island. They had close ties to Zürich through their work and analysis with Jung, helped to found the Analytical Psychology Club of New York, and in 1941 created this journal, which makes *Spring* the oldest Jungian psychology journal in the world.

Spring would like to honor the anniversary of Jung's lectures by publishing in this issue Richard Brown's "The Origins and Development of Carl Jung's Relationship with Wolfgang Pauli" and in our next issue Brown's "Carl Jung's Bailey Island, Maine, and New York City Seminars of 1936 and 1937."

In subsequent issues *Spring* is very excited to have the opportunity to publish three papers that were presented at a special event honoring the 75th anniversary of the Bailey Island lectures. This September 2011 event was held at the Bailey Island Library and organized by the Jung Center of Maine. The papers that *Spring* will publish are one about Dr. Esther Harding (1888-1971) by psychologist and Jungian analyst Polly Armstrong, another about Dr. Kristine Mann (1873-1945) by Vassar professor and Jungian analyst Beth Darlington, and a third about Dr. Eleanor Bertine (1887-1967) by Chris Beach, a Jungian analyst in Maine.

Oddly, Jung's Bailey Island lectures themselves have never been published. Fortunately for us readers, they are in preparation for publication now through the Philemon Foundation as part of its Philemon Series and are being edited by Suzanne Gieser.

The Origins and Development of Carl Jung's Relationship with Wolfgang Pauli

RICHARD P. BROWN

By way of a letter dated 4 November 1932, Carl G. Jung, opened a thought-provoking, intellectual, and theoretical correspondence with the Nobel Prize laureate in physics Wolfgang Pauli. It was a correspondence that was to continue for 26 years, until 2 months before Pauli's untimely death on December 15, 1958 at the age of 58.[1] Within a short time after the initial letter, Jung and Pauli expanded beyond the professional relationship and began—and continued throughout the years—to exchange articles, thoughts, and ideas that reflected their common interests in the relation between depth psychology and quantum physics.

Both men gained from this long relationship. This article explores the origin, basis, and catalyst for their relationship—the existence of common ideas that could have shaken the pillars of science.

Richard P. Brown, J.D., Ph.D., teaches at Bellarmine and Spalding Universities in Louisville, Kentucky, and also has a private practice specializing in growth and development. He has Ph.D. from Saybrook University and a J.D. from the University of Louisville.

A THEORY CRITICIZED

Jung's form of psychology was subject to the criticism of not being demonstrable in scientific reductionist terms. However, Jung strongly felt that his form of depth psychology was scientific. He simply believed that the reductionist stance taken by the majority of scientists was too narrow in its interpretation of what designated an area of study as scientific and what constituted scientific proof.

The crux of the problem for Jung was the difficulty that arose from the inability to produce experimental models with quantitative measurements. At the same time Jung believed in and vociferously argued that his depth psychology was scientific, he begrudgingly acknowledged certain limitations in proving his theories in what was considered scientific terms. In the English translation of *Traumsymbole des Individuationsprozesses*,[2] Jung pointed out that he had understood the dilemma created by his seeming lack of proof, and had remained consistent on this matter throughout his writings by continually advising, "We do not yet possess a general theory of dreams that would enable us to use a deductive method with impunity... There is no theoretical argument to prove beyond doubt that any causal connection necessarily exists between [the psyche and consciousness]".[3]

Later in his career, Jung took a different tack. This less accommodating position argued that sufficient evidence for a designation of science is gained if an experiment showed a repetitive nature of observation and provided applicability to specific events.[4] For example, the repetitive presence of archetypal imagery in tens of thousands of patient's dreams that he had analyzed over his career and, likewise, their presence in the mythologies and art of ancient cultures throughout the world constituted scientific proof of the existence of archetypes. Applicability, therefore, was the best and most important indicator of the scientific nature of a theory.[5] Jung used the example of the migration instinct in birds to support this position. "There is also no 'scientific proof' for the existence of the migration-instinct, for instance, yet nobody doubts it".[6]

No matter the position taken, Jung's ideas continued to fall on the deaf ears of other psychologists—many of whom were fighting to establish their own theories. Throughout his life, he remained adamant in his defense of the scientific nature of his depth psychology.[7] In 1960, he suggested that the uniqueness (and resultant limitation) of his depth psychology, one that bridged the natural and human sciences, lay in the psyche's inability to adequately observe itself.[8] By viewing it in this way, Jung felt his psychology should be raised in certain respects, above the other sciences:

> It is evident that [a Jungian form of] psychology has the claim of being "scientific," even where it is not only concerned with (mostly inadequate) physical or physiological methods. Psyche is the mother of all our attempts to understand Nature, but in contradistinction to all others it tries to understand itself by itself, a great disadvantage in one way and an equally great prerogative in the other![9]

Before the above position was adopted, in the1920s and early 1930s Jung was still vacillating between a strong conviction in the science of his depth psychology and doubt in the ability to ever prove it in acceptable scientific terms. At some point, a juncture appeared and Jung realized that he had two avenues open that could be taken in an effort to gain the acceptance he desired. One direction was to find proof that would be acceptable in existing scientific terms. The other direction was to change the definition of science itself so that the current proof became acceptable in an expanded concept of science. In 1932 Jung discovered that he had found a possible source of proof that could be responsive in the confines of the former and a kindred spirit to pursue the latter. Both arrived on his doorstep in the form of Wolfgang Pauli. Pauli offered his dreams as an independent source that Jung believed would help to prove his dream theory in the current arena. Pauli also brought with him a new, quantum perspective from one of the basic sciences—a perspective that acknowledged the need to amend the rules of science.

Jung's ideal—of the broad acceptance of his depth psychology as a science—was no small issue to him or would it have proven to be to the world. If the definition of science expanded and his goal was accomplished, it could have shaken the foundations of psychology and science in general. It would have demanded the adoption of much broader perspective by scientists and possibly shifted the basic tenets that modern science had held sacred since the time of Kepler. The desire to foster a new scientific paradigm was a view that Jung and Pauli shared.

His introduction to Pauli quickly caused Jung to accurately surmise that quantum physics offered a very real and possible solution to his problem of proof.[10] At its core, quantum physics exhibited a similar problem to the one Jung had identified in his concept of psychology. While the laws of quantum physics held that observation affected the observed, Jung noted that depth psychology lacked "a base outside of its object" from which to view the psyche.[11] These acknowledgements showed the element of uncertainty with regard to an objective stance—fundamental to the conventional scientific perspective—that was common to both disciplines. While Jung was looking for positive proof of his theories, it appears to have come in a backhanded manner from Pauli in the form of proof-in-the-negative from a new branch of one of the oldest, and most respected sciences—physics.[12] It was an argument that said, "Maybe my depth psychology cannot offer scientific reductionist experiments as proof, but quantum physics cannot offer absolutes either. It can only offer mathematical rules of probability. In both cases, the ability to stand outside and not influence the observation is impossible." In an effort to quiet criticism, Jung proposed Pauli's dreams as an independent form of scientific proof of his dream theory.

The relationship between Pauli and Jung was rare in the annals of the history of science. With its origin in Pauli's personal crisis, the relationship soon moved far beyond this particular impetus to a much more interdependent relationship which lasted over 26 years. From the beginning, Jung sought to employ the dreams of Pauli as examples of his dream theory at work. To that end, he initially limited his contact with Pauli for the first eight months by having him analyzed by a new therapist[13] for five months and then did not see Pauli for another three months after that.[14] During that 8-month period, Pauli produced 400 dreams or other unconscious products.[15]

It appears as though Jung fully recognized from the beginning the possibilities that could arise from some kind of relationship with Pauli that went beyond therapy. In a letter to M. Fuss dated 20 February 1932 (approximately one month after Pauli's initial contact with Jung), Jung was already comparing the problem of proof in psychology to the new laws of probability fostered by quantum physics—laws that replaced the unambiguous and observable experimental results of classical physics.[16] He continued with that thought process, expanded it, and published (after comments and review from Pauli) *Der Geist der Psychologie* in 1946.[17] This particular paper by Jung went into detail outlining what he saw as the similarities between psychology and physics, as well as explaining psychological issues in terms of physics.[18]

In the end, the fortuitous meeting of Pauli and Jung provided Jung with three extremely important things:

1. The direction and focus to explore his ideas of proof for his theories from a different perspective;

2. An unimpeachable source of support (by Jung's high standards) that—through the anonymous use of Pauli's dreams—might demonstrate the validity of Jung's dream theory;[19] and

3. Support from another field of science with which Jung could identify and which he could offer publicly as evidence of the stature of his depth psychology as a true science.

With this foundation, one can shift focus to the individuals in the relationship.

Jung and Pauli

Jung, is a well known figure in the world of psychology. Much has been written by and about him over the years, but what of Pauli? A short biography will provide an illuminating picture of the man.

Wolfgang Pauli: The Conscience of Science[20]

Wolfgang Ernst Friedrich Pauli was born on April 25, 1900, in Vienna, Austria. The middle name of Ernst was given in honor of his godfather—Ernst Mach. Pauli's father, Wolfgang Josef, had moved to Vienna in 1898, and changed his name from "Pascheles" to "Pauli" upon his arrival in the city. In just over a year there, he married, converted to Christianity (baptized Catholic) from Judaism, and welcomed Wolfgang Pauli, Jr., into the world. The name change[21] and conversion, it is assumed, were the result of the rise of anti-Semitism in Europe and had nothing to do with beliefs. Wolfgang Pauli, Sr., wanted only to continue his work in chemistry and medicine.[22] Pauli, Jr. was the first of two children; his sister, Hertha, was born in 1906.

From an early age, the younger Pauli appeared gifted. He was raised in a highly stimulating and intellectual environment, and as his abilities appeared, his father hired first a high school teacher and then a university professor to tutor him in mathematics.[23] In 1918, Pauli went to the University of Munich where he attended classes taught by Arnold Sommerfeld, one of the early authorities on quantum theory. As gifted as he was, Pauli did not often attend classes, but as he recalled later, he realized that the intellectual atmosphere was essential for his scientific development.[24] Recognizing how gifted Pauli was and the fact that the classes bored him, Sommerfeld asked the 19-year-old to write a paper on Einstein's Theory of Relativity. The paper took 2 years to write and ran 250 pages. It impressed all who read it, including Einstein, who said of it:

> No one studying this mature, grandly conceived work would believe that the author is a man of twenty-one. One wonders what is most to admire, the psychological appreciation for the development of ideas or the reliability of the mathematical deduction, the deep physical insight, the ability of clear, systematic interpretation, knowledge of the literature, the factual completeness, the trustworthiness of the criticism.[25]

Einstein's regard for Pauli continued throughout his life, in fact. On the occasion of a party held in Pauli's honor after he had been awarded the Nobel Prize in Physics in 1945 for his Exclusion Principle,[26] in a speech Einstein described Pauli as "his intellectual successor".[27]

From the earliest days of his professional career, Pauli was recognized as one of the brightest in the field of theoretical physics, even though his name might not have been as well known as those of others.[28] He received his Ph.D. from the University of Munich at the age of 21 and became a full professor at Eidgenössische Technische Hochschule (ETH) when he was 28.[29] Besides the Nobel Prize for his development of the Exclusionary Principle and his prediction of the neutrino 30 years before technology was able to discover it, Pauli's curriculum vitae included: Professor of Theoretical Physics at the Federal Institute of Technology in Zürich (part of ETH); Visiting Professor at the Institute for Advanced Study, Princeton, at the University of Michigan, and at Purdue University (1942). Elected to the Chair of Theoretical Physics at Princeton in 1940, he returned to Zürich at the end of World War II.[30] In addition, he was an invitee to all of the Solvay Conferences from 1927 on, a guest lecturer often in demand, and he received several of the most important awards in physics, including the Lorentz Medal (1931) and the Max Planck Medal (1958).[31] Several universities bestowed on him honorary degrees: Stockholm, London, Upsala, Lund, Copenhagen, Boston, Munich, and Bangalore. In 1955, Pauli presided over the conference in Bern on the occasion of the 15th anniversary of the Theory of Relativity. Shortly before his death, he received an honorary doctorate from the University of Hamburg.[32]

This list of accomplishments is provided in order to highlight Pauli's brilliance and the high regard in which he was held in a field known for its intellectual giants. However, the success that he attained in the field of physics was not matched early on by success in his adult personal life.

The Origins and Foundation of the Relationship

Pauli had always been known for his acerbic wit, biting criticism, and intolerance for a lack of perceptive thinking. At night, he was also known to wander around the bars until the early hours, and had a propensity for getting into fights.[33] Problems began to arise in his young adult life when Pauli experienced three great traumas in rapid succession, beginning with the suicide of his mother in 1927. Shortly thereafter, his father married a woman near Pauli's own age.[34] Years later Pauli still resented this woman and in a letter to Jung called her his "wicked stepmother".[35] The last of these traumatic events was the dissolution of his marriage within a year of his wedding to his first wife, Käthe Deppner, an actress who left him to marry a chemist. The marriage appears to have been doomed from the start. According to Enz, Deppner had apparently fallen in love with the chemist even before she married Pauli. Five months after the marriage, a friend of Pauli, Hermann Weyl, wrote in a letter to Erich Hecke:

> With respect to marriage, Pauli is not well; for the moment his wife lives again together with her former friend in Berlin, but surely will soon again come to be with him a little, I am not close enough to him to be able to judge how threatening the whole is. Anyhow—in spite of his theories he is, like other mortals, at times vehemently plagued by jealousy.[36]

As for Pauli, he wrote on February 10, less than 2 months after his December 23, 1929, wedding, "In case my wife should at one time run away, you (as also all my other friends) will receive a printed notice".[37]

The combination of these events led to a personal crisis for Pauli.[38] According to personal conversations that took place in anticipation of an authorized biography of Wolfgang Pauli, Charles Enz, Pauli's assistant at the time of his death, was told by Pauli's widow, Franca Pauli, that Pauli's father had recognized the need for his son to seek help and suggested that he go to see Carl Jung.[39] In conformity with his scientific penchant, it appears that, prior to contacting Jung personally, Wolfgang Pauli attended some of Jung's lectures and read his *Contemporary Problems of the Soul* and *Transmutations and Symbols of the Libido*.[40]

Variously referred to as a "complete" disintegration and "acute depression", this crisis and his reasons for approaching Jung are perhaps best described in two letters that Pauli wrote: one, in 1931, before he undertook analysis, and the other reflecting back on the psychoanalytic experience from his viewpoint in 1934.[41]

> With women and me things don't work out at all, and probably it also will never succeed again. This, I am afraid, I have to live with, but it is not always easy. I am somewhat afraid that in getting older I will feel increasingly lonely. The eternal soliloquy is so tiresome.[42]

> [At the time] I had great fear of everything concerning the [*sic*] feeling and therefore have expelled it. This finally caused an accumulation in the unconscious of all claims concerning the [*sic*] feeling and a revolt of the former against an attitude of the consciousness that had become too one-sided, which manifested itself in discord, loss of value and other neurotic phenomena.[43]

From these two letters one can appreciate the difficulties that Pauli confronted in his personal life: first, through his expression of hopelessness in the letter of 1931, and second by way of the self-analysis in his letter of 1934. As expressed in his own words and as his therapy would bear out, Pauli appeared to have fine-tuned his extraordinary intellect at the expense of his emotions and to have had difficulty in his interactions with women as a result.

There remain two general issues in Pauli's life that have bearing on his relationship with Jung that should be addressed before moving forward. First is the issue of the "Pauli effect." The Pauli effect was a phenomenon that was recognized by most of Pauli's colleagues. Noticed originally in 1925 in Hamburg, Markus Fierz recalled the effect in these terms:

> Even quite practical experimental physicists believed, e.g., that his [Pauli's] mere presence in a laboratory produced all sorts of experimental mishaps, he so to speak tricked the objects. This was the "Pauli effect." For this reason, his friend Otto Stern, the famous artist of molecular beams never let him enter his laboratory. This is not a legend, I knew Pauli and Stern both very well! Pauli himself thoroughly believed in his effect. He once told me that he sensed the mischief already before as a disagreeable tension, and when the suspected misfortune then actually hit—another one!—he felt strangely liberated and lightened. It is quite legitimate to understand the "Pauli effect" as a synchronistic phenomenon as conceived by Jung...[44]

Enz recalls that Pauli believed that one of the characteristics of the Pauli effect was his own immunity from its effects. He remembers an occasion near Lake Como where he, Pauli, and another individual had had some spare time and decided to take a taxi up one of the mountain roads and then walk a short distance in order to capture a panoramic view of the lake and mountains. Upon their return to the taxi it would not start. Enz remembered that he had cautiously whispered to the other person present, "The Pauli effect", whereupon Pauli, having overheard him, strongly shook his head in disagreement because he was inconvenienced by the event (C. Enz, personal communication, February 12, 2010).

Perhaps this "Pauli effect," which even Pauli confirmed, prompted his interest in and discussions with Jung regarding the common subject of matter and psyche—the second issue to be raised here.[45] It is a subject that interrelates with the concept of synchronicity—a subject on which Pauli pressed Jung to publish. Pauli used his own considerable intelligence to explore the similarities between the unknowable processes and interactions on the quantum level, on the one hand, and the unconscious processes on the other, in an attempt to find a commonality—a root. On the occasion of Jung's 80th birthday, Pauli expressed the perplexity of the problem by observing:

> Since the unconscious is not quantitatively measurable, and therefore not capable of mathematical description and since every extension of consciousness ("bringing into consciousness") must by reaction alter the unconscious, we may expect a "problem of observation" in relation to the unconscious.[46]

His attempt to discuss this issue in scientific terms (i.e., addressing it as partially analogous to the conundrum of the "observer-object" in quantum physics) is perhaps the result of couching it in a way that was most comfortable to him. However, his natural reluctance did not hide his overall goal, which was to seek an even larger postulate. In a lecture at the Zürich Philosophical Society, Pauli asked for no less than a "renewed agreement of the physicists and philosophers on the epistemological foundations of the scientific description of Nature".[47] He believed that the route to this integration involved the entry of the subjective psyche into the equation.[48] In his paper, "The influence of archetypal ideas on Kepler's Theories," Pauli decried the movement toward the one-sided perspective that science was taking. He pointed out the need to return to a more holistic approach in order to get past the inconsistencies that were then plaguing physics and to find the common ground that seemed to him to exist now between psyche and matter.

> The possibility of bridging the antithetical [quantitative and qualitative] poles has become less remote [since Kepler]. On the one hand, the idea of complementarity in modern physics has demonstrated to us, in a new kind of synthesis, that the contradiction in the applications of old contrasting conceptions (such as particle and wave) is only apparent; on the other hand, the employability of old alchemical ideas in the psychology of Jung points to a deeper unity of psychical and physical occurrences. To us ... the only acceptable point of view appears to be the one that recognizes both sides of reality—the quantitative and the qualitative, the physical and the psychical—as compatible with each other.[49]

And later: "It would be most satisfactory if *physis* and *psyche* could be understood as complementary aspects of the same reality".[50]

One can see the thrust of Pauli's arguments as highly ordered and intellectual. Pauli described himself as influenced by the philosophy of Mach, whom Pauli described as "antimetaphysical." Although

Sommerfeld, Bohr, and Jung broadened his horizons in later years, in a letter to Jung dated March 31, 1953, Pauli wrote that he still remained self-labeled as "of antimetaphysical origin"—a label that he could never quite totally remove.[51] Perhaps, if it was an existential crisis that Pauli had undergone, the ability to discuss the issue fully on an ongoing basis with Jung—a fellow traveler and questioner—was the best therapy. Perhaps his relapse into depression and drinking toward the end of his life was a result of the loss of that relationship, as Jung's own health was diminishing (evidenced by Jaffe, Jung's secretary, taking over some of the letter writing duties for Jung and by the extended gaps in correspondence).[52]

The Implications of the Jung-Pauli Relationship

To many, the Jung-Pauli relationship focuses on two issues: (a) Jung's use of Pauli's analytical process and dreams as evidence of his theories; and (b) Pauli's influence on Jung in finally publishing the latter's work on synchronicity.[53] However, they explored much broader issues than just these. They shared an interest in the relationship of matter to the psyche,[54] the limitations of scientific reductionist thinking,[55] a fascination with numbers,[56] and the inability of language to adequately explain or explore the conceptualizations both of the psyche and of quantum physics.[57] This last issue encapsulates the quandary in which each of them found themselves in their respective fields. Visualization of concepts was a problem for both Jung and Pauli (i.e., archetypes that could never be formed but only expressed through archetypal images, and the inability in physics to visualize and express the exact model of the quantum universe). At the quantum level in physics, normal analogical processing is replaced by mathematical formulas and probabilities. The same difficulty arises in psychology when one attempts to address not only the depth and breadth of the unconscious (which by definition is unknowable) but also the transition from the physical to the metaphysical—from brain to mind.

It is also clear from the correspondence between the two that Pauli used their relationship to explore psychological concepts and metaphysical issues that he could not discuss with many of his colleagues in his own discipline. Pauli's depth of understanding of the philosophical issues that confronted physics after the Copenhagen interpretation of quantum physics is still unparalleled (H. Primas, personal communication, February 4, 2010; C. Enz, personal communication, February 4, 2010). He was haunted by the seemingly insurmountable problem of how to approach a definition (or even a reframing) of reality beyond the confines of empiricism, yet still finding evidence (or maybe even proof) thereof within the current structural limitations of the natural sciences. He felt alone in this sense. Not known for his tact, at one point he bemoans—directly to Jung—the lack of someone to talk to who has Jung's depth of psychological understanding and "who also has a background in mathematics and physics".[58] This, he writes, "drives me into spiritual loneliness".[59] Taking all the above as a whole, Jung and Pauli had embarked on a journey that questioned (from each of their perspectives) our view of reality.

In many ways, Jung was shifting our perspective of reality with the idea of the way that our consciousness interacts with the unconscious. Jung, as has been discussed, saw an autonomous unconscious that on a deeper level contains archetypes that carry forward an imprint or pattern of thinking that has existed over the history of humankind. These archetypes impact our conscious thoughts—the way that we perceive the world. For his part, Pauli came to Jung with a long abiding interest in reality as its conception had been changed after the Copenhagen interpretation of quantum physics. At the time the interpretation was presented by Bohr, and accepted in 1927 at a conference in Como, Italy, most physicists did not truly appreciate its reach.[60] Heisenberg (in agreement with Pauli) advised afterward that our whole concept of reality had to change. Cartesian dualism needed to be abandoned.[61] They realized that the only thing that is being measured in physics is an empirical reality.[62] This fact seemed to catch hold at the time, as leading physicists agreed that reality was not what was being measured. Bohr said, "It is wrong to think that the task of physics is to find out how nature is. Physics concerns what we can say about nature".[63] Toward the end of his life Einstein offered his own view on the subject: "It is basic for physics that one assumes a real world existing independently from any act of perception, but this we do not know. We take it only as a programme in our scientific endeavors".[64]

Pauli wanted to get past the limitation imposed by accepting an empirical reality, and then, just letting the issue drop. His curiosity demanded an exploration of the issue of what it would take to see beyond the empirical world. Although a mathematician, he "saw clearly that the method of logical analysis was not the only way of comprehending reality.[65] Scientific reductionist thinking had to be abandoned. In a letter to his friend Markus Fierz on August 12, 1948, he wrote, "When the layman says 'reality' he usually thinks that he is speaking about something which is a self-evident known; while for me working on the elaboration of a new idea of reality seems to be precisely the most important and extremely difficult task of our time".[66]

The distinction that Pauli found in his appreciation of the field of physics (and his incorporation of psychology into his worldview) is readily evident from his way of interpreting the influence of the observer on the observed object in quantum physics. Whereas Bohr was convinced by traditional physicists to treat the observer as a detached observer[67], where the "observation is an interaction between the object and the instruments"[68]; Pauli treated the "observation [as] an interaction between the object and the psyche of the observer".[69] This is a critical distinction in viewpoint between the two physicists. Over time, Pauli appeared to fully adopt Jung's concept of psyche and the unconscious (including the collective unconscious and its contents). To his critical way of thinking, Pauli had to accept this view. It conformed to and explained in part the conundrum that was being encountered in physics—the loss of a real world and the creation of a statistical one. To Pauli, it was quite patently a fact that observation is nothing more than a psychic event, and, therefore, answers must lie in that mechanism or process. Pauli began to realize that psyche and physics were two sides of the same coin—two different approaches to the real reality. He believed "there was an inner as well as an outer way of connecting to reality, and that these two options needed to be harmonized".[70]

Pauli's method for bridging the two approaches to reality required a broader usage of the term complementarity.[71] He wished to clearly expand its use outside of the world of physicists. In a letter to Jung, Pauli said, "It actually seems to me that in the *complementarity of physics*, with its overcoming of the wave particle duality, there is a sort of *role model or paradigm of that other, more comprehensive conjunctio*".[72] Pauli believed that the characteristics of the perceptual world were created from a common origin of ordering principles (his way of looking at archetypes) and that these ordering principles were at the base of (his concept of) a regressive "background physics" and also found in Jung's idea of the collective unconscious. This belief in the commonality of symbols arose from his own dreams[73] and, among other things, the commonality of those symbols with "treatises of the 17th century, especially Kepler, where scientific terms and concepts were still relatively undeveloped, and the physical considerations and ideas were interspersed with symbolic concepts".[74] Pauli believed a new neutral language was needed to describe the emergent aspects originating in these ordering principles of our perceptual reality without losing the breadth of his new reality. He also believed that when the correct methodology was applied to both physics and psychology one could reach common ground. To him, the psychological aspect of Jung's idea of the archetype was only half of the story: "The other half is the revealing of the archetypal basis of the terms actually applied in modern physics".[75] In this way psychology and physics were intertwined—one approaching the subject matter from the outside and one approaching it from the inside.

Carrying this idea further, in a letter dated August 12, 1948, Pauli wrote to Fierz, "On the one hand a symbol is a product of human effort, on the other hand it is a sign for an objective order in the cosmos of which man is only a part".[76] Clearly, Pauli had taken Jung's archetype and expanded its use for application in his discipline.[77] Whereas Jung's theory said that the archetypes were "motifs [that] presumably derive from patterns of the human mind,[78] Pauli took this definition to another level by showing that he understood the role of the archetype to be a connector to reality itself, beyond perception. In a letter to Fierz on January 6, 1952, Pauli wrote:

> The symbol is symmetrical with respect to "this side" and the "beyond," that is to say, dual in the sense of your suggested view of the process of perception; it has a relationship to "observing" and to "comprehending," it can be mathematical or also even more primitively picture-like. The symbol is like a god which exerts an influence on man but which also demands from man that he have a back effect on him (the God Symbol). It seems to me that only in this manner does the "this side" obtain any sense.[79]

Still later in his article published in *The Interpretation of Nature and the Psyche*, Pauli wrote:

> As ordering operators and image-formers in this world of symbolical images, the archetypes thus function as the sought-for bridge between the sense perceptions and the ideas and are, accordingly, a necessary presupposition even for evolving a scientific theory of nature.[80]

These last words of Pauli take on a deeper meaning, as the former quote helps to clarify the extent of Pauli's intent. Pauli was reaching for an understanding of a new reality—beyond scientific empirical reality. He hinged his concept for this new reality on the archetype. In 1954 Pauli wrote:

> Personally I see in [the evolved definition of archetype by Jung] the first indications of the recognition of ordering principles, which are neutral in respect of the distinction psychical-physical, but which ... are ideal and abstract, that is, of their very nature irrepresentable.[81]

He further explained that the attempts to bridge mind and matter at an earlier point in time, in medieval alchemy, had failed because of their use of "concretistic psycho-physical unified language".[82]

All this work referred to above by Pauli finds its roots in the depth psychology of Jung. Originating there, Jung was able to expand his theories as Pauli tested the concepts from another perspective. In the end, Pauli's view blended with Jung as the latter re-conceptualized the archetype as psychoid in nature. Perhaps influenced through his conversations with Pauli, Jung began to see the archetype as something beyond the individual.[83] The term had evolved over many years and eventually Jung saw it as a connecting principle between mind and matter[84] that could aid in one's understanding of the *unus mundis*—"that the multiplicity of the empirical world rests on an underlying unity".[85] This redefinition created a shift in the landscape not only in the idea of the archetype, but also in his model of the psyche.[86] Jung began to believe it "fairly probable ... that psyche and matter are two aspects of one and the same thing".[87] He came to this conclusion at a time when further refinement of theories and new discoveries in physics confirmed uncertainty's reign and reinforced matter and energy's interchangeability. So the "matter" that Jung refers to is, in its most basic form, energy. Jung, in other words, was listening to Pauli. For his part, Pauli agreed by saying, "It would be most satisfactory of all if physis [matter] and psyche could be seen as complementary aspects of the same reality.[88]

CONCLUSION

In the end, it is nearly impossible to sort out the interrelated influences that Jung and Pauli had on each other. Each brought their own perspective, education, and personal interests into the relationship. They created a symbiotic and synergistic relationship as they fed on each other and attempted to move science forward. Taken as a whole, there is an attempt by Jung and Pauli to reach more deeply into the perceived reality and discover what lay behind. Pauli had adopted Jung's concept of archetypes and combined it with his view of a "general order in the cosmos ... [expressed] … both in the laws of nature and [now] in the functioning of the psyche".[89] Pauli made this leap as a result of his belief in the psyche's role as observer in this perceptual world. Jung's depth psychology was, in turn, influenced by Pauli's scientific approach to psychological issues. He gave strength where needed by proofing, commenting, and augmenting Jung's papers and ideas. As Gieser says, "Pauli is constantly broadening his perspective and Jung is obliged to sharpen his conceptual apparatus".[90] It could equally be said that Jung created and expanded a conceptual apparatus that Pauli constantly tested in the hopes of providing a framework for his ideas. Much was gained in the relationship as "Pauli's conceptual thinking [came] into conflict with Jung's more imprecise and intuitive thinking".[91]

Perhaps the commonality of what Pauli and Jung sought can be expressed more clearly by using a variation of a model of Jung's theory of the psyche.[92] From the model one can visualize the psyche that contains the entire individual—both consciousness and the unconscious. Consciousness (represented in an inner circle) is surrounded by the personal unconscious (next layered concentric circle), and then that is surrounded by the collective unconsciousness (with no outer limitation or barrier). This last area stretches out into an unknowable. From Pauli's perspective that unknowable—which Jung believed reached to the spiritual aspect of the psychoid—also reached the reality that he was seeking. But the movement was not unidirectional: the psychoid or spiritual element of the archetype residing there reached back, bridging to the mind of the observer.

Looking Forward

Since the deaths of the founders of the Copenhagen interpretation of quantum physics, the rift between science and psychology has expanded rather than diminished. Modern physicists are too well grounded in the "belief that physics describes an objective reality which is independent of any observers and observations. Today physicists transfer such problems to philosophers".[93] Pauli had written "he belonged to a generation who saw really deep problems in modern physics but was not able to solve them".[94] He and others grappled with this problem, whereas the newer generations have ignored it. Hans Primas has suggested that this type of creativity is imperative in the field of physics (personal communication, December 12, 2009). New energy must be thrust into it in order to recapture the direction in which it was going and rescue it from reductionist thinking.

Likewise, much of psychology has taken the route of reductionist thinking. For the most part, it is on a parallel road with all other science. In both fields, the basic assumption reigns that this empirical world *is* the reality and that nothing else exists or can interact with it.

Jung and Pauli came the closest to achieving a forum for creating a new view of reality. They did not totally agree on what that view was;[95] but crucially, they did believe that the way to it was through a recombination of the mind and matter, much as alchemy had attempted in the past, albeit ineffectually. Only through this holistic approach was true reality to be found.

As Primas says, it is not important that they did not succeed. What is important is that they tried and that we are still talking about it. As long as the dialogue continues the idea never dies (H. Primas, personal communication, December 12, 2009).

NOTES

1. C.A. Meier, (ed.), *Atom and Archetype: The Pauli/Jung Letters, 1932-1958* (Princeton, NJ: Princeton University Press, 2001).

2. Originally a lecture, it was translated into English in 1939 (1940 in England) as *Dream Symbols of the Process of Individuation*. It was modified and added to by Jung and published again as *Psychologie und Alchemie* in 1944 (revised in 1952). Eventually this material was

translated and included in C.G. Jung, *The Collected Works of C.G. Jung* (Princeton, NJ: Princeton University Press, 1968) vol. 12, § 44. Further references to Jung's *Collected Works* (hereinafter "*CW*") will be by volume number and paragraph number.

3. C.G. Jung, *The Integration of the Personality* (New York: Farrar & Rinehart, 1939), p. 98.

4. E.A. Bennet, *C.G. Jung* (London: Barrie and Rockliff, 1961), p. 97.

5. *Ibid.*, pp. 95, 97. In furtherance of his position, Jung even suggested that the real roadblock to the acceptance of his psychology by the mainstream was that *scientific* means something different in mainland Europe than it does in England or the United States. "On the Continent ... any kind of adequate logical and systematic approach is called 'scientific'; thus historical and comparative methods are scientific." *Ibid.*, p. 102.

6. *Ibid.*, p. 101.

7. Further evidence is seen in Jung's use of statistical analysis in his work on synchronicity even though Pauli and his colleague, Markus Friez, who actually prepared the statistical analysis for Jung, disagreed with its applicability (H. Primas, personal communication, February 11, 2010). Pauli had cautioned Jung regarding this in a letter of 30 November 1950 when he observed that "'statistical correspondence' [does not] characterize ... synchronicity [because it] ... only applies when there is a large number of individual cases" not when there are only small numbers involved, Meier, (ed.), *Atom and Archetype*, p. 59.

8. Sonu Shamdasani, *Jung and the Making of Modern Psychology* (Cambridge, UK: Cambridge University Press, 2003), p. 94. This is a classic issue in physics and can also be seen in pure mathematics where problems arise when a system is self-referencing. Seth Lloyd, *Programming the Universe* (New York: Random House, 2006), p. 34. The importance here is that with such mathematical proofs, the ancillary is that "self-reference leads automatically to paradoxes in logic." Lloyd, *Programming the Universe,* p. 35.

9. Bennet, *Jung* (London: Barrie and Rockliff, 1961), p. 102.

10. Suzanne Gieser noted in her book, *The Innermost Kernel* (New York: Springer, 2005), that Jung's knowledge of physics prior to Pauli was "rather superficial ... [and that his] ... references to science became

more numerous and changed character after 1932 … becoming more explicit, clear and reflective", pp. 227-228.

11. Jung, *CW* 8, § 429.

12. In a commentary to Jung's paper, *Der Geist der Psychologie* (1946), Pauli expressed his understanding of the shared dilemma. "As a matter of fact the physicist would expect a psychological correspondence at this point, because the epistemological situation with regard to the concepts 'conscious' and 'unconscious' seems to offer a pretty close analogy to … the 'complementarity' situation in physics. On the one hand, the unconscious can only be inferred indirectly from its (organizing) effects on conscious contents. On the other hand every 'observation of the unconscious', i.e., every conscious realization of unconscious contents, has an uncontrollable reactive effect on these same contents (which as we know precludes in principle the possibility of 'exhausting' the unconscious by making it conscious). … It is undeniable that the development of 'microphysics' has brought the way in which nature is described in this science very much closer to that of the newer psychology: but whereas the former, on account of the basic 'complementarity' situation, is faced with the impossibility of eliminating the effects of the observer by determinable correctives, and has therefore to abandon in principle any objective understanding of physical phenomena, the latter can supplement the purely subjective psychology of consciousness by postulating the existence of an unconscious that possesses a large measure of objective reality", Jung, *CW* 8, § 439, footnote 130.

13. According to Enz, Franca Pauli (Pauli's second wife) described the novice practitioner, Erna Rosenbaum, as "a young Austrian, pretty, fullish, always laughing." Charles Enz, *No Time to be Brief: A Scientific Biography of Wolfgang Pauli* (New York: Oxford Press, 2002), p. 240.

14. Pauli sought out Jung in January of 1932 and appears to have first contacted the analyst Jung recommended to him—Erna Rosenbaum—in a letter dated 3 February 1932. Enz, *No Time to be Brief*, p. 241, contained in *Pauli, Letters to Erna Rosenbaum*, 1932, WHS ETH-Library, Hs 176.

15. Jung, *CW* 12, § 45.

16. C.G. Jung, *C.G. Jung Letters* (Princeton, NJ: Princeton University Press, 1973), p. 87-88.

17. Subsequently revised, edited, and published in *CW* 8, § 343 under the title *On the Nature of the Psyche.*

18. *CW* 8, §§ 434-442.

19. A source, however, that he could not identify (other than in cryptic terms regarding Pauli's extreme intelligence) in the context of his seminars on patients' dreams, yet one that appeared to increase Jung's own level of confidence.

20. This brief biography relies in large part on an interpretation of the original German in two works by Charles Enz, *No Time to be Brief : A Scientific Biography of Wolfgang Pauli* (New York: Oxford Press, 2002), a biography authorized by Pauli's widow, and *Wolfgang Pauli: Writings on Physics and Philosophy* (New York: Springer, 1994), for which Enz was a co-editor and penned a short introductory biography of Pauli in the opening pages; Suzanne Gieser's *The Innermost Kernel*; Kalervo Laurikainen's, *Beyond the Atom* (Berlin: Springer, 1988), and *The Message of the Atoms* (Berlin: Springer, 1997); as well as information from the ETH Zürich, where Pauli held a faculty research position as Chair of Theoretical Physics for most of his career. Enz was Pauli's last assistant, having served as such for the summer semester of 1956 and the winter semester of 1958, until Pauli's death in December. Over time, Enz became good friends with Pauli and his wife Franca. In fact, after Pauli's death it was Franca who requested that Enz write Pauli's official biography. Since most of the research material and Pauli's letters are in German, this author has relied on Enz, Gieser, Laurikainen, and ETH for the translations.

Pauli signed his correspondence in some cases as GG, indicating *der Geissel Gottes*, the scourge of God. He was also called *Zwei Steine*, "two stone" to Einstein's one stone (R. Schulmann, physics historian, personal communication, October 4, 2009). The reference to *Geissel Gottes* is also found in David Lindorff, *Pauli and Jung: The Meeting of Two Great Minds* (Wheaton, IL: Quest Books, 2004): "The letters between the two men reveal a wily humor in which Ehrenfest addressed Pauli as 'der Geissel Gottes' (the scourge of God) or 'der fürchterliche Pauli' (the frightful Pauli). Pauli reciprocated by signing letters to Ehrenfest as 'der Fürchterliche' or simply 'G.G.'" *Ibid.,* p. 12.

21. Although there is no certainty about the matter, it has been suggested that Pauli, Sr. chose his new name to tie his history to the family home in Prague. The house there had, at one time, been home

to a Catholic order of nuns known as Paulans. Enz, *No Time to be Brief,* p. 8.

22. *Ibid.*, pp. 7-8.

23. ETH (Eidgenössische Technische Hochschule), *Wolfgang Pauli and Modern Physics.* Exhibition of the ETH-Bibliothek on the occasion of the 100th birthday of Wolfgang Pauli. Retrieved July 22, 2009, from http://www.ethbib.ethz.ch /exhibit/pauli/index_e.html.

24. Charles Enz & Karl von Meyenn, (eds.), *Wolfgang Pauli: Writings on Physics and Philosophy* (New York: Springer, 1994), p. 14.

25. Lindorff, *Pauli and Jung,* p. 11. Translated from S. Richter, *Wolfgang Pauli: Die Jahre 1918-1930* (Frankfurt: Verlag Sauerlaender, 1979), p. 18.

26. Pauli won the Nobel Prize for answering a problem regarding the specific multiples in the electron orbits. He discovered that when a 4th value (a spin value) was applied to the electron state, it allowed for a rule to be created that said "two electrons in an atomic structure can never have all four quantum numbers in common." ETH, *Wolfgang Pauli and Modern Physics.* The work that this prize was based upon was done in 1924. In 1930, Pauli once again shocked the world of physics by theorizing the existence of a new particle without mass—a neutrino. Thirty years later, this particle was discovered.

27. ETH, *Wolfgang Pauli and Modern Physics.*

28. Letters from Pauli were famous in the field. They could run into many pages in a critique of an idea or concept, or in exploring new ground. They were known to be posted on bulletin boards at the institutions that received them. It was recalled that when Bohr received a letter from Pauli, he would carry it around for days showing it to many and carrying on imaginary conversations with Pauli, as if Pauli were right there. A. Hermann, Karl von Meyenn, & Victor Weisskopf, (eds.), *Wolfgang Pauli: Scientific Correspondence with Bohr, Einstein, Heisenberg, Volume I: 1920-1929* (Berlin: Springer, 1979), p. 58.

29. Enz & von Meyenn, (eds.), *Wolfgang Pauli,* p. 17.

30. Wolfgang Pauli, in *Nobel Lectures: Physics 1942-1962* (Amsterdam: Elsevier, 1964). Retrieved July 19, 2009, from the Nobel Foundation Web site: http://nobelprize.org/nobel_prizes/physics/laureates/1945/pauli-bio.html.

31. Founded by the industrialist Ernest Solvay and starting in 1911, Solvay's continuing series of conferences brings together the

leaders in the fields of physics and chemistry. They have continued to attract renowned physicists over the years. It is a very exclusive, "by invitation" only, conference, Niels Bohr, *Quantum Theory of Fields* (1961). Retrieved June 25, 2009, from http://www.solvayinstitutes.be/AboutUs/OpinionBohr.html.

32. ETH, *Wolfgang Pauli and Modern Physics.*

33. Gieser, *Innermost Kernel*, p. 14-15.

34. Enz, *No Time to be Brief*, p. 162; Enz & von Meyenn, (eds.), *Wolfgang Pauli*, p. 18. Enz's version of the events surrounding the suicide leaves the question open as to whether or not Pauli's father had remarried prior to his mother's death. Suzanne Gieser in *The Innermost Kernel* says that Pauli's mother killed herself "after his father had left her and married a younger woman." Gieser, *Innermost Kernel*, p. 18. Beverley Zabriskie, in Meier (ed.) *Atom and Archetype*, says that the suicide was "in reaction to his father's involvement in an affair." (p. xxxii).

35. Meier, (ed.), *Atom and Archetype,* p. 151.

36. Enz, *No Time to be Brief*, p. 210.

37. *Ibid.*, p. 210.

38. It should be noted that Pauli left the Catholic Church in May of 1929. Enz & von Meyenn, (eds.), *Wolfgang Pauli: Writings on Physics and Philosophy* (New York: Springer, 1994), p. 18. Although this would not in the normal sense be considered traumatic, it does suggest an existential issue.

39. Enz, *No Time to be Brief*, p. 240.

40. *Ibid.,* p. 240. Copies of these works, heavily marked by Pauli's hand, are kept in the Pauli Room at CERN. CERN is the European Organization for Nuclear Research. Founded in 1954, its name is derived from the French: *Conseil Européen pour la Recherche Nucléaire. Contemporary Problems of the Soul* was published in 1931 under the German title *Seelenprobleme der Gegenwart*, and *Symbols of the Libido* in 1925 as *Wandlungen und Symbole der Libido*. Based upon his personal relationship with Pauli, Charles Enz believes that Pauli would have researched Jung thoroughly prior to approaching him. Enz, *No Time to be Brief*, p. 240.

41. C.G. Jung, *Dream Symbols of the Individuation Process, Vol. 1* (Unpublished manuscript of the September 20-25, 1936, Bailey Island Seminar, 1937), p. 6; Gieser, *Innermost Kernel*, p. 142.

42. Enz, *No Time to be Brief*, p. 240. This letter was originally dated "3. August" by Pauli and was included in the correspondence of 1940-1949. Further research caused the editor to emend the date to 1931 with the notation "*Die Datierung ergibt sich eindeutig aus dem Zusammenhang* [the date is clear from the context]", von Meyenn, (ed.), *Wolfgang Pauli: Scientific Correspondence with Bohr, Einstein, Heisenberg, a.o., Volume III: 1940-1949* (Berlin: Springer, 1993), p. 754.

43. Karl von Meyenn, A. Hermann, & Victor Weisskopf, (eds.), *Wolfgang Pauli: Scientific Correspondence with Bohr, Einstein, Heisenberg, Volume II: 1930-1939* (Berlin: Springer, 1985), p. 340. This letter was written by Pauli to one of his early assistants and friends, Ralph Kronig, on 3 August 1934. It clearly reflects the adoption of Jungian language in his self-analysis.

44. Enz & von Meyenn, (eds.), *Wolfgang Pauli*, p. 17. Translated from M. Fierz, *Naturwissenschaft und Geschichte. Vorträge und Aufsätze* (Basel: Birkhäuser, 1988).

45. Jung had had similar dramatic and synchronistic occurrences in his life but did not consider them to rise of the level of an "effect". In *Memories, Dreams, Reflections* he recounts how, while visiting home from school during the summer holidays, first a table split on its own and then 2 weeks later, a knife in a cupboard had "snapped off in several pieces." C.G. Jung, *Memories, Dreams, Reflections* (New York: Random House, 1989), p. 105. He also remembered that while meeting with Freud he "had a curious sensation.... And at that moment there was such a loud report in the bookcase ... that we both started up in alarm (*Ibid.*, p. 155).

46. Enz & von Meyenn, (eds.), *Wolfgang Pauli*, p. 23.

47. Jagdish Mehra, (ed.), *The Physicist's Conception of Nature* (Dordrecht, Holland: D. Reidel, 1973), p. 789.

48. Enz &von Meyenn, (eds.), *Wolfgang Pauli*, p. 24.

49. C.G. Jung & Wolfgang Pauli, *The Interpretation of Nature and The Psyche* (New York: Pantheon Books, 1955), pp. 207-208. "Complementarity" is a term in quantum physics that reflects the apparent conflicting aspects of certain properties of objects in the nature of the micro when an analogy is conceived in the macro. Bohr coined the term as an adjunct to Heisenberg's uncertainty principle and in an attempt to quell the turmoil created by the proposed and seemingly

contradictory wave-particle properties of electrons, C.A. Meier, (ed.), *Atom and Archetype*, p. xix.

50. *Ibid.*, p. 210.

51. Meier, (ed.), *Atom and Archetype*, p. 103.

52. See Marie-Louise von Franz, "Letter to the editor", *Psychological Perspectives: A Semiannual Journal of Jungian Thought* (1988), 19(2), 377, for reference to Pauli's return to drinking, and Meier, (ed.), *Atom and Archetype* for evidence of the later letters being answered by Jaffe. It is also notable that Franca, Pauli's wife, advised Enz that she ended up listening to Pauli's dreams at the breakfast table and that "this activity occupied an increasing space towards the end of Pauli's life" Charles Enz, *Of Matter and Spirit: Selected Essays of Charles P. Enz* (Hackensack, NJ: World Scientific Publishing, 2009), p. 220.

53. Jung traces his interest in synchronicity to two incidents: a meeting with Einstein early in his career, and Richard Wilhelm's presentation to him of a Chinese alchemical interpretation of "The Secret of the Golden Flower", Meier, (ed.), *Atom and Archetype*, p. xxx. It was not until 1948 that Pauli and Jung began addressing the issue in their correspondence. The exchange culminated in the joint publication of *The Interpretation of Nature and the Psyche* in 1952 (in German), which contained Jung's essay "Synchronicity", and Pauli's essay "The Influence of Archetypal Ideas on the Scientific Theories of Kepler", published in English as C.G. Jung & Wolfgang Pauli, *The Interpretation of Nature and The Psyche* (New York: Pantheon Books, 1955).

54. In a letter of 31 March 1953, Pauli expresses the desire to "once again take up the discussion of the question that is so important to me—namely, the relationship between spirit, psyche, and matter." Meier, (ed.), *Atom and Archetype*, p. 60. Jung also addressed this issue in many of his writings. See *On Psychic Energy*, *CW* 8, § 1-130; *Psychology and Alchemy* in *CW* 12; and, *Alchemical Studies* in *CW* 13.

55. Pauli directly addresses the issue of scientific reductionist thinking in his essay, "The Influence of Archetypal Ideas on the Scientific Theories of Kepler". In that essay, he points to the intellectual dispute between Kepler and Fludd as a turning point in the de-animization of the world and the rise of scientific rationalism, Jung & Pauli, *The Interpretation of Nature and The Psyche*, p. 154. Jung's works

are filled with his view of the necessity to reach beyond reductionist thinking in order to reach a life of deeper meaning.

56. Pauli and Jung also shared a common interest in numbers—Jung expressing the significance of numbers that appear in dreams in C.G. Jung, *Dream Symbols of the Individuation Process, Vol. 1.* (Unpublished manuscript of the September 20-25, 1936, Bailey Island Seminar, 1937), pp. 95-96, 123, 139-140, and Pauli discussing the mystical value that was placed on numbers by Pythagoras, Plato and Theaetetus, in Enz & von Meyenn, (eds.), *Wolfgang Pauli*, p. 141. They also were in agreement with their interpretation of the movement from the 3 to the 4 as an indication of wholeness in Meier, (ed.), *Atom and Archetype*, pp. 115-124.

57. Pauli writes of the need for "a new ('neutral') psycho-physical standard language, whose function is to symbolically describe an invisible, potential form of reality that is only indirectly inferable through its effects" (*Ibid.*, p. 81); for "a correct conceptual language ... that is not yet known" (*Ibid.*, p. 107); and the ability to translate dreams if one has the correct "lexicon" (*Ibid.*, p. 110). In many places, Jung addresses the constricting role of language when attempts are made to explore the psyche. For a good discussion, see *Two Kinds of Thinking* in Jung, *CW* 5, § 4-46.

58. Meier, (ed.), *Atom and Archetype*, p. 123.

59. Pauli seems to have depended upon his friend and fellow professor of physics, Markus Fierz, to some extent for inclusive discussions in mathematics, physics, and philosophy. Fierz had met Pauli and accepted the position as his assistant in 1936. In 1938 they collaborated on the "the 'Pauli-Fierz model' of a nonrelativistic electron coupled to the radiation field." Peter Minkowski, *Markus Eduard Fierz-Biber, 20.06.1912-20.06.2006.* Retrieved February 2, 2010, from http://www.mink.itp.unibe.ch/data/Fierz4.pdf., p. 6. Fierz went on to hold the position of Professor of Theoretical Physics at Basel University. They remained friends thereafter, meeting as often as they could and exchanging correspondence over the years. That correspondence is one of the few limited sources where Pauli can be found to freely discuss "philosophy and history of ideas." Kalervo Laurikainen, *Beyond the Atom* (Berlin: Springer, 1988), p. 3. It is unfortunate that when he was approached to write a biography of Pauli, Fierz (at the same time that he made suggestive comments regarding

the depth of their conversations aside from their correspondence) refused the opportunity, stating that that chapter is closed (H. Primas, personal communication, February 11, 2010). Perhaps the reason for the close relationship and freedom of expression that Pauli felt (as seen in the correspondence) comes from the fact that Fierz was no stranger to Jungian psychology. Fierz's mother had consulted with Jung in 1918, Peter Minkowski, *Markus Eduard Fierz-Biber, 20.06.1912-20.06.2006.* Retrieved February 2, 2010, from http://www.mink.itp.unibe.ch/data/Fierz4.pdf, p. 4; and Fierz, although he was not in agreement with a statistical proof of synchronicity (a position with which Pauli concurred), provided the mathematical analysis to Jung that the latter used in his published work, *Synchronicity: An Acausal Connecting Principle,* in Jung & Pauli, *The Interpretation of Nature and The Psyche.* (H. Primas, personal communication, February 11, 2010).

60. Kalervo Laurikainen, *The Message of the Atoms* (Berlin: Springer, 1997), p. 2.

61. *Ibid.*, p. 44; Werner Heisenberg, *Philosophical Problems of Quantum Physics* (Woodbridge, CT: Ox Bow Press, 1979), p. 25. The Copenhagen school of thought created its own "duality of a mutually contradictory (but 'complementary') pictures", Bernard d'Espagnat, *Veiled Reality* (Boulder, CO: Westview Press, 2003), p. 14.

62. Laurikainen, *Message of the Atoms*, pp. 18-20.

63. Harald Atmanspacher & Hans Primas, (eds.) (*Recasting Reality* (New York: Springer, 2009), p. 1.

64. Laurikainen, *Message of the Atoms*, p. 148.

65. Laurikainen, *Beyond the Atom*, p. 6.

66. *Ibid.*, p. 193.

67. Enz, *Of Matter and Spirit: Selected Essays*, p. 156.

68. Laurikainen, *Beyond the Atom*, p. 177.

69. *Ibid.*, p. 177. See a translation of an excerpt of Pauli's letter to Bohr on the subject in Laurikainen, *Beyond the Atom*, p. 176.

70. David Lindorff, *Pauli and Jung: The Meeting of Two Great Minds* (Wheaton, IL: Quest Books, 2004), p. 81.

71. Bohr first used the word in 1927 at a lecture in Como, Italy to describe the fact (as he put it in 1934) that "any given application of classical concepts precludes the simultaneous use of other classical concepts which in a different connection are equally necessary for the elucidation of the phenomena", Harald Atmanspacher, & Hans Primas,

"Pauli's Ideas on Mind and Matter in the Context of Contemporary Science," *Journal of Consciousness Studies,* 13(3) (2006), p. 14.

72. Meier, (ed.), *Atom and Archetype*, p. 91.

73. Jung disagreed with Pauli's view on this issue and suggested that the content (symbols from physics and math) was merely an indication of Pauli's conscious focus or an unconscious avoidance of psychology. "Your dreams are physical because this is your natural language, on the principle *canis panem somniat, piscator pisces* (dogs dream of bread, fishermen of fish)....[or]...the unconscious has the tendency to confine you to physics...because psychology, for whatever reason, is not appropriate", Meier, (ed.), *Atom and Archetype*, p. 113.

74. Meier, (ed.), *Atom and Archetype*, p. 179.

75. *Ibid.*, p. 180.

76. Laurikainen, *Beyond the Atom*, p. 193.

77. Pauli's refinement of the archetype, expanding his own concept of it, and assisting by helping to fine-tune Jung's proposed expansion 4 years later, is detailed in three lengthy letters, as Jung was preparing to write *Synchronicity: An Acausal Connecting Principle* (the title itself reflecting Pauli's input, casting synchronicity as an additional law of nature other than causal connecting principles, *Ibid.,* pp. 53-70). Pauli was discussing the breadth of his idea of the archetype with Fierz in 1948. The correspondence with Jung dates from 1952.

78. Jung, *CW* 11, § 88.

79. Laurikainen, *Beyond the Atom*, p. 194.

80. Jung & Pauli, *The Interpretation of Nature and The Psyche*, p. 153.

81. Enz & von Meyenn, (eds.), *Wolfgang Pauli*, p. 159.

82. *Ibid.*, p. 159.

83. Jung, *CW* 8, § 419.

84. *Ibid.*, § 420.

85. Jung, *CW* 14, § 767.

86. This idea was published in 1947, in German, under the title *Der Geist der Psychologie,* in Jung, *CW* 8, § 343.

87. Jung, *CW* 8, § 418.

88. Jung & Pauli, *The Interpretation of Nature and The Psyche*, p. 210.

89. Laurikainen, *Message of the Atoms*, p. 145.

90. Gieser, *Innermost Kernel,* p. 171.

91. *Ibid.*, p. 171.

92. Laurikainen, *Message of the Atoms*, p. 147.

93. *Ibid.*, p. 3. After Pauli and Bohr died, "criticism by the younger generation of the Copenhagen interpretation became the dominant feature in the discussion concerning the foundations of quantum theory". Laurikainen, *Message of the Atoms*, p. 3.

94. *Ibid.*, p. 3.

95. For example, Pauli had trouble understanding Jung's concept of synchronicity. Laurikainen, *Beyond the Atom*, pp. 82 & 203. The difficulty lay in the distinctions that Pauli placed on causality. "When causality is statistical, it presupposes an indeterminism alongside the determinism of events. Causality achieves only statistical mean values. Pauli looked at the indeterminism of the individual events as a kind of 'road sign' to something new, which Jung, on the other hand, aimed at reaching on the basis of the concept of synchronicity", *Ibid.*, p. 143. Jung attempted a statistical proof of an acausal property of reality. Pauli saw this as an impossible task.

When "One" becomes "Two"
The Vocational Character of the Mediating Other: An "Enterview" with Greg Mogenson

ROBERT HENDERSON

Greg Mogenson was born in Saskatoon, Saskatchewan. A graduate of The University of Western Ontario, he did his family therapy training at The California Family Study Center and his analyst training through the Inter-Regional Society of Jungian Analysts. A long-time contributor to *Spring*, Greg is the editor of the Studies in Archetypal Psychology Series of Spring Journal Books and a founding member of The International Society for Psychology as the Discipline of Interiority. The author of many articles in the field of analytical psychology, his books include *A Most Accursed Religion: When A Trauma becomes God*, *Greeting the Angels: An Imaginal View of the Mourning Process*, *The Dove in the Consulting Room: Hysteria and the Anima in Bollas and Jung*, *Northern Gnosis: Thor, Baldr, and the Volsungs in the Thought of Freud*

Robert S. Henderson is a pastoral psychotherapist in Glastonbury, Connecticut. He and his wife, Janis, a psychotherapist, are co-authors of *Living with Jung: "Enterviews" with Jungian Analysts*, Volumes 1, 2 and 3 (Spring Journal Books, 2006, 2008, and 2009). Many of their interviews with Jungian analysts have also been published in *Spring Journal*, *Quadrant*, *Psychological Perspectives*, *Harvest*, and *Jung Journal: Culture and Psyche*.

and Jung, and (with David L. Miller and Wolfgang Giegerich) *Dialectics and Analytical Psychology: The El Capitan Canyon Seminar.* For more information see the website: www.gregmogenson.com.

Robert Henderson (RH): I understand that you were born in Saskatchewan and have roots in the rural life of that Canadian province. What impact do you think that may have had on your later life and career as a Jungian analyst and marriage and family therapist?

Greg Mogenson (GM): Both of my parents grew up on farms in Saskatchewan during the "dirty thirties" of the Depression era. The first in generations to leave the farm and to become educated, I think they felt a debt to the lives and the relatives they left behind. In my father's case this was especially strong. It was only because his older brother was adamant about not wanting to go to high school (which involved living away from home and boarding in a town some distance away that had a school) that my father, the next oldest, had had the opportunity to go at all. Much to his credit he made the most of this happenstance, finishing high school by sixteen, teaching grades one to ten in a one room school house while obtaining a Bachelor's degree by correspondence, and then after attending graduate school establishing a very interesting and productive career as a research scientist and high-ranking university academic! Oddly, though, considering the role educational opportunity had played in my parents' lives (my mother, too, had had a professional career as a nurse), there was little encouragement or expectation that I would be educated. On the contrary, there was bizarrely an attitude of antipathy from my father with regards to this for me even though for my generation higher education had become par for the course. Almost as if in payment of a debt, I spent most of my summers growing up billeted away from home on an uncle's farm as soon as school let out, and sometimes a month or so before that to help with seeding. Fortunately for me, I loved my uncle, his family, and the large mixed prairie farm. There I had many adventures, both in the actual work of planting crops, summer fallowing, harvesting and caring for the animals, and in the life of the wider community in the late hours carousing with my wild cousins. For most of my childhood right up into my late adolescence I was very much identified with this life, and even wanted to be a farmer. Though this was gradually to give way to my going on to university and graduate school with the aim of becoming a Jungian analyst (I should explain that I had learned something of Jung in high school and that my interest in him greatly helped me in overcoming my father-complex enough to see university education as a prospect for my own life as well), I continued to work on farms right through into my Master's training which was in family therapy. And even then, after graduating, the rural connection continued through my practicing as a family therapist in a children's mental health center in a rural community in Ontario for ten years. For this work my farming experience was a great asset. I could easily relate to the children and families that I had to treat and could readily couch all that I had to say in the language of the barnyard, a proficiency that is still with me when needed, all these years later in my work as an analyst.

RH: How did you become interested in Jung?

GM: When I was in the tenth or eleventh grade of high school—I think I was sixteen years old at the time—a teacher of world religions gave a lecture on Jung's concept of the archetype and the collective unconscious. Freud, the teacher had explained by way of contrast, saw the psyche reductively and personalistically as being a function of the laying down and lingering on of the vicissitudes of one's childhood and early family experience. Well, by sixteen I had had quite enough of that, or so I liked to think, and for this reason as well was all the more taken with Jung's vision of a transpersonal psyche. There was grandeur in the notion of the archetype, grandeur and transcendence. I loved the idea that I was more than what the external contingencies of "time, place, circumstance, cause and effect" had made me. Though I had not yet read in Jung about the star in man, I had in my puerile exuberance already hitched my wagon to it.

The other path that led me to become interested in Jung I found by way of the novels of Herman Hesse—*Demian*, *Steppenwolf*, *Narcissus and Goldmund,* and the rest. As I recall it now, I was introduced to this author on the same day that I was introduced to Jung. Immediately upon leaving my World Religions class, my head still reeling with the thought of a psyche that is as "fathomless as the abysms of the earth and vast as the sky" (*CW* 11, § 758), I walked into the classroom of a favorite teacher and spied a copy of Hesse's *Demian* on his desk. Noticing my interest, and having just finished the novel himself, my teacher generously offered that I might like to borrow it. Later that day, thumbing through the pages, my eye fastened upon a highlighted section in the Prologue, "But every man is not only himself; he is also the unique, particular, always significant and remarkable point where the phenomena of the world intersect once and for all and never again. That is why every man's story is important, eternal, sacred; and why every man while he lives and fulfils the will of nature is a wonderful creature, deserving the utmost attention." These lines were then followed by another which has haunted me ever since: "In each individual the spirit is made flesh, in each one the whole of creation suffers, in each one a Saviour is crucified." Once again, I felt that same chord struck in me that had been struck earlier that day when I heard about the collective unconscious. Whatever Jung may have meant by that concept (and I certainly intended to find out more about that!), I felt an inward certainty that it had do with a great truth, whatever its merits as a scientific hypothesis might be. And then there were those marvellous characters from Hesse's novels—Emil Sinclair, Max Demian, and Pistorius; Harry Haller, Hermina, and Pablo; Narcissus and Goldmund; Peter Camenzind. Communing with these troubadours of a questing spirit in the meeting place of my daily reading, a good deal of the atmosphere and ethos of Jungian analysis was imparted to me before I even really knew there was any such thing as Jungian analysis.

RH: In contrast to your experience in meeting Jung through a classroom lecture and through insightful novels, some of the early first generation Jungians we have "enterviewed" discovered Jung when they were in the midst of a personal crisis. For example, Jane and Jo Wheelright met Jung while in the midst of a marital crisis. What difference do you feel it makes as to how a person first meets Jung and his psychology?

GM: Maybe the ways of meeting Jung and his psychology which you contrast are not mutually exclusive alternatives, but two sides of the same coin. We know from their own reports that the first generation Jungians who were treated by Jung got a good many lectures from him during the course of their analyses! Joseph Henderson, for example, has described how Jung would pace about in the consulting room pontificating about abstruse topics, on occasion even drawing his attention to material from old books from his library. And we know from the Wheelrights that in the lecture hall of their marital crisis Jung taught them his ideas concerning typology. As for the other side of the coin, I think that one's being introduced to the depth psychological tradition generally and to Jungian psychology in particular through classroom lectures, books, and insightful novels may also ramify as a crisis through one's self-understanding inasmuch as that one's former, merely personalistic or ego-psychological framework may be radically torn asunder. One learns, to say it with Jung's words, that one is not the master of one's own psychological house. This is a key point. Pushing it a bit I would even go so far as to doubt whether one has really been reached by Jungian thought if one's encounter with it, however this is mediated, has not shaken one up and brought about an inner crisis of sorts.

Now this being shaken up, I should add, has also another important aspect. It indicates that the idea by which you have been struck is not only an external idea, but one that your own soul reverberates with, finds more of itself in, or makes itself with. So there is a vocational aspect to such encounters, vocational in the sense of what is meant when we speak of one's having a calling. Until you are shaken up or brought to crisis you are only superficially in yourself and not really in psychology yet.

I remember in this connection a dream I once had after reading a radical and mind-blowing book. I dreamt that a creek behind my home had spilled over its banks washing my house off its foundations! And there have also been dreams, after having been exposed to various ideas that were new to me, that my office has been trashed by invaders while at the same time, in another moment of the dream, I discover that there is now a new hallway and door leading into my office—a new approach to my practice, in other words.

The upshot of these reflections is that whether one comes to psychology by way of some sort of personal crisis or to crisis by way of psychology, the important thing as far as a specifically Jungian approach in psychology is concerned is that the mediating other—be it the Jung who the first generation Jungians worked with, a symptom, a dream, a lecture, novel or life event—is grappled with as an *internal* other. In one of his books, Jung avers that "We meet ourselves time and again in a thousand disguises on the path of life" (*CW* 16, § 534). This statement aptly indicates what is meant when we refer to the figure of the other as the soul's own other, itself as other. Theoretically considered, the heuristic of our soul-making that Jung provides with this line is nothing else than a lively reiteration of his psychology-constituting insight that for psychology there is no Archimedean vantage-point outside the psyche to view it from objectively. "No Archimedean point" in this context means that nothing is external to the soul. It means that all that presents itself as other is none other than the soul itself, consciousness *per se*, in another of its facets. "All perception is apperception," as the saying goes. Or as the Chandogya Upanishad has it, "Thou art that."

A passage of Jung's beautifully spells out what I am describing here:

> When a summit of life is reached, when the bud unfolds and from the lesser the greater emerges, then as Nietzsche says, 'One becomes Two,' and the greater figure, which one always was but which remained invisible, appears to the lesser personality with the force of a revelation. He who is truly and hopelessly little will always drag the revelation of the greater down to the level of his littleness, and will never understand that the day of judgement for his littleness has dawned. But the man who is inwardly great will know that the long expected friend of his soul, the immortal one, has now really come, 'to lead captivity captive,' that is, to seize hold of him by whom this immortal had always been confined and held prisoner, and to make his life flow into the greater life—a moment of deadliest peril! (*CW* 9i, § 217)

Along with the powerful description that Jung provides in this passage of the figure of the other as the soul's own other, he also emphasizes the challenge character of the encounter. As strange and alien as it may seem, the figure of the other is always and only the mediator of a more comprehensive self-understanding. Or perhaps it is better to say that it already is this self-understanding, albeit in a posited, projected, and often menacingly incisive form. Of course, the more ensconced we are in the definitions we have already assigned to everything or been recruited to the more we will tend to tighten up against this new truth as against some terrible threat. But the challenge, as Jung rightly suggests, is to transcend its seeming externality by realizing that the way it appears is wholly and self-critically a function of one's own psychological position, identity, or stance. "Who am I," writes Jung in a somewhat different context (*CW* 12, § 152), "that all this should happen to me?"

These reflections bring me back to my story about having immediately identified with Jung's concept of the collective unconscious at age sixteen. At that youthful summit of life it was a true and wondrous thing to meet the friend of the soul in that notion. And in hindsight I can say that the transference of that time was such a positive and even idealizing one because the challenge that had been posed fit well with my age and stage. I felt an affinity with Jung and readily understood that to grow up with his help I had only to throw myself into learning more. Never mind that I could only understand a small percentage of what I read of his *Collected Works*. Very gradually an understanding began to take shape and along with this the plan to eventually train as a Jungian analyst myself.

But, of course, there are other junctures of life, other summits. And at some of these the challenge posed by the soul's unfolding has more to do with emancipation via seeing through. In *Treasure Island*, for example, the youthful protagonist Jim Hawkins has to learn that the mentoring friend of his soul who he had met up with in the course of his voyage, Long John Silver, is actually a treacherous pirate! I mention this to say that my identification with and esteem for Jung's concept of the collective unconscious has since that time gone wholly under for me into quite other notions. While I remain a dedicated Jungian, I am a (happily!) disillusioned one. I no longer believe in the collective unconscious. And Jung, too, has been largely stripped of his *mana* for me.

RH: I would guess that for many Jungians the collective unconscious is one of the most important aspects of Jungian psychology. Talk about your no longer believing in it.

GM: Freud once declared the Oedipus-complex to be the shibboleth of psychoanalysis, its avowal serving to distinguish adherents of the movement from its detractors. If the concept of the collective unconscious is in much the same way the shibboleth of analytical psychology, well then I guess I have some explaining to do! For these days I find myself stuttering over that watchword even as in a dream I had a few years back I found myself stuttering the name "Ca-ca-ca-ca-ca-aarl Ju-Ju-Ju-Ju-Ju-Ju-ung." I guess you could say that my youthful identification with both Jung and his signature concept have been broken apart through their having become subject to critical reflection.

But before I discuss this any further I want to return to the implicit understanding of the concept which struck me so powerfully and won me over so completely when I first learned of the collective unconscious back in that classroom at age sixteen. Thinking about this now I am put in mind of a passage from one of Emerson's journals that was written a good many decades before Jung came up with his concept of the collective unconscious.

> Were you ever instructed by a wise and eloquent man? Remember then, were not the words that made your blood run cold, that brought blood to your cheeks, that made you tremble or delighted you,—did they not sound to you as old as yourself? Was it not truth that you knew before, or did you ever expect to be moved from the pulpit or from man by anything but plain truth? Never. It is God in you that responds to God without, or affirms his own words trembling on the lips of another. (Oct 27, 1831)

This is a marvellous passage. Expressive of the soul, it serves in our context to bring the similarly expressive aspect of Jung's concept of the collective unconscious to light. This is not to imply, however, as many Jungians would be inclined to assume, that the experience described by Emerson "comes from the collective unconscious." It is much rather the other way around. The concept of the collective unconscious is but a later stanza of Emerson's poetic journal entry (if I may put it that way), a stanza, however, that lapses unpsychologically into the prose of explaining the soul.

The problem I am pointing out has to do with what might be called the expression/explanation difference. The soul and its truths are not such that they could ever be explained from without. On the contrary, like works of art that disclose the inner logic of life events and sometimes even the truth of an Age, they can only be expressed. Jung, as we already discussed, knew about psychology's lack of an Archimedean vantage-point. He knew that everything that is theoretically stated about the psyche is internal to the psyche, a participating expression of its on-going phenomenology. And yet he exempted his concept of the collective unconscious from this critical consideration and presented it as a scientific hypothesis and timeless explain all. Perhaps, however, far from being the explanation of the soul which he intended it to be, Jung's hypothesis of the collective unconscious was itself an expression of the soul, an expression in the medium of scientific explanation. But even if this is so, and I think that it is, the question arises as to whether such an explanation, however plausible it may seem, is adequate to the expression of the soul that it self-constitutively gives at the same time. And the answer, I believe, is that it is not. Psychology is not explanatory in the manner of science. Explanations proceed from the outside of what they claim to be about. Firmly ensconced in the subject-object distinction, they bring to bear an external mode of reflection. For this reason alone they can never do full justice to the inwardness, autonomy, and creativeness of the soul.

It surprises me just now to find myself critiquing Jung's concept of the collective unconscious for being a reductive interpretation in the sense of its not being up to the truth that it wants to express. But I say this as one who was instructed by Jung as by a wise and eloquent man! What mattered to me at sixteen and since then is that his words resounding in my blood sounded to me as old as myself, to say it with reference to Emerson's phrase. What more proof did I need of "the collective unconscious" than this event of its expressive meaning!

I realize, of course, that this is a very anima-enthused manner of knowing. It is what poets like Keats mean when they speak of something being "proven upon the pulses." Or moving on to psychology, it recalls the muse-like role that hysteria and its symptoms played in inspiring the analytic thought that became psychoanalysis. And this being so we are invited to inquire: wherein does such effusive and symptomatic anima-knowing find its animus-other? Or again: how does that which first announced itself by bringing blood to the cheeks unite with its inherent *logos* to become psych-*ology*? I have already pointed out that it cannot be by way of external explanation. No, the expressive soul's true other is the animus of immanent criticism.

Now, with this in mind, let us return to the passage of Jung's I cited earlier about the one becoming two such that at the various summits of life one meets the long-expected friend of the soul. If Jung's giving the collective unconscious out as a scientific hypothesis to be proven by means of comparative research led him, as I claim, to fall out of psychology into an external mode of reflection, this text—so similar to Emerson's!—sets us back on the right track again. As a truly psychological notion, the collective unconscious is not a realm or place existing in addition to or alongside our real world, but merely a more or less adequate expression for those soul-making encounters in which consciousness illuminates its world-situation from within even as it immanently and self-critically grapples with itself as other.

So you see it is the conventional view of the collective unconscious as a psychic substratum or superstructure in us that I am rejecting. I don't think that we can just turn the telescope around and point it at the inner constellations of the soul, as the poem by Coleridge appearing in the front of *Memories, Dreams, Reflections* puts it. For such a maneuver leaves the observing consciousness behind the telescope untrammelled, unscathed. No, it is the concrete universality of those consciousness-seconding figures in whose friendly and sometimes not so friendly light we know and experience the world that matters psychologically. And rather than abstracting these from their contexts and locating them, at the expense of *their* souls (!), in the supposedly trans-historical, trans-cultural depths of *our* collective unconscious, what Jung called the collective unconscious should be thought of in these more phenomenological terms. For there is another side to his wonderful insight about the greater figure which always implicitly was appearing with the force of a revelation. On the heels of paying his tribute to such figures Jung states by way of a warning that "He who is truly and hopelessly little will always drag the revelation of the greater down to the level of his littleness, and will never understand that the day of judgement for his littleness has dawned." Is this not a description of what happens to our sense of soul when the collective unconscious is conceptualized as an existing entity, realm, or power *in us*? The world in miniature in me, the gods residing in the human breast, the archetypes as constants of our human nature, the objective psyche as a matter of personality development—this view I submit, so prevalent in Jungian psychology, amounts to a dragging down of the greater to the level of our own littleness!

Fortunately, however, there is another way of approaching this whole topic. Emerson's reference to the words of a wise and eloquent man sounding to us as old as ourselves does not have to mean that our souls are literally age-old and that as inheritors of a treasury of archetypal images we are born with silver spoons in our mouths. I see his reference as having more to do with the vocational moment I spoke of earlier. If the words of a wise and eloquent man sound to you as old as yourself it is because the challenge and imperative of your own coming of age is being heard at the same time. And here I should immediately add that one's coming of age is not simply one's own in the sense of being merely personal. Our coming of age is only worthy of being designated as such if at the same time it is the coming of age of consciousness-at-large again and again through us. It is a manner of one's existing and speaking *as universal*, and a nice emblem of this moment is Jung's statement in *Memories* about that point at which, as he put it, "… I ceased to belong to myself alone…" (p. 192).

RH: "The coming of age of conscious-at-large again and again through us." Can you take this idea a little further?

GM: What I am trying to get across here may become a little clearer with the help of an anecdote concerning Jung's reaction to being asked by a correspondent if he believed in life after death. Irked by the question, he answered that his beliefs in such manners had worth only for him alone and that each person must rise to the challenge of finding *his own* answers. It is the same, I submit, with Jung's concept of the collective unconscious. To simply take over this great concept on the basis of Jung's authority and findings is not enough. That only lands us in the Church of Jung, shielded and protected from the soul by an abstract notion of it. But psychology, as Jung rightly said, only exists *extra ecclesiam*, and this is so even in relation to its own institutionalized pieties. Each of us must weigh in with answers of our own to the conundrums of the soul that we face in our life and time.

It is a matter of leaving home! The concept of the collective unconscious in which Jung housed his psychology is the home that we who follow after must set out from to come into our own. This is not to lose sight of the many insights and helpful formulations that we may draw upon from Jung in the course of our own psychologizing efforts. I have already shown something of this with my references to that passage in which Jung talks about meeting the long-awaited friend of the soul and the challenge of letting one's own life flow into that greater life. And in addition to this passage there are many others which are expressive of the same dynamic, albeit in different imagery. Perhaps, the earliest of these is a little text having to do with the challenge that the soul self-constitutively presents to itself by way of a son's apperception of his father. "For the boy," writes Jung, "the father is an anticipation of his own masculinity, conflicting with his wish to remain infantile" (*CW* 4, § 737). Here again we see the two aspects, the progressive unfolding of the one into two via the mediating figure of a greater other and the regressive tendency that would drag the revelation of the greater down to the level of one's incorrigibly self-identical littleness by remaining infantile. Turning to other writings of Jung's we find passages in which this consciousness-critiquing encounter with one's greater other is mediated by the culture-relativizing encounters of one's worldly travels and scholarly reading. In *Memories,* for example, Jung gives an account of how while travelling in North Africa the sight of a majestic horsemen prompted him to subsequently dream that he was in a life and death struggle with a similar figure in the mote of a citadel or casbah, even as in the bible Jacob had to wrestle with the angel at the ford of a river. Of this we can say (by way of another line in which he refers to the alien mentality of the "unexpectedly dark brother" which the European meets on his travels in Arabia and India): "and though I deny it a thousand times, *it is also in me*" (*CW* 18, § 1472). And then there is that statement from his "Commentary" to *The Secret of the Golden Flower*: "A growing familiarity with the spirit of the East should be taken merely as a sign that we are beginning to relate to alien elements within ourselves" (*CW* 13, § 72). Common to all these passages is the aforementioned soul-making encounter in which the one has become two such that from the lesser the greater emerges with the consciousness-critiquing force of a revelation. Or to put it in the terms of our Emerson quote, in each of these passages there is an encounter with a wise and eloquent otherness which, by sounding to us as old as ourselves, calls us to come forward with relevant and more compendious insights of our own.

So, if I reject Jung's concept of the collective unconscious it is because it reifies and externalizes the dialectic of consciousness which it is more deeply about and places a sort of seal of prophecy upon it. But just as Jung stated that "for the boy the father is an anticipation of his own masculinity, conflicting with his wish to remain infantile," so is the collective unconscious an anticipation of our own (by now long-present) future consciousness within a global world context, conflicting with our regressive wish to remain bound to myth, religion, and God.

RH: In your treatment of Jung's collective unconscious concept you say that it is not up to what it truly means as an expression of the soul. Can *you* weigh in, as you said one must, with an answer of your own to the question of what the concept of the collective unconscious expresses of the soul?

G.M: I see that my remarks thus far have something in common with that old novelty song of from the 1920's "Yes! We Have No Bananas"! In a manner similar to that song it is as if I've been singing, "Yes! We Have No Collective Unconscious"! Pondering this for a moment I think that the "no" in this phrase can be linked up with *negation* in the sense of that term which Giegerich has lately been introducing into analytical psychology. Contrary to Jung and drawing upon Giegerich, I would say that the collective unconscious is *not* a positivity or thing-like entity. Rather, it is an interpretation or theory that gives logically negative expression to the soul even as at the same time it invites the kinds of criticism that I have given above.

But you asked me what Jung's concept of the collective unconscious, if not taken literally in the substantial sense that Jung intended, might mean as a soul-expression. My answer today is a two-fold one. On the one hand, I think it is significant that Jung's psychology of individuation and the collective unconscious appeared at a time in history in which novels of the *Bildungsroman* type were becoming popular. Just a century prior to Jung's birth, Goethe paved the way for this type of novel with his *Wilhelm Meister's Apprenticeship* and *The Sorrows of Young Werther*. And the novels of Herman Hesse that I mentioned earlier, appearing alongside Jung's own works, are important for their seeming to actually present Jungian psychology by way of stories concerning the education and coming of age of a young man. My point, however, is not to stress the novelist's debt to the analyst—on the grounds, for example, that Hesse's *Demian* is known to have been based upon his analysis with the Jungian analyst Josef Lang. Rather, it is to suggest that Jung's psychology can itself be claimed as an example of this literary genre. This, let us call it the *Bildungsroman* character of depth psychology, is quite obvious in the diminutive sphere of psychotherapy and analysis. Why, it might even be possible to show that the creation of the role of "patient" in the analysand sense of that term probably owes a great deal to the unwitting mimesis of Werther, Peter Camenzind, Emil Sinclair, and many more. Or maybe, on second thoughts, it would be better not to derive the one from the other, but to see both the fictional characters created in those novels and the patient role created by psychology as expressions of the culture-critiquing challenge that is posed by the generational difference as it made itself felt at that time. "What you have inherited from your forefathers," writes Goethe, "grasp it and make it your own." Is Jung's concept of the collective unconscious not true to the adage of this wise and eloquent man? But beyond the level of analysis which the individual as patient is the addressee and beneficiary of, I would want to stress that the history of consciousness in a greater, generation and even aeon-spanning sense has also the character of a *Bildungsroman*. Again and again in the course of its history, consciousness itself has been challenged by changes in its world-situation (as by a greater other) to come of age anew. Considered in this light, Jung's concept of the collective unconscious may be expressive of the soul in this greater sense of its unfolding life through time. Far from transcending time and place by being rooted in a common human substrate of psychic similarity below and in back of these, the concept expressively and creatively speaks from a time and into a time in which the Western mind was meeting its greater other in the mighty figures of world history and trans-cultural geography which had then become subjects for it as never before.

I can now turn to the other aspect of what I think the concept of the collective unconscious reflects as an expression of the soul. Thinking about how this may most succinctly be conveyed, I am put in mind of some imagery from the popular Hollywood movie, *The Bourne Identity*. Based on the best-selling novel by Robert Ludlum, the film begins with the protagonist of the story, played by Matt Damon, having been rescued from the ocean by a fishing trawler. As the rescued man suffers from a condition of total amnesia, the drama begins with his quest to discover who he is. Following up on various clues (such as his ability to speak various languages, and a bank account number sewn into his skin), his search leads him to a safety deposit box in a bank in Zürich—of all places! Opening the box he finds a passport with his picture in it. The enigma of his identity would seem to be solved—except that in the next instant he discovers that it is not, for there are four or five more passports with his picture in them, each one certifying him as a citizen of a different country and identifying him by a different name! And then he notices, along with the passports, that there are also substantial wads of money in the box, again in various world currencies. Quite an image, this! Without subscribing to Jung's theory of the collective unconscious, we can nevertheless say that it seems to be well-figured in this imagery of multi-national amnesiac world-citizenship. Jung, as we know, saw the collective unconscious as being mediated cross-culturally. As I mentioned earlier, that is what his travels were mainly about. And with regards to how our film's amnesia reference may figure into this mix we have only to connect Jung's having addressed himself to the scholarly equivalent of this condition in his early essay "Cryptomnesia" with his own having been awash in an ocean of erudition and amplification throughout most of his adult life. But, then, here is the thing: far from suggesting that there is a common denominator in us which has expressed itself in various ways in various times and places, the film simply shows the truth of our actual world-situation today. Far-flung places have become immediately accessible, the world a global village. What began with the great sea-faring explorations of earlier centuries has become fully integrated into our consciousness today, the touchstone of this being our modern high-speed travel and telecommunications technology. Now it might well be that in presenting its hero as an amnesiac with multiple passports and various world currencies those responsible for the film were making use of Jung's concept of the collective unconscious, just sort of applying the concept in a Hollywoodizing manner. But I think it is less contrivedly the other way around—that the film may be regarded as bringing out into the open what that concept, for all its inadequacy in other respects, shows with respect to the state of consciousness today. Having long encountered itself in other cultures, consciousness is challenged to push off from the remissive tribalism of its national interests. But of course this is easier said than done and it is everywhere the case that the revelation of the greater has been brought down to the level of our nationalistic littleness. And yet, while this is everywhere the case, we also know that the day of judgement for this littleness has dawned. Indeed, our knowledge of this is so integrated that it can even be represented in a Hollywood film.

Along with those numerous passports and diverse world currencies, the protagonist of our film finds a gun in the Swiss bank box as well. Attacked by various CIA agents who are attempting to assassinate him, he discovers that he has uncanny combat savvy himself. From these and other hints he is finally able to realize that he is a CIA agent whom that organization is intent upon decommissioning by lethal means. Fighting both for his identity and his life, he must pit himself against this agency of American domination, his individuation as it is played out upon the big screen amounting to an immanent critique of the *Pax Americana*.

So much for my film example. I should mention as well that from time to time in my practice I have heard dreams which present what I take to be the same truth. I recall, for example, a dream that was set in *a global village clothing exchange* and another in which there was a tap that issues drinking water which is drawn from all the cities and villages of the world. Dreamers have found themselves in international airports, noticing the names of diverse places and even time periods on the flight gates. And I have also heard dreams of multi-cultural festivals and World Fairs in which pavilions from many nations are depicted. Is this what the passing of the Oedipus-complex looks like today?! Psychology in the Freudian mode knows all about childhood and family life. But what about the psychology of adulthood and of the coming of age of consciousness in our own time? This, it seems to me, has as its *mise-en-scène* the vaster horizons that the film I mentioned and these dreams show.

RH: When I first saw your book, *God Is a Trauma*, I was prepared to hear your view of God. What is your view of God?

GM: I am aware in hindsight that the titles of several of my books may give the impression that God is a big topic for me and that I, perhaps, am a religious person. This, however, is not the case. It is strictly as a psychologist that I have been interested in God and religion. Throughout the vaster part of its history, consciousness has been religious, the soul a function of its gods. It thus behooves us as psychologists to take the history of religions into our purview. But the deaths of the gods and of God have been equally significant events in the spiritual life of mankind. And psychology, it could be said, has arisen in the wake of the religions that preceded it. Expressing this in terms of my earlier discussion of the one becoming two, we could say that when consciousness was not yet conscious of itself its potential to be so took the form of its gazing and being gazed upon by itself as divine other, as God or the gods. When, however, at a much later date consciousness became more fully aware of itself, its symbolization as God became effete.

The footnote owed to Jung in this connection is to his ideas concerning the death of symbols. In Jung's view, a symbol is alive and necessary only so long as it is an "expression for something that cannot be characterized in any other or better way." When, however, "its meaning has been born out of it," when, that is to say, "that expression is found which formulates the thing sought, expected, or divined even better than the hitherto accepted symbol, then the symbol is dead, i.e., it possesses only a historical significance" (*CW* 6, § 816). Now, applying this insight in a more thoroughgoing way than Jung did, I think that it has been constitutive of modern consciousness that those greatest of all symbols, God and the gods, have succumbed to the same process. Jung, of course, worked mightily to avert this process. He attempted to re-evoke and re-valorize God as the immanently transcendental God within. He did not see, as I claim, that his insight concerning the death of symbols has provided the starting point for a Jungian analysis *post mortem dei.* But the soul-historical basis of this was right there in the Christianity that he struggled with in forging his psychology. Wholly present in each person of the Trinity, the Christian God is conceived of as having died as a man on the cross, or so the apex of Christian thought avers. And here I am also put in mind of those lines that Jesus spoke at the Last Supper to reassure his disciples just hours before his death:

> It is for your own good that I am going
> Because unless I go
> The Paraclete will not come to you;
> But if I do go,
> I will send him to you.
>
> John 16:7

In this passage the going under of religious consciousness into its successor form is figured. What Christ refers to as the Paraclete (the advocate, comforter) corresponds to that determination of consciousness that has become conscious of itself, in other words, to consciousness *per se* or psychology as such. Now on the heels of stating this I must hasten to add that by psychology I do not mean the personalistic psychology that everywhere prevails and which, when it deigns to take on religious topics at all, reduces them to the dynamics of the Oedipus complex, as does Ernest Jones with his grotesquely reductive analysis of the Holy Ghost and Christopher Bollas with his conflation of the Holy Family with the family of the hysteric. These are examples of psychologies that have fallen below the *niveau* of the religious consciousness that preceded them. No, by psychology I mean a psychology that is up to the level of its religious other and which contains its religious precursors within itself as what Giegerich would call sublated moments—psychology in the tradition of C.G. Jung.

You mentioned in the course of posing your last question my early book, *God Is a Trauma*. This book, which was re-issued some sixteen years later in a revised and expanded version under the title, *A Most Accursed Religion: When a Trauma becomes God*, is not a book about God *per se*. Rather, it simply works with metaphors of God along with various other religious tropes as a way of insighting or seeing through what psychology has struggled with under the heading of trauma. Just as God has been described as having "made us in His image after His likeness," so I suggest do those events that we regard as traumatic due to our difficulty in assimilating them. There are, of course, many passages in the bible that lend credence to this comparison. One of my favorites is Job's crying out, "Even after my skin is destroyed, Yet from my bones I shall see God" (Job 19: 26). But whereas Job distinguished himself by remaining pious, our patients may have to take the opposite approach. For, indeed, when it is a matter of being held in thrall by some trauma-god, it may be the more heretic moments of our soul-making that bring healing. This, at any rate, was the view I put across in that book.

A moment ago I said that I am not a religious person, despite what the titles of my books might seem to imply. Likewise, I would now like to add that I have no particular interest—or belief!—in the trauma concept either. To my mind Freud and Jung made the right move in abandoning trauma theory, and the return to trauma in so much of clinical practice today I regard as a disheartening loss of theoretical nerve that has gone hand in hand with a regression into unpsychological modes of thought. Consciousness (and this is a point I made even as early as *God Is a Trauma*) is *self-traumatizing*. Its incisive action of self-critically cutting into itself at those junctures at which it already knows more than it is ready to admit and take responsibility for is mediated from without by all manner of arrows and slings, untoward events and happenings. And here again I would point out the dialectic of the one becoming two. Existing as both subject and (subjectively apperceived) object, the inwardness or consciousness of our world-relation is perpetually challenged with having to realize that the apparently impinging, external other which it has pictured itself as being menaced by is not really as external as it had at first maintained.

RH.: I bet there are people who read this "enterview" who will find it very intellectual, academic, and difficult to understand. And they might wonder why doesn't Greg write in such a way that we can understand what he is saying. What would you say to such people?

GM.: The challenge of such a question, when one is functioning as an analyst, teacher, lecturer, or author, is to not be seduced into identifying with what the questioner is resistantly trying to foist off from him or herself onto you. Freud said that in his practice he always worked so as not to take on the roles he was being recruited to by his patients, but to stay with the sober work of psychology. This, it seems to me, is good advice. Even though it may work out that we have to wear what is put onto us for a while before this can come home to the patient as their own, the point about not colluding with this process, but standing ready to analyze it, is well taken. Now with this in mind, I would try to reply to the kind of question that you mention in such a way that the tension in it between the wish for a simplistic psychology, on the one hand, and the fended-off insight that psychology is a complex and challenging business, on the other, is borne intra-psychically by the person asking it and not allowed to remain distributed interpersonally between us.

It all comes down to what I said before about all perception being apperception. Though my questioner is not completely making me up or misperceiving me (for, obviously, I do make a lot of effort with respect to the intellectual clarification of the topics I discuss), I nevertheless believe with Jung that he is also meeting himself in me. So it is an important moment. Unbeknownst to himself my hapless interrogator may be setting himself up to reap more than he bargained for. For packed into his question a subtle version of the classic flight-from-a-pursuer dream may be playing itself out. Clinging to ideological commitments and familiar selves, it is regularly the case that people run away from new insights. In our dreams, this can be a very frantic action, as if we are running for our very lives. At the end of a lecture, however, this same dialectic can seem very lazy and laid back. He who very possibly will be running away from himself in a nightmare only a few hours from now saunters up to the speaker and asks him why he makes it all sound so difficult, why doesn't he express himself more simply so that others can understand. But I think that when such a question is asked the innocence of the person posing it has already been wounded by his having gotten more from the lecture or article than he wants to let himself in for. He got it in his soul and with his question is only mounting an ego-psychological defense. But like all such defenses, even when they seem to work for a time, this one comes too late. The unwanted insight has been thought, the comfort of the Jungian pew ruined forever, the quest for a truer conception already begun (even if, as is so often the case, this beginning has the form of one's running the "wrong" way at first).

But I continue to talk like a book and have not yet told you what I would say if such a question were put to me! Well, here is how I imagine one possible response. Tilting my head back and fixing my questioner with a look which already conveys that while I appreciate his clever con-game, I am not falling for it, I would chide him with a smile,

> "So you want psychology to be easy, eh?! Want me to say it all more simply, maybe even to do your homework for you, to boot?! Nice try!"

Following upon this, I would then probably try to find out something about him, and drawing upon this information, direct him to some even weightier books and writers. Or, if I really took a liking to him—let's say this was at a wine and cheese party at the conclusion of a lecture—I'd probably use the challenge posed by his supposed ignorance as a foil and passionately launch into a two or three minute crash course on the topic of my talk, with the likely outcome (I say "likely," here, because this has again and again been my actual experience!) that my new friend would be drawn along with me as I relish for myself the edifying boon of having just now come up with analogies and distinctions I'd never thought of before.

RH: Wonderful response. I would like to end our time with one last question, Greg. I appreciate your thoughtfulness and time in doing this "enterview." You have been generous with your responses and I thank you.

A lot of the world often wants "quick," "simple," and "positive." Whether it be the positive psychology movement, the seemingly quick cures that medication offers, the fundamentalist movement, or the appeal of short-term therapy, many in the world today are adverse to a healing process that takes time and hard work. Some have wondered if depth psychology (like Jungian psychology) will fade from the scene soon. How do you react to this?

GM: An adage comes to mind. I think it was first uttered in a more formal version many years ago by the British psychoanalyst, Masud Khan. He said that it is not so hard to cure a neurosis; it's hard to cure a cure. This, I believe, is an important insight. Again and again in our practices we meet patients for whom the crux of the treatment has to do with their coming to see that the problems they complain of are hand-in-glove with some phoney self-cure which they defensively indulge in, cling to, or collude with. Why, just the other day the discussion I had with a young man about his particular version of this ruse led to his having to make the still somewhat testy confession that he'd rather live the perfect lie than the imperfect truth!

But let us leave our patients out of it for the moment. Khan's idea about the difficulty of curing a cure has also another addressee: Psychology itself. In the "highly competitive market-place" that we live in today, psychology is big business. From pop-psychology to life-style magazines, the counselling hour to the analyst's armchair and couch, it has learned to cater to such needs as the patient I just mentioned admitted to. Or perhaps it would be truer to say that it is not a matter of merely catering to such needs, but of having invented them in the first place! I refer to the fact that like everything else in our epoch, psychology has become a commodity, its patients consumers. In your question just now you mentioned some of its featured products—short-term therapy, medication for everyone, fundamentalism, and the positive psychology craze. While concurring with you about this list, I would not see Jungian analysis and other long-term depth psychologies as being essentially any different, for are they not just high-end boutiques in which such ritzy cures as "wholeness," "individuation," "the feminine," "personal growth," or some new-age God may be purchased? What an embarrassment of riches psychotherapy has become!

So, again, let's leave aside the too easy focus upon the patient. It is the physician—Psychology—that must heal itself. But what in its case does it mean to cure a cure?

I can only hint at this with the help of a few lines from Jung. The first of these suggests the self-critical application of the talking cure to itself. "We should never forget," writes Jung, leaving the psycho-babble of the analyst and his patients behind, "that in any psychological discussion we are not saying anything *about* the psyche, but that the psyche is always speaking about *itself* (*CW* 9i, § 483). Read in relation to the present context, I take this to mean that in any truly psychological discussion, as in any truly transformative therapy, the concepts of the cure, far from being routinely applied, are themselves subject to the treatment, subject to themselves, as I shall explain a little more about in a moment.

The second line that I want to quote has to do with the problem of the transference, but here again the emphasis is not on the patient and analyst *per se*, but on "the third of the two," as it has been called, psychology and its concepts, the soul and its truths: "Psychological induction," writes Jung, "inevitably causes the two parties to get involved in the transformation of the third and to be themselves transformed in the process" (*CW* 16, § 399). This is a most important recognition. That the "two parties get involved in the transformation of the third" and only then, through this effort, are themselves transformed, suggests that it is "psychology" or "the soul" that is in treatment through us.

What I am getting at here is more readily understood by means of an analogy to the judicial system. In a court of law, the process of discernment is not totally focussed upon applying established laws to those who are charged with having contravened them in some way. While this, to be sure, is its workaday concern, the Law itself, the very notion of Justice, is also on trial. I refer here to the existing prospect that any case, even the most petty from a human point of view, may lead justice to new distinctions and insights, to redefine itself through new precedents even. And so it is, or at least potentially may be, with psychology. Just as the law places its notion, "Justice," again and again before the bar of its own self-redefining judgement, so, too, must psychology place its notion of itself, its notion, "the soul," again and again into its own scales.

So to return to your question, it is not the difference between short-term counselling and long-term analysis that concerns me (both of which may be equally shallow or deep), but of the difference—referred to by Giegerich as "the psychological difference"—between the psychology that people *have* and can talk *about*, and the recursive, new precedent-setting conversation of the soul with itself. Now with this distinction in mind we may return to the two who, perhaps unbeknownst to themselves, are "involved in the transformation of the third," that is, of psychology itself. I am not suggesting that the patient and therapist should indulge in meta-psychological discussions, or that the word "soul" should be bandied about. Rather, in a most down-to-earth manner, and as if time and again from scratch, it is through the most compelling issue of each session that "the third" is engaged and transformed. In one hour or one case, the marriage concept may be the face of "the third" that is being grappled with; in other hours or cases it may be any of a host of others such as, "Honesty," "Devotion," "Responsibility" or what have you. Of course, these are usually brought at first in the form of empirical realities, as the wife, the kids, the boss, and little old me. And it may take some time for the realization to dawn that it is actually the universals that these particulars concretely exemplify that are "the third" that the work is about. And here I am reminded of the insight that led Jung to overcome his childhood neurosis. Overhearing his father's worry that he might be incurable and unable to earn his own living, the fainting and indolent boy suddenly realized, "Why, then, I must get to work!" (*Memories, Dreams, Reflections*, 31) And so it is each day in our practices. The young father who has lagged behind his having become a father goes under and across into the concept-expanding and perhaps even new precedent-setting recognition, "Oh, so *that* is what it means to be a father!" Likewise, the jaded playboy, rattled by having been impotent with the woman who has for the first time in his life really quickened his love, comes to realize, "Oh, so that is what "Love" is, what a "Girlfriend," a "Fiancé," and a "Wife" are. And now he simply has to be different. No need for a string tied around the finger reminding him to implement a behavioral strategy drawn from some rule-book of appropriate living. He now *is* fiancé and husband even, his symptoms and struggles having resulted in a freshly acquired and possibly transformed *conception* of what these soul-truths are.

But here now, on the heels of presenting these examples of what I like to call "Notional Practice," I am prompted to take this characterization of psychotherapy a whole lot further by mentioning those moments in which the interpretative rapport of the two is fully up to "the dispassionate gaze of the soul." All at once, "in the twinkling of an eye," the ordinary figures and topics of the life-world that I just mentioned may be released from being merely what they are literally about to the ego and appear in a wholly different light on the mind's stage as the *dramatise personae* through which consciousness or "the soul" is staging, producing, and enacting a completely new conception of its truth. Interpretatively speaking, such insight is a matter of our making that same move from *Vorstellung* (picture-thinking) to the notion when hearing the imbroglios of our patient's social lives, the melodramas of their object relations, or a dream that Hegel made when he moved from the imagery of religious faith to its philosophic comprehension.

But you wanted to know my reaction to its seeming to some that depth psychology will fade from the scene soon. In my opinion, this has already happened, already long ago, but as the opposite of itself, i.e., in what Philip Rieff, already in 1966, called "the triumph of the therapeutic." In my remarks about this above I touched upon the topic of this demise in terms of the commercialization of psychology, its big business and commodity fetish character. Borrowing a figure from

Hegel this same problematic could also be discussed under the heading of "the positivity of psychology." It is a fatal situation, *fatal but not grave*. Depth psychology, as I illustrated earlier with my references to the death of Christ and the sending of the Paraclete, began with the going under of the religious consciousness that preceded it. In something of the same spirit, it must now tarry with its own demise, going under and across into that concept of the cure that is making itself anew through our lives, and loves, and times. It is a matter of our facing what the cure has become in our day, and of being humbled by how facile and phoney it has in so many ways become. True, as the decades pass a certain adroitness may be achieved. The therapist becomes an old hand. Psychology, however, should never become so old hat for him that a patient or the wind could not knock it from his head at any moment. And here again, with this mention of the two whose work, as Jung rightly said, most deeply "involves the transformation of the third," I am again put in mind of those lines from Hesse that I cited at the outset, "... every man is not only himself; he is also the unique, particular, always significant and remarkable point where the phenomena of the world intersect once and for all and never again. That is why every man's story is important, eternal, sacred; and why every man while he lives and fulfils the will of nature is a wonderful creature, deserving the utmost attention. In each individual the spirit is made flesh, in each one the whole of creation suffers, in each one a Saviour is crucified."

The Wanderer: Curse or Capacity to Live in Between?

ANN BELFORD ULANOV

"Archetypes are like riverbeds which dry up when the water deserts them, but which can find it again at any time".[1] The archetype of the wanderer is such a riverbed, and many of us find the water of life flowing again into its deep channel. Perhaps for some of us here, coming to Ireland is part of our wandering. We will try to draw a map of this primordial image in it many meanings and directions we take when we find ourselves impelled by its energies. It will be a map that is also not a map because the imagery goes backwards into endings and forwards into beginnings, as well as the reverse, backwards into hidden beginnings that lead us forward into endings. The map slides all over between forth and back, even sideways, like the mercury we tried to catch in science class as schoolchildren

Ann Belford Ulanov, Ph.D. L.H.D., is a Jungian analyst in private practice in New York City and Christiane Brooks Johnson Professor of Psychiatry and Religion at Union Theological Seminary. She lectures in the States and abroad and has authored many books and articles. The most recent of those, with her late husband Barry Ulanov, is *Transforming Sexuality: The Archetypal World of Anima and Animus*, and by herself, *The Unshuttered Heart: Opening to Aliveness and Deadness in the Self.*

This paper was first presented in Ireland as part of a March 2010 program led by Aryeh Maidenbaum, Director of the New York Center for Jungian Studies.

that must not be grabbed at or it proliferates into miniscule particles that can poison.

IMAGES OF WANDERERS

Let us then for a beginning wander among images of the wanderer. Mercury/Hermes touches this theme as the messenger at crossroads, the one in between gods and humans, combining, like Coyote, male and female, trickery and rightness, conductor of souls to the abyss and generator of new life.[2] Norse mythic Gyfil, in the form of an old man called Ganglerei, the wanderer goes to Asgard the residence of Aesir, the race of gods, to find out if they are so cunning because it is their nature or because it is ordained by divine powers. Putting three questions to three kings as forms of Odin, he is told about the different worlds of gods, giants, dwarfs, and humans. Odin disguises himself as a wanderer in long grey cloak, blue tunic, wide-brimmed hat, sometimes a hood, and his hair falling over the lost eye he gave in exchange for the runes and their wisdom. Wotan too wanders the earth to find Siegfried his free hero who will not know fear to forge the sword of Nothung. And with him, like Odin, come secret musings, but also storm, wind, fury, uprooting everything that is not deeply rooted, gripping citizens in a state of fury, "an elemental Dionysus breaking into the Apollonian order."[3] Odysseus and Ulysses on their epic journeys explore the geography and characters in the world and in the psyche. Elissa, Queen of Phoenicia, traveled to North Africa after the death of her husband and changed her name to Dido and founded Carthage.

In religions wanderers abound, from the Buddha to the contemporary His Holiness the Dalai Lama. Francis of Assisi, like Jung, knew the security of worldly position, wealth, fame, and renounced it to go in search of the soul and its maker. Jung writes in *The Red Book*, "Like a tired wanderer who had sought nothing in the world apart from her, I shall come closer to my soul....[and] learn that my soul finally lies behind everything....".[4] Brother Klaus of Switzerland combines berserker fierceness and honey-filled devotion as his religious vision sets him on his journey. Cain, banished into the fugitive's life with nowhere to lay his head (Genesis 4:14), links with Jesus who says the same of himself. But Cain is cursed to restlessness and unquiet, feeling a victim of Divine punishment, whereas Jesus, put to actual death, offers it for everyone's salvation.

The element of air associates with the wanderer image. Etymologically, wanderer links to opening a door for air to enter, to blow, to fly.[5] Such airy currents put us on the move, stirred, filled by " the mighty rushing wind" of Wotan who "is not only the god of rage and frenzy who embodies the instinctual and emotional aspect of the unconscious.... [but also shows] its intuitive and inspiring side...for he understands the runes and can interpret fate".[6]

The cowboy with his song, "Give me land, lots of land and the starry skies above; don't fence me in!" sings the free space the wanderer inhabits, in contrast to the knight's quest for the Grail. Even the hobo, aimlessly wandering, the vagabond, the bad boy, the nomad, all leave the safe confines of the normal on an unknown path to the unknown. Or we wake up to find ourselves in our mid-life crisis, like Dante facing a dark wood, losing his way, beginning a revolutionary journey. But unlike Dante, no Virgil appears with a planned guided tour. The wanderer wanders, going by way of ignorance to arrive at what he does not know.[7] Kerouac's *On the Road,* the song "On the Road Again", and the television series *Route 66* catch both the adventure and the compulsion to keep on the move.

Johnny Cash sings, "I went out walking in a city without a soul, in tears when I said goodbye; Jesus I'll be home soon." And Mary Travers, of Peter Paul and Mary, sings, "leavin' on a jet plane, don't know when I'll be back again", "hate to go", "I've let you down", "played around", "every place I go, I think of you", "I sing for you", "wait for me, hold me like you'll never let me go." A contemporary movie, *Up in the Air*, features George Clooney whose whole life is on a plane, a wanderer in the air, flying to business companies to fire people and thus initiate their wandering. And the intergalactic wanderer, flying the vast spaces of our galaxy, testifies to the relevancy of this archetype to our twenty-first century.

Archetypes pair opposites that span the continuum from one extreme to the other—negative to positive, instinctual to spiritual, one image contrasting with its opposite. Recalling the paired opposite of an archetypal image helps us grasp its emotional quality. We are relational beings, never only one half, not a monad, but a couple. The wanderer image calls up the opposite pictures of home, community, belonging, thus casting into bas relief the wanderer's loneliness, solitary searching, even isolation in his rootlessness, outcastness, with nowhere to lay his head.

Looking at wandering from an archetypal view reminds us of what the Blues and Spirituals sing—no permanent home exists for us here below. Together we are all wanderers, exiled from God's garden, with no way back to paradise, on our journey toward death. Our personal images of home get layered onto the archetypal hearth and onto woman as its keeper, mother and apple pie, she who puts fresh linen on the bed, prepares favorite meals as welcome, provides space and time for us to let down, let go, sleep, rest, renew. I suggest it is in part because of that projection onto women of the one who takes care of others that we find fewer female images of the wanderer.

Origins of Wandering

Wandering begins from different origins. We are set adrift, cast out by trauma. Our journey henceforth goes out to other sources of life than those we now label "before": before the traumatic event; before the gang rape; before the brain injury; before the accident; before the war; before the baby died; before the divorce; before expulsion from school; before falling addicted; before the mugging; before the economic collapse; before my son became one of the disappeared, and on and on the examples.

Wandering can initiate from inner eruptions such as Jung's lava stream of fantasies in 1913 that disrupted his sense of achievement in gaining his profession, marriage, five children, fame, financial security, and made him go looking for his lost soul. The different stages of his attending to these powerful images, recording them, painting them, entering conversations with them, transformed his fear he was descending into psychosis. He discovered seminal ideas applicable to all of us, to our human psyche. He spent the subsequent decades of his life bringing these ideas into the world through his clinical practice, his writings, his public lectures.[8]

Wandering, then, can begin in collapse, the end of the road, crises of faith and of belief in our self, but also in a sense of summons. Something addresses us. We may not know what it is exactly, yet have the conviction we must follow it, set loose from the known to go to this other country, other job, different school, new relationship. We go into the unknown—we know not where, only that we must set out. And remember, the archetypal constellation that ejects us from our established schedule pairs with its opposite. Thus in the midst of collapse may hide a creative imperative; in the midst of the summons may hide a danger of the madness of inflation. What stands out about St. Francis, for example, is he did not become his God but poured out himself to his God. Devotion to otherness trumped identification of it with himself.

When the waters of life flow again into the wanderer riverbed, their currents are powerful, compelling. How to keep our feet? How to drink a cup without being washed away in its rushing currents? How to acknowledge this is real without going crazy? How to respond without splitting off from the waters into obligatory formulas, clichéd phrases? Why do we seek the living among the dead?

Types of Wandering: as Nowhere

Wandering can start by feeling it is imposed on us. Loosed from our moorings, our sense of meaning in ruins, held no longer within a coherent universe, we feel adrift and it makes no difference where we are. We have lost our bearings. One analysand described being overcome by this feeling on her way to an analytic session: "I am on the train coming to the session but it makes no difference. I might as well get off at the next stop and wander around in the airport because I don't belong anywhere: nowhere to go or return to."

Like the *I Ching* hexagram 56 called "The Wanderer," the mountain (Ken) on the bottom stands still and the fire (Li) on the top flames up and does not tarry; the two trigrams "do not stay together and "strange lands and separation are the wanderer's lot;" "a wanderer has no fixed abode and his home is the road".[9] "The Wanderer means great dispersion;" "it is time when all creatures lose the place where they dwell".[10]

One way nowhere sets us wandering arises from our experience of never having been anywhere. We never coagulated into a coherent self, so we wander, looking for how to come into being, to lodge in a self that is our own. All of us as adolescents know some of this lack of I-ness, of subjectivity that is ours, of a voice we are discovering that is our very own. But some of us live in this nowhere zone as if permanently. So our wandering expresses our drifting, our fragmentation, but also bespeaks our looking, looking everywhere for this evasive selfness. We both defend against fitting in anywhere by floating from group to group, and avoid belonging in one group with the task of differentiating who we are in relation to them. We dodge the inevitable conflicts of sorting out where we are like the others and where we differ.

If this meandering never meets up with an other who wants to know who we are, then we may move into hobo life, the vagabond, the loner, even the ne'er do well. What we miss is the precious sense of realness. Realness always demands roots to nourish an ongoing real self, real relation, real work. One such boy told his mother he never felt real except in dangerous situations. Sensational life-death crises, extravagant spectacles, can be the closest we get to this precious aliveness we call the real.

Another way we are set loose to wander, feeling we dwell nowhere, erupts as the consequence of violence. Cain's story exhibits the violence not only that we do, but, as a result, the violence that we introduce now into the world. We are back again in the garden with the mysterious appearance of the serpent from whose temptation unfolds action and denial, hiding and exposure, confession and punishment. Punishment means exile. The door is closed behind us; we are banished from the garden paradise where we dwelt with God, and set on a journey that includes pain to find our new way.

Similarly, Cain, who tries to speak when the Lord rejects his offering and accepts his brother Abel's, finds his speaking aborted, and the Lord says to him, "Sin crouches at the door, and for you is its desire" (Genesis: 4:7). Cain loses his voice, his words, and his behavior speaks instead: he rises up and slays his brother. His violence is answered by banishment. He is driven out from the land, losing the ground on which he stands before God, and given over to restlessness, unquiet. He loses his place to incarnate a life of his own in relation to the whole, and becomes a fugitive and wanderer on earth (Genesis 4:14). He loses his place and his words in relation to the whole, to speak, to pray to God.[11]

When we commit violence against another, we introduce violence into our world. As a consequence we suffer exile from relation to those others we wrong and to the self we were before we committed such crime. We feel that banishment in our fear of another entrapping us. We assert ourselves by leaving relationship, electing wandering as our version of freedom. We do not engage, nor plant, nor embody. Rising up as if on currents of air, we forsake the ground and our chance to incarnate. A chilling detachment imbues even our shows of warmth and interest. In extreme cases, we do not even know what we have lost, having forfeited our language to speak to ourselves about it. Enactment replaces words to our self and to others. We do not take up residence in life—with our self and with others. We remain a tourist, merely visiting, passing through. If we lose our voice to our self, then others do not hear us. A dream motif expresses this plight: a man sees a danger and warns others, alerting them to action. But they pay him no heed, do not believe him, do not credit what he says. His voice is not heard.

This lostness of self and of relation to others exposes a failure to link our capacity for human destructiveness to our capacity for human love. They stay split apart and then cannot transform. We lose the connection between being attracted and cherishing. Lasting intimacy escapes us and we flee it to avoid our dread of falling captive to someone or something outside our self. Hence a larger container, a universe of meaning and relationship, a wholeness in which we dwell eludes us. We feel cast out. If we believe in a God, that God's face is hidden from us. We lose our capacity to see there is no lasting home for us here below that increases the preciousness of the home we do have.

The evil intent, mysterious like the serpent suddenly appearing in the garden, from which spring murderous actions—killing the moment of communication, refusing another reaching out to us, fighting what Freud called the procrastinating function of thought to slip into the mania of destructive violation of another's body or mind—these feel like active crimes that we know and remember.

Equally destructive is what Bollas calls innocent violence.[12] There we deny the destructiveness we vent. We absent our understanding of the adamant mood we inflict on the other. We disavow understanding what the other says and thus disembowel its meaningfulness. We revise the history of what happened and act as if the other imagined it, or exaggerated it, or misremembered it. We withhold emotional response, as if what is happening to the other is not important, does not involve us, is merely the other's experience of what happened, that somehow belongs only to their manufacturing it and has nothing to do with what we have done or not done. Aloof, rising above or removing our self from the interaction with another, we strip it of meaning, in effect act as if it had not happened. Such denial, in its many guises, appears innocent while it unloads violence on the other, spreading confusion about what is going on, doubt about one's memory or understanding, loss of confidence about meaningful communication and the existence of truth. Such a stance cuts us loose from human company among which we wander. Like the *I Ching* hexagram of "The Wanderer," where the higher trigram, flame, goes upward and the lower trigram, mountain, presses downward, we, too, pull apart inside, and find no place outside as our own incarnate link to existence.

Wandering that arises from feeling nowhere and the despair that we are in fact no one, not really in being, or that arises from intentional violence toward another, or from innocent violence that denies its happening as it is happening, leaves us in a gap. Our feeling of nonconnection to self, other, a shared universe of meaning, expresses itself in our wandering, not belonging anywhere, going to sleep on our lives, or suffering acute anguish. We feel a divide between us and everyone else; a puncture in the whole surround, and we fall through as if into a crevasse, hanging there on an edge of the abyss, the void, straying close to the edge, meandering, deviating, digressing, going nowhere.

Transition

Yet we may fall into our destiny, right there in the gap between us and society, between us and a symbolic universe of meaning. A curse of feeling exiled from others, may transform into space of discovery. A transition begins in our wandering from distress to anticipation, from lostness to acceptance, from an old way of knowing to a new one emerging. What feels like being the proverbial lost sheep wandering in the wilderness, but this time with no one looking for us, so that we despair of bonds to others, may transform into a different kind of connectedness that roots us to others so firmly that the bond transcends even the separation of death. Such a connectedness plants us in an expanding universe of meanings that destroy and yet emerge from and hence link to previous bounds of knowing. I think of the great shifts in art when new ways of seeing destroy old perspectives, and yet, and yet, emerge from that opposite.

John Berger interprets Monet as sorrowful in his discovery and invention of impressionism in painting. Lost is the former way of painting interiors whose unchanging endurance we, the viewing subjects, can enter and return to enter into again as "an alcove to the world...." Such a painted scene, for example, of Vermeer painting himself painting *The Girl with the Pearl Earring*, grants us time and space outside our mortality, as if an acceptance of death shows in the steadfast reality of objects in the room or in the face in the portrait. In contrast, the passing impression of a scene in the outer world is "an image of homelessness...its very insubstantiality makes shelter in it impossible" for we must recognize that everything dissolves into and is indivisible from the colors.[13] But we discover an emergent meaning that Monet describes: "what I want to represent is what exists between the motif (of the painting which he says is "secondary") and me".[14] The axis of meaning shifts to our relation to what the world gives us in nature, in color, in transparency of light, in the radiant flesh of the nude. We do not create the meaning, but find it; yet our finding it brings it into being in the interplay between us and the painted impression. Meaning is neither lodged solely in the subject nor in the object, but found and created between them.[15] Now we are both inventor and receiver of meaning; phenomena of the world are given and layered with humanly created meaning. Thus scenes of passing impressions of extravagant colors and shimmering light gather into themselves all our memories of other sunsets, cathedral entrances, haystacks, poppies, and flowers with their reflections in water, in ripples, shadows, sunlight, surfaces, and depths.[16]

Contra Berger, I suggest we are not left shelterless by Impressionism, but housed in new ways in the space between what we see and what we remember, visions that gather into the exuberance of life the mortality of death. Impressionism is hardly decorative or inconsequential. It exhibits the preciousness of ordinary lived life in the café, at the waterside, eating at the outdoor table, seeing the sea through the curtained window, its flash of color changing in the moving light of nature. We feel the impact of the giveness of life, its priceless treasure. We, the gifted, cherish it, all the more because we see it in its passing splendor.[17]

We come to this new way of seeing from our stance between us and the rosy apple, us and the multicolored Cezanne bather, between us and the tree, instead of us separate, looking at the tree. We see the tree and we create the tree in our seeing, for the tree we are looking at, is not the tree, but the impression we contribute to its coming into being. This new seeing lies before the wanderer too and may ripen into our taking this new placement in between self and other. The gap of lostness, outsiderness, changes into a space of immediacy and intermediacy, of a new third out of the opposing two. How do we get there in our wanderings?

It begins in longing. Our own longing and the longing of the unconscious that Jung describes as "its unquenched and unquenchable desire for the light of consciousness." We are so easily captured by our own insights, ideas, and proposals for what will fix problems, our own—like our schedules, our irritations, our bus route—and big ones we share—like healthcare, economic loss of jobs, war, educational problems that beset us from all sides. Yet, as Jung adds, "consciousness, continually in danger of being led astray by its own light and of becoming a rootless will o' the wisp, longs for the healing power of nature, for the deep wells of being and for unconscious communion with life in all its countless forms".[18] How can the two realms meet up? join? integrate? We long to leave the spirit of contemporary times and find again what Jung calls the spirit of the depths revealed to him and recounted in his recently published *The Red Book, Liber Novus.*[19]

This longing spurs wandering not only as a necessity, but as a courageous act, a liberation, a hope of discovery, a surprise at finding the new that may unite all that is separated in our old ways of being. Then we discover the joys of going away from the old grayness into technicolor, like Dorothy, and all the movie viewers since, in the *Wizard of Oz.*[20] We are on the way to find the home we will make, the society we will construct. Longing leads us to uncover in ourselves deep structures for human motivation and meaning that evoke in us deep feeling. Thus we can brave loneliness, and solitary, spiritual searching to find our own voice, our own calling to put into the world our small contribution of good.

Wandering in this spirit does not mean a careless lightness, an escape from society. (I think of Ulrich in Robert Musil's *A Man Without Qualities* as the pivotal example of wandering as looking for new ways of connectedness.) Right away wandering means meeting up with monsters—the untameable, "those chthonic powers that have always been recognised as dangerous and frightening yet essential to all life".[21]

Chief among such dark powers is "sudden, monstrous death", the just-so fact of our mortality, of the killing and eating to maintain life among us, including plants, animals, celestial planets, throughout the fabric of the universe and the inhumanity we add on top of that by inflicting death on our neighbors.[22] Our religions enact the age-old god's sacrifice in the beginning to incarnate in the world.[23] Communities engage in ritual acts to maintain their identity through mirroring the immortal sacrifice.[24] The legend of the Wandering Jew Ahaseurus, which is a Christian not a Jewish tale, tries to deal with the monstrous by dumping it all into this figure who wanders because he rejected the actual redeemer. Such a projection of unconscious contents is no help, no cure, but leading only to barbaric enactment of debased sacrifice acted out in Christian persecution of Jews.

The monstrous is an intractable element we do not like to admit—an animal side of God, an unredeemed human element, a restlessness, a panting of the heart to find its rest in the wholeness of reality. This ungovernable element "attracts to itself the new light, the energy of the new symbol....it arouses all the repressed and unacknowledged contents".[25] Thus, when wandering we must have the right attitude that the *I Ching* describes as unpretentious, modest, not meddling in controversies that do not concern us, nor busying with trivial things. Not losing touch with our inner being, we are reserved, preserving our inner dignity. We defend our self not by attacking but by remaining true to our self, even to our wandering. Conscious of being a stranger, we do not give way in careless jest nor insistent rigidity, but yield, keep still, and adhere to clarity.[26] Yet the monstrous death of consciousness must be included too. We feel it in two ways (at least).

One way is the very leaving of our father's house—the accepted norm of truth, knowledge, culture. And we leave the mother's house, the sense of home, whether good or bad, the small plot of earth where we were grounded, even if stuck. By wandering instead, we in effect destroy those originating places by rendering them not ultimate, but to be left, not preserved. We demolish them by making a space between us and them. No longer wed to them, no longer acknowledging them as the central axis of the universe from whose vantage point we understand about life, we open to the unsubdued, the uncultivated. No longer residing in the inherited known, we wander forth into the unknown, the not yet known. Our language is not lost, but as the poet

Paul Celan wrote, "it had to pass through its own lack of answers, through terrifying silence, through the thousand darknesses of murderous speech answerlessness...through...falling mute, pass through a thousand darknesses.[27]

A second way we include in awareness monstrous death is moving into a new way of knowing that changes our sense of what consciousness is. We are not venturing forth on a quest. Great gusts of Odin set us in motion by irrupting powers of the unconscious that bypass consciousness, so there is no sense of setting out for a goal. Jung's *Red Book* began in a streaming forth of images, affects, dreams so powerful he feared he would be swept away into psychosis. With brute strength and creative power, he took the impact and climbed into the event, letting himself surrender to the force of the unconscious. Gradually, and "only by extreme effort," "violent resistance," "distinct fear," he also found a way to study what was appearing.[28] He discovered that what he thought was his own psyche's disturbance was a collective phenomenon: he was in it, not it in him. What he unearthed about the psyche—how it speaks to us, what it says and our process of interacting with it—applies to all of us, not just to himself:[29]

> the years...when I pursued the inner images, were the most important time of my life. Everything else is to be derived from this....My entire life consisted in elaborating what had burst forth from the unconscious like an enigmatic stream and threatened to break me....Everything later was merely the outer classification, the scientific elaboration, and the integration into life. But the numinous beginning, which contained everything, was then.[30]

Wandering: Capacity or Curse

Jung's wandering yielded not to a goal but to a process, to a rhythm of being in that in-between-space, a present that engenders the future. Improvisation leads, not knowledge. A space, an interval, opens to contemplate what is, respond to it, see what happens, be surprised by entry into consciousness of what was left out by our former ever-vigilant ego. Wandering means unfinishedness, abandoning closure as premature, as imposition of certainties, as refusal of new meanings. Jung's experience gives a clue to the pattern of our wanderings, to those of us touched by this pattern of becoming our beingness.

A shift occurs. We are not solely in our subjective self, nor solely in the objective world, but in a forthing and back in between, uniting and separating subject and object, so that the line between them blurs and reality emerges in that intermediate zone Winnicott wrote about as transitional, and Jung wrote about as subtle body, and religions speak of as mystical body, even as resurrected body, that is, an ephemeral zone that proves stronger than destructiveness and death and is embodied in definite form and substance, but not like what we have meant by those terms before.

Paradoxically, this serious shift in meaning in such a process of wandering induces a sense of play. Aware of opposite pulls within that process, we uncover our capacity to live in between, related to both opposing pulls, of, for example, destructiveness and generativity. If we are not aware, we feel tossed back and forth like a ping-pong ball, not held within the game. Our wandering then feels like a curse, a banishment to outsiderness. Each of us is different so the accents of opposing pulls vary, but we share in common the pattern. The line between inside and outside moves back and forth, as if both are part of a larger wholeness. Our fantasy of who we are displaces to this space in between, and our discovery of the world as other, not something we created, reveals itself, not so much as insult but more as potential partner in play. We separate from our illusion that we create our sufficiency, and separate from the world as inflicting its indifference upon us, or as co-opted by our illusions. Instead, both self and world (including people) stand linked in their realness. And we move back and forth between them, finding and creating them, yet not exhausting either by our knowing. Each shows a core of mystery, as does this generative space between them.

The untameable comes within the rituals of playing—playing imaginatively, playing ritualistically, playing prayerfully. We feel our capacity for adventure, for not knowing what will happen and meeting that unknown with excitement. We endow what happens with emotion, possibility, inner challenges that we transfer to outer events.

This capacity for imagination opens our heart to meet what is, what arrives, what is before us and endows its just-so quality with anticipation—what will the assignment of jury duty bring us? Who will our child grow into? Where does our dread take us? We bring curiosity to the daily—what meaning assembles in this event of having to speak in class, of having to go on this job interview? Like the child with the favorite stuffed animal that symbolizes experiences of union with the one who held him or her in being, we play with what happens in a day, the odd message across the email, the person we unexpectedly run into, the sharp cold air in the sunset, the unexpected invitation. They bespeak experiences of union with living that we elaborate in our present response, thus linking our past to the emerging future. Even boredom becomes a spacemaking for desire to emerge into form, into feltness.

Such psychic wandering allows emergence of thoughts outside the familiar, just like a stranger entering a strange city. We see connections that were eclipsed before, now made more visible because not tethered to set ways of thinking and perceiving. We allow anger to surface, before prohibited by moral constraints. But the gap maintained by our wandering, that is, our awareness we have no permanent home where we can just discard our emotions for others to pick up, forces us to look into our anger, not act on it. Because of the gap wandering introduces, we cannot fall into identifying our mood with God's intent, thus justifying taking out that mood on others. Wandering keeps us humble, modest, as the *I Ching* advises, and thus we escape the "madness of omnipotence".[31]

Wandering can mean the evenly hovering attention of Freud's free association where we are surprised by what comes up when freed from censoring. Our awareness of what specifically evokes our response in Jung's method of directed association makes us feel the object in the world or the person in our dream addresses us, says something to us we would not have said to our self. Cracks, fissures in what we know appear; voices not heard before can reach us because we have wandered away from inherited assumptions. We may have lost a former stability, but our wonder at what is given prompts us to notice the unknown. The commonplace and the strange are inextricably mixed.[32] Mystery underlies the ordinary, evoking a sense everything is possible. Our leaving, absenting, leaves space open and recognizes there is no closure this side of the grave. Wandering allows hints, scraps, memory links, unexpected connections.

Such passage between mind and body may become freer, so that the ache in the knee, albeit actually physical, may also bespeak our emotional attitude of being unwilling to kneel, to yield; or it insists it is high time to get off our knees. Psyche and soma, usually in separate compartments now together, comment on, embroider our experience, giving a lilt and a gravity, a weighty message we can heed. Before I had to give up, much to my sorrow, daily standing on my head due to neck issues, for several months I knew fear every morning as my legs lifted upwards. This new fear announced a sacrifice I was yet to make at doctor's orders. Or, a woman in turmoil about the end of a relationship exclaims, "This is the third time driving my car I have skidded into the guardrail!" She hears questions that uncover the connection between her inner self and this outer happening. What needs guarding? What am I slipping up on? What is this outer accident saying to my inner way of driving, conducting my life?

A different kind of body of experience grows, not anchored to the one right way things should be done, anymore than to one specific place. Wandering frees us to see what our process ploughs up, trips over, leads to. We do not know in advance. Gradually this passage between our physical senses and psychological apprehension converse. We accumulate body that is subtle, evanescent, but unmistakable—a whole zone of thoughts, feeling perceptions, embodied intuitions that root us in current events and liberate us to their meaning. Wandering turns out to be a space of living, a preview of dying, for we see that all of us essentially are wanderers, not permanent inhabitants in our thought-forms, our physical placement here on earth. What Jung calls the psychoid joining of physical and psychical, of outer happening and inner realization of meaning, of empirical and spiritual experience, acculmulate body, that is, definite shape and weight, so that no matter our circumstances we know this realm and receive its communications. Winnicott says even the bedridden or the withdrawn schizophrenic can live creatively in their breathing.[33]

Christians speak of the mystical body composed of the divine in us (God in Christ) and the mortal us, and composed of all people who know the spanning of this bridge of eternal into the historical. This mystical body is individual and social, personal and corporate, here and now and piercing right through to the beyond.

This transgression of empirical and transcendent reaches a climax in the Christian belief in resurrection body—that the transient, wounded, decaying, physical matter of us will be a new and spiritual body (1 Corinthians. 15:35-54), raised above the limitations of the earthly body yet recognizable as the same personality. Wandering would seem to be the opposite of such a realized state. But insofar as wandering ushers us into this process of living between, in the relationship between us and what we behold both inside our self and out in others and in the world, and insofar as wandering previews our mortal state that indeed we are all, finally, wanderers on this earth destined to death and the hereafter, this belief in resurrected body gives us a view of the whole from the other side.

Wandering and Individuation

Where do we experience this other view while still here on earth in this ordinary life? Jung tried to capture it in his notion of individuation—always in process, never finished, never complete in being done, accomplished. Any effort toward wholeness brings us back ever again to what is missing, what is inadequate, wounded, and even more forcefully, the wild ever present in us, the leopard that would enter the temple.[34] Reckoning with the ungovernable must be faced in individuation, with what Jung calls "The brutal coldness of feeling that the saint requires to separate himself from woman and child, and friendship, is found in the animal kingdom. Thus the saint casts an animal shadow...." He cites the vision of God's wrath of the Swiss saint Brother Niklaus von Flüe: "this wrath applied to he [sic] who had betrayed his dearest ones and ordinary people for the sake of God".[35]

Three things stand out in Jung's notion of individuation in relation to our theme of wandering: first, coming to our self, all of I, nothing left out, is a process, not a finished state of being. Second, only through our particular idiosyncratic idiom, genius, weirdness, whatever word we choose to mark the ineradicable specific form of our own lived experience, is the space, the place, the hut, the house in which the All and the Vast manifests. We are the site of transcendence and each of us must respond. That is how vision moves into ethics. In religions, God speaks to persons, not in position papers, or through new theories. The human heart is sought as the place of incarnation; standing within Torah is the space in which the Holy makes itself known. Are we willing? Third, such a process and such an address to us that we must answer in our particular ways, means recognizing our dependence. We do not make it happen; it happens to us and we make it our own by responding, working it, finding words, forms of reflection and musing, the right color.

And we need others to find those symbols, words, gestures of interpretation. We feel this dependence when the crown on our tooth falls out and we have a dentist to call; when the car skids and there is a guardrail some worker constructed; when a tradition of looking into dreams exists and we can call upon it to understand our own. We feel our dependence in the absence of others to rely on, when we wander homeless, caught in nowhere, aware of no oneness as if we have lost our self because we feel lost to any others. Yet, and yet, a poem, a pop song, even a huckster sermon, let alone a painting or string quartet, tells us this other knows of nowhere and shows us its hidden springs of desire.

Wandering includes the collective. We might discuss whether our country, perhaps our world, has entered a wandering phase. That new consciousness, characterized as awareness of serious play, as subtle body, as mystical body, as resurrection body, includes a collective dimension too. Winnicott's transitional space of play for the young child grows into the location of culture in which we live and on which we depend as adults. Jung's subtle body means synchronicity, an additional "law" of connectedness that exceeds causality, and time and space. Christians' idea of the mystical body describes a community across the ages, gathered into a people in their revolution around the same center. The resurrection body, though specific to Christian belief, extends to all of us who come through death-dealing experiences in this life, reborn in spirit, and offers to all of us the extraordinary possibility in the hereafter that love proves stronger even than death.

Wandering leaves open that space in which we may recognize in each other's particularity, through the ownmost self of each other, the universal patterns we share in common. What archetypal patterns appear as foremost in our child, our mate, our teacher, senator, president, and how does that pattern concur or conflict with the patterns operating in our self? Which patterns move our favorite painter, actor, poet, or neighbor? Perceiving them, we perceive that together we are joined one to another in our wanderings and in our asking about the central axis of our living. With Rilke we may say:

> I am circling around God,
> Around the ancient tower,
> And I have been circling for
> A thousand years
> And I still I don't know if I am
> A falcon, or a storm,
> Or a great song.[36]

NOTES

1. C. G. Jung, "Wotan," in *Civilization in Transition,* vol. 10 of *The Collected Works of C. G. Jung*, trans. R.F.C. Hull (New York: Pantheon, 1936/1964), § 395. All future references to the *Collected Works* (hereinafter "*CW*") will be by volume number and paragraph number.

2. Joseph Campbell, *The Masks of God: Primitive Mythology* (New York: Viking, 1959), pp. 416-17.

3. Jung, *CW* 10, §§ 384, 387, 391.

4. C.G. Jung, *The Red Book*, ed. Sonu Shamdasani, trans. Mark Kyburz, John Peck, Sonu Shamdasani (New York: W.W. Norton, 2009), p. 223.

5. Eric Partridge, *A Short Etymological Dictionary of Modern English* (New York: MacMillan, 1903).

6. Jung, *CW* 10, § 389 and § 393.

7. T.S. Eliot, "East Coker," *The Four Quartets* (New York: Harcourt, Brace and Company, 1943), p. 15.

8. Jung, *The Red Book.*

9. *I Ching Book of Changes,* orig. trans. Richard Wilhelm, English trans. Cary F. Baynes (New York: Pantheon, 1980).

10. *I Ching Book of Changes,* trans. Richard John Lynn (New York: Columbia University Press, 1994).

11. Avivah Gottlieb Zornberg, *Genesis: The Beginnings of Desire* (Philadelphia: The Jewish Publication Society, 1995), p. 21.

12. Christopher Bollas, *Being A Character* (New York: Hill and Wang, 1992), pp. 165-192.

13. John Berger, *The Sense of Sight* (New York: Vintage International, 1985), p. 191 and cited in Avivah Gottlieb Zornberg, *Murmuring Deep, Reflections on the Biblical Unconscious* (New York: Schocken Books, 2009), pp. 141, 305.

14. Berger, *The Sense of Sight,* p. 193.

15. D.W. Winnicott, *Playing and Reality* (London: Tavistock, 1971), chapters 1 and 7; see also Ann Belford Ulanov, *Winnicott, God, and Psychic Reality* (Louisville, Ky.: John Knox/Westminster Press, 2001), pp. 14-16.

16. Berger, *The Sense of Sight,* p. 196.

17. Jean-Luc Marion, *The Crossing of the Visible,* trans. James K.A. Smith (Stanford, Calif: Stanford University Press, 2004), p. 92 n.6, p. 97 n.2; see also pp. 25, 26, 33, 35, and 37.

18. Jung, *CW* 5, § 299.

19. Jung, *The Red Book,* pp. 229-231.

20. See Ann Belford Ulanov, *The Feminine in Jungian Psychology and in Christian Theology* (Evanston, Il.: Northwestern University Press, 1971), chapter 12.

21. Joseph Campbell, *The Masks of God: Creative Mythology* (New York: Viking, 1968), p. 118.

22. Campbell, *The Masks of God: Primitive Mythology,* p. 177.

23. *Ibid.,* p. 182.

24. See Jung, "Transformation Symbolism in the Mass,"*CW* 11. See also Rene Girard, *Violence and the Sacred,* trans. Patrick Gregory (Baltimore: John Hopkins University Press, 1972).

25. Jung, *CW* 6, § 454.

26. *I Ching,* trans. Richard Wilhelm (1980), pp. 233-234, 235.

27. Paul Celan, "Bremen Speech", *Collected Prose,* trans. Rosemarie Waldrop (Manchester: Carcarnet Press, 1986), p. 34.

28. C.G. Jung, *Memories, Dreams, Reflections,* ed. Aniela Jaffe, trans. Richard and Clara Winston (New York: Pantheon), p. 178.

29. *Ibid.,* p. 199.

30. Jung, *The Red Book,* p. vii.

31. Avivah Gottlieb Zornberg, *The Murmuring Deep, Reflections on the Biblical Unconscious* (New York: Schocken Books, 2009), p. 331.

32. Alan Fournier, *The Wanderer,* trans. Francoise Delisle (New York: Doubleday Anchor Books), pp. 13, 83.

33. D. W. Winnicott, "Living Creatively", in *Home Is Where We Start From* (New York: W.W. Norton, 1986), pp. 42-43.

34. Franz Kafka, "Leopards in the Temple", *Parables and Paradoxes* (New York: Schocken Books, 1961), p. 93, cited in Zornberg, *The Murmuring Deep*, p. 232.

35. C.G. Jung, letter of 2 May 1945, *Letters*, vol. 1 of 2, eds. Gerhard Adler and Aniela Jaffe, trans. R.F.C. Hull (Princeton: Princeton University Press, 1973), p. 364, and cited in Marie-Louise von Franz, "The Transformed Berserker, The Union of Psychic Opposites", *Archetypal Dimensions of the Psyche* (Boston; Shambhala, 1997), p. 43.

36. Rainer Maria Rilke, "I live my life", *Selected Poems of Rainer Maria Rilke,* trans. Robert Bly (New York: Harper & Row, 1981), p. 13.

BOOK REVIEWS

Dennis Patrick Slattery. *Day-to-Day Dante: Exploring Personal Myth Through the Divine Comedy*. Bloomington, IN: iUinverse, 2011.

REVIEWED BY SUSAN ROWLAND

"Knowing is an act of loving…"

Day-to-Day Dante explores the great medieval epic poem, *The Divine Comedy*, by the Florentine Dante Alighieri (1265–1321) in terms of a sophisticated appreciation of literature and a rich harvest from Dennis Patrick Slattery's career in depth psychology.* What his marvelous *treatment* of the poem most immediately supplies is the extraordinary fertility of more than one perspective, as analysis from literary studies and psychology are blended to enable a modern reader to penetrate the depths of a canonical poem from another age.

**Eds.' Note:* Dennis Patrick Slattery Ph.D., is a core faculty member at Pacifica Graduate Institute. He has been teaching for 40 years from elementary to secondary, undergraduate, and graduate programs. He is the author of several books including: *The Idiot: Dostoevsky's Fantastic Prince; The Wounded Body: Remembering the Markings of Flesh; Grace in the Desert: Awakening to the Gifts of Monastic Life; Harvesting Darkness: Essays on Literature, Myth, Film and Culture* and *A Limbo of Shards: Essays on Memory, Myth and Metaphor.*

Susan Rowland, Ph.D., a Professor of Literature and Jungian Studies, is author of several books on Jung, theory, gender, and the arts, including *C.G. Jung in the Humanities* (Spring Journal Books, 2010).

It has long been my suspicion that depth psychologists make some of the best literary critics for this century. After all, the problem of how to approach art from another era has formed the spine of the academic discipline of literary studies from its origins in the modern academy, a moment that is contemporary to the evolution of psychology in the late nineteenth century. Where depth psychology begins with the problem of knowledge as it relates to the unconscious, so literary studies began with the issue of the significance of the long history of texts to be received by the psyche of the modern person. How can a reader of the twenty-first century comprehend a three-tier world of Heaven, Purgatory, and Hell from the fourteenth?

Day-to-Day Dante is a superb answer to this perennial problem. Slattery postulates a psychology that suggests an historical collective depth in the human psyche. This enabling theory adds something extra to the literary critic's sensitivity to the specifics of the poem. Archetypes denote the possibility of similar structures of meaning in very different cultures. This very idea forms a framework that acts as a doorway into another world. Here the author becomes a psychopomp whose doubled lens of psychology and literary criticism provides an intense engagement with the poem. With such a guide the reader becomes the initiate.

The structure of the book provides a deceptively simple four-part division of each page, recalling C.G. Jung's predilection for patterns of four. Divided into one page per day over a year, each opens with verses from the poem, followed by an explanatory commentary of the specifics. A further paragraph moves the historical weight of the poetry into an alchemical transformation of psychological imagination. The last section of each page is a suggested meditation formed by questions to the reader. Slattery suggests that this could be completed in writing, or in a dialogue with a reading group. In this way *Day-to-Day Dante* makes *The Divine Comedy* into a mediator across time, between Dante and Slattery and between both authors and their readers.

Of course the key enabling term of this remarkable time travel is "myth." Slattery argues at the start that literary classics are varieties of myths that contain protean qualities to speak to different cultures (p. 1). The hypothesis of archetypes allows a notion of "personal myth" to be a framing and meaning-making device in an individual life. In this way, a great narrative poem such as *The Divine Comedy* can be read as *an analogy* for individual struggles today (p. 4).

Going deeper, *Day-to-Day Dante* shows how an archetypal analogy can revise the relationship between history and fiction. Dante's poem is fiction. It describes a journey through Hell, Purgatory, and Paradise that, although it never occurred in actuality, is full of historical personages, and even bears traces of Dante's life in Florence. It is imagination become liminal to history in a lived life. In the poem, the psyche's archetypal truth spans centuries. It never happened, yet it became *real* in the imagination of the poet who is embodied in time and place. More powerfully yet, *The Divine Comedy,* through the analogical presentation by *Day-to-Day Dante,* is imagined against and for the first time in the soul of every reader.

Here is an argument defending poetry that gives embodied form to archetypal constants across time. It enables being in the imagination.

> In a very real way [the poem] is true, for as we read it, we are recollecting it as something that once existed and now exists for us for the first time. (p. 85)

The archetypal backbone of poetry gives it the substance of a myth. Poetry such as *The Divine Comedy,* says Slattery, gives an aesthetic dimension to archetypal myth. In bridging the collective world of literature with the individual psyche of the reader, literary myth energizes and expands our personal myth. Here history becomes imagination, and vice versa, for our own stories in time dance outwards into mythical patterns.

> Here the imagination is history. In its personalness our own history spirals out to something much bigger than itself, more archetypal and essentially true. The imagination creates history even as it fabricates its own historicity. (p. 107)

In tracing the arc of the poem from Hell's depths to Paradise, *Day-to-Day Dante* is a stunning achievement of literary, psychological, and, ultimately, spiritual exposition. Again, the dual lens of art and archetype enables the sacred role of poetry to be recovered for a new age. Dante's epic is both historically acute and woven into the fabric of a perspective of eternity. In opening the gates to this text from another world and time, Slattery gives the reader an opportunity for spiritual initiation.

Effectively, *The Divine Comedy* is a journey of personal myth in another age. *Day-to-Day Dante* allows the modern person to engage with the poet as a fellow pilgrim. Slattery's book is therefore multifaceted. Beginning by its appreciation of a sometimes opaque work of art, excavating its spiritual properties, *Day-to-Day Dante* becomes an initiatory web of revelation. Here are the truths of history's saturation of the imagination, of the creative psyche's passion for eternity, and for our fragile life in time.

BOOK REVIEWS

The Jung-Kirsch Letters: The Correspondence of C.G. Jung and James Kirsch. Ed. Ann Conrad Lammers. Trans. Ursula Egli and Ann Conrad Lammers. London and New York: Routledge, 2011.

REVIEWED BY PAUL BISHOP

Bit by bit, Jung's correspondence is beginning to be published. Everyone knew that the two-volume (in German, three-volume) selection of letters edited by Aniela Jaffé and Gerhard Adler and published as supplements to the *Collected Works* represented only the tip of the iceberg and, over the last quarter of a century or so, at least eight further selections of correspondence have appeared. These include (ordered by date of publication) Jung's correspondence with Freud (1974), with Sabina Spielrein (1980), with Hans Schmid-Guisan (1982), with Wolfgang Pauli (1992), with Emil Medtner (1994), with Eugen Böhler (1996), with Ernst Bernhard (2001), and with Victor White (2007). Of these, the important exchange between Jung and

Paul Bishop, Dr. Phil., is professor of German at the University of Glasgow. His books include *Reading Goethe at Midlife: Ancient Wisdom, German Classicism, and Jung* (Spring Journal Books, 2011); *Analytical Psychology and German Classical Aesthetics,* vol. 1, *The Development of the Personality* (Routledge, 2007) and vol. 2, *The Constellation of the Self* (Routledge, 2008); and (as editor) *The Archaic: The Past in the Present* (Routledge, 2012).

the English Dominican priest and theologian, Father White, was co-edited by Ann Lammers, author of a study of that correspondence entitled *In God's Shadow* (1994), and she is now responsible for bringing to press the letters, or those that have survived, between Jung and the analytical psychologist, James Kirsch.

Born in Guatemala City in 1901 as a son of a Jewish businessman and brought up in Berlin, Kirsch studied medicine in Heidelberg, before returning to Berlin to work in a psychiatric hospital. He began a Freudian analysis but discontinued it, before reading Jung's *Psychological Types* (1921), beginning an analysis with Toni Sussmann, and then entering an analysis with Jung in Zürich in 1929. (In 1946 Kirsch recalls how he was told by a palm reader that there had been two major influences on his life: his mother, and someone he had met when 28 years old [p. 110]—his age when he first met Jung.) This analysis, followed by sessions with other analysts (including Toni Wolff, whose correspondence with Kirsch has been published in part), constituted his professional training, and Kirsch's private practice in Berlin acquired a Jungian orientation. The correspondence between Jung and Kirsch, drawing on materials in the C.G. Jung Archive of the ETH-Bibliothek in Zürich and the James Kirsch Archive in Palo Alto, California, follows Kirsch from Berlin to Tel Aviv, then London, and finally Los Angeles. (Both Kirsch's first wife, Eva, and his second, Hilde, also practised as psychotherapists or analysts.) As well as lecturing on such subjects as the novel *Moby Dick* (pp. 251 and 264) and the American writer Jack London (see Appendix C in this volume), Kirsch published two books, *Shakespeare's Royal Self* (1966) and *The Reluctant Prophet* (1973) (an analysis of the dreams of the late-nineteenth-century rabbi and Palestine émigré, Hile Wechsler). Although (or perhaps because) Kirsch never obtained a medical license, in Los Angeles he played, together with Hilde, an important role in promoting Jungian ideas in southern California (and their son, Thomas B. Kirsch, lends a personal note to this volume in the shape of a preface). James Kirsch died in LA in 1989.

Across these letters between 1928 and 1961, a number of important *aperçus* emerge. For instance, we understand better one of the psychological functions, intuition, when Jung tells Kirsch that it "does not say what things 'mean' but sniffs out their possibilities" (p. 21), while Jung's definition of synchronicity as "a factor inherent in

Nature", "accounting for the existence of teleological arrangements", the existence of which explains why "man forever thinks in terms of gods" (p. 180), sheds some useful light on this notoriously elusive concept. In response to Kirsch's invitation in 1953 to become an honorary member of the Society of Analytical Psychology of Southern California, Jung (who seems to have been genuinely touched by this gesture) defines the psychological system that bears his name as its label. Jungian psychology, he tells Kirsch, is "a movement of the spirit which took possession of me", which "I had to and was allowed to serve all my life" (p. 159), a "great cause" whose service had brought him a "glad *serenitas*" (p. 159, cf. p. 162); although other parts of the correspondence might make the reader sympathize with Kirsch's statement, made in a much earlier letter of 1931, that "analysis is very close to black magic" (p. 19).

At the same time, this correspondence crystallizes around a number of themes, some of them (for varying reasons) difficult to assess or discuss. The first of these themes concerns Jung's attitude to Judaism in certain remarks made in the 1930s and the accusations against him to which they have, ever since, given rise. Following his acceptance of the presidency of the AAGP/IAAGP in 1933, his assumption of the editorship of its house-journal, the *Zentralblatt für Psychotherapie und ihre Grenzgebiete*, and the publication in its December edition of his editorial "Geleitwort," Jung had been accused in the pages of the *Neue Zürcher Zeitung* by Gustav Bally of anti-Semitism. (The background to these institutional developments is clearly set out in Appendix D of this volume.) When one reads Jung's "Geleitwort" (with its distinction between "Germanic" and "Jewish" psychology), his essay in the first 1934 issue, "The State of Psychotherapy Today" (with its comments about the Jew as a "relative nomad" without his own form of culture), and his interview with Adolf von Weizsäcker for Radio Berlin on 26 June 1933, one can see Bally's point. In his letter to Jung of 7 May 1934, sent from Tel Aviv and written "from the heart," Kirsch challenges Jung directly on this matter.

Jung's reply is, frankly, astonishing. Referring to these "amusing rumors," he dismisses the charges against him, yet he does so in a way that suggests he did not really understand what was at stake. "This sensitivity is simply pathological and makes every discussion almost impossible," he writes, going on to declare that, "with this readiness to sniff out anti-Semitism everywhere, the Jew directly evokes anti-Semitism"; whereas, he insists, "in the great majority of cases, I've been getting along very well with my Jewish patients and colleagues" (p. 46). It is, even by Jung's standards, a remarkable performance: he gives every impression of being a rhetorical bull loose in a china-shop of political incorrectness; but why did Jung get it so wrong? In part, I think, the answer lies in the discursive context into which this correspondence gives us insight. In the summer of 1931, Kirsch had sent Jung an essay entitled "The Jewish Image of the World," reproduced in this volume (pp. 15-16), and later in 1934 he published an article in the *Jüdische Rundschau* entitled "The Jewish Question in Psychotherapy," in which he publicly took issue with Jung's remarks in "The State of Psychotherapy Today." (Appendix A in this volume contains another paper by Kirsch on the subject of Judaism, written in Tel Aviv in 1934.) What Jung did not (or could not) understand, it seems, is that, while it was one thing for Jews to distinguish between "Jewish" and "German" culture or psychotherapy, it was another thing entirely for a non-Jew to do so, especially in the context of racial policies in Germany, which led in 1935 to the Nuremberg Laws (and, ultimately, to the Holocaust). It is also interesting to note that, on at least one occasion, Jung expressed the wish that he did not want any of his followers to write in his defense (p. 102); one has the impression that Jung's remarks on Judaism constitute almost a kind of *acte manqué*; in this instance, an unconscious desire for censure.

A second theme in the correspondence is alchemy: at first sight, a topic totally unrelated to the first, but in one letter we find that Kirsch speaks of alchemy, Jung's 1936 essay on "Wotan," and his introductory remarks on the *Tibetan Book of the Dead*, all in the same breath (p. 90). Jung's interpretation of alchemy, expounded in the papers later included in *Psychology and Alchemy* (*Collected Works*, vol. 12), saw that "the Self appears under many names, such as gold, stone, divine water, the squaring of the circle, etc." (p. 81); this sparked numerous associations in the mind of Kirsch. His letters, like Jung's, frequently weave alchemical sayings into his remarks, and it was thanks to Kirsch's intervention, so we learn, that Jung acquired a copy of the sixteenth-century Hermetic text, the *Poimandros*.

Third, this correspondence demonstrates how important the Kabbalah was for Jung. In a letter to Kirsch written after he was recovering from a cardiac condition in 1952, Jung explains how the sefirot tree "contains the whole symbolism of a Jewish development parallel to the Christian idea" (p. 143). A full understanding of Jung's interest in the Kabbalah has been recognized as a major scholarly desideratum (not least by Sanford L. Drob in his *Kabbalistic Visions: C.G. Jung and Jewish Mysticism*), and it is to be hoped that this correspondence acts as a stimulus for further research into this topic. A related interest, which constitutes a fourth theme, is Kirsch's enthusiastic reception of Jung's late, great works, *Aion* (1951) and, in particular, *Answer to Job* (1952). In fact, Kirsch went so far as to translate the book, and he was disappointed when Hull's translation was chosen to appear in the *Collected Works.* (Kirsch used his own translation for his seminars on *Answer to Job* given in LA in 1952-1953, and in 1959 he prepared a series of lectures for a public radio station, KPFK.) Jung's letter to Kirsch of 16 February 1954 shows how *Answer to Job* arose directly out of his analysis of Judaism and his interest in the Kabbalah (p. 195).

Fifth, and more contentiously, there is Jung's interest in a phenomenon that came to grip the public imagination in the 1950s and 1960s: flying saucers. This topic, on which Jung published two short articles in *Die Weltwoche* in 1954, is probably more of an embarrassment than anything else for most Jungians today, but Jung makes it clear that he himself had not seen in anything in the skies. That is, unlike Kirsch,—who, to judge by a letter dated 23 January 1955, claims to have watched a saucer for over an hour in California in 1955. (In response to Jung's—almost sceptical—question as to "why almost no photographs are taken, even though every trifle gets photographed" [p. 217], Kirsch replied—somewhat archly—that although his camera, "loaded with film," had been in the next room, the idea of photographing the UFO had "never occurred" to him, an "unconsciousness" on his part for which he had "no explanation" [p. 218] ...)

Finally, there is a sequence of letters that give a flavor of the environment that grew up around analytical psychology in southern California. Kirsch reports to Jung, for instance, on the visits to Los Angeles by the giants of the Zürich analytic scene: in 1953 Marie-Louise von Franz, whose trip was a "big success" (p. 161); in 1954 C.A. Meier, whose month in LA was "a great success" (p. 211); and in

1955 Father Victor White, to talk about good and evil (p. 218); while, in the Fall of 1953, Jolande Jacobi's visit led to tensions between her and Kirsch (p. 182). (Other visitors included Rivkah Schärf, Barbara Hannah, Gerhard Adler, Michael Fordham, and Margaret Ostrowski.) Among the American analysts, Joseph Wheelwright, Elizabeth Whitney, John Weir Perry, and Joseph Henderson are among the names that form an alternative roll call to the list of European analysts (aside from the Zürich circle) mentioned, including Wolfgang Müller Kranefeldt, Johannes Heinrich Schultz, Jakob Wilhelm Hauer, Bruno Klopfer, Gustav Richard Heyer, Fritz Künkel, Ernst Bernhard, and Siegmund Hurwitz, although several of these, too, subsequently moved to California. By the same token, two letters from 1958 in which Kirsch tells Jung about his visit to Japan and his interest in Zen demonstrate a concern on his part to relate analytical psychology to the traditions of the East.

Taken as a whole, this correspondence provides us with fresh insights into the role that analytical psychology once played (and, indeed, continues to play), not simply as a therapy, but as a cultural praxis. To this extent, it is a significant contribution to the gradual piecing-together of the vast mosaic that is the intellectual history of analytical psychology. As an edition, its presentation is scrupulous, and detailed footnotes carefully document the sources of most quotations. (Two exceptions to this are the omission to note the source of an allusion to Goethe's *Faust* [= Part Two, line 6275] on p. 36, and one to Nietzsche [= "Amid Birds of Prey," from the *Dithyrambs of Dionysos*] on p. 96.) The translation, prepared by Ursula Egli with assistance from Lammers, reads consistently and smoothly; in a few places, however, it would interesting to know the original German (as when Jung refers to himself in one letter as a "Swiss bourgeois" [p. 47], or when a letter from Aniela Jaffé to Kirsch talks about a "common pre-condition" [p. 240], or when Jung comments that Gershom Scholem is "all wet" on a point about Jewish gnosis [p. 144].) But let us set these niggles—and some issues, such as Kirsch's "relationship to his anima," which apparently was "a lifelong struggle" (p. xi)—to one side: for this reviewer, one of the greatest delights of this volume was to learn that, at a Christmas party held (probably in 1958) by the Psychological Club in Zürich, its participants took the time to sign a copy of the menu card and send it to James and Hilde Kirsch. For some reason (and the origins of the joke are now presumably lost), all the analysts present chose to sign themselves as a kind of dog: including Liliane Frey-Rohn as a St. Bernard, Marie-Louise von Franz as a chihuahua, Dora Kalff as a cairn terrier, Fritz Baumann-Jung as a hunting dog, Aniela Jaffé as a schnauzer, and Kurt Binswanger as a fox terrier, while Jung discovered a new identity as a pointer for game birds… This signed menu documents the intensely human sense of community that established itself in the Zürich analytic circle, while the correspondence between Jung and Kirsch shows how the ideas that sustained that community were able to take root and to develop on another continent (a fuller account of which can be found in Thomas B. Kirsch's study, *The Jungians: A Comparative and Historical Perspective* [2000].) *Habent sua fata libelli!* "Little books have their destinies!" as one of Jung's favorite sayings puts it (pp. 174, 208), and *this* book's destiny must surely be to count as a further step on the long road to appreciating the historico-cultural achievements of analytical psychology.

BOOK REVIEWS

Jay Sherry. *Carl Gustav Jung: Avant-Garde Conservative*. New York: Palgrave Macmillan. Palgrave Studies in Cultural and Intellectual History. 2010.

REVIEWED BY MURRAY STEIN

In this study, Jay Sherry sets his sights on capturing Jung's general social and political leanings by using the polar designations, avante-garde and conservative. With this pair of binoculars (familiar to Jungians as the puer-senex dyad), he attempts to focus our attention on Jung's basic attitudes toward society and its governance.

More specifically, however, what Sherry is really most intent on investigating is Jung's attitude toward Germany and the Germans in the 1930's and his alleged antisemitism: "This book will document for the first time a complete and accurate account of what Jung wrote about Jewish psychology and Nazism while placing his opinions in the wider intellectual context of the period."[1] This is an ambitious claim. While the work is long and detailed, it cannot be said to be exhaustive,[2] and Sherry's methodology also raises many reservations about accuracy.

Murray Stein, Ph.D., is a training analyst at The International School of Analytical Psychology in Zürich, Switzerland, and since 2009 the President. He is the author of many articles and several books, including *Jung's Map of the Soul* and *The Principle of Individuation*, and the editor of the recently published *Jungian Psychoanalysis*.

Happily, however, Sherry is successful in correcting Richard Noll's "sensationalist protrayal of Jung"[3] regarding his position vis-à-vis the Nazis and their racist philosophy and thereby offers an important critique of the picture that has been widely disseminated and accepted as historically valid.

First, about the general characterization, then to the specific items of interest.

Jung, an Avante-Garde Conservative?

There are several basic positions that serious thinkers may choose from as they reflect on society and politics. They may advocate maintaining a deep connection to the spirit of the past at all costs, thereby insuring essential continuities with "tradition" (the conservative-to-reactionary position, classically (and moderately) expressed by Edmund Burke (1729-1789) in his reflections on the French revolution). At the other end of the political spectrum, they may opt for some type of ideology —perhaps to promote greater social justice or to purify the state—that would set out to create a new political and social structure on a platform of reform or revolution (the progressive-to-revolutionary position, classically expressed by Thomas Paine (1737-1809) in his enthusiastic support of the ideals of the French revolution, radically expressed later by Karl Marx (1818-1883) and Vladimir Lenin (1870-1924) in their vision of a communistic state, also by Adolf Hitler (1889-1945) in his idea of a racially pure Aryan nation). A third option is to seek to discern the Will of God, who governs and creates history, either by studying a Holy Scripture (or Bible) for guidance or by examining signs, visions, oracles, or other forms of direct communication from the Deity to humans, and then to line up one's intentions and actions accordingly (the religious position, classically espoused by St. Augustine (354-430) and John Calvin (1509-1564) and recently by religious fundamentalists of many faiths). Or they may simply look for practical solutions to immediate problems and muddle through in an ad hoc fashion without reference to the past, ideology, or religious guidance (the pragmatic position, a quite frequent political posture of many contemporary politicians). There are, of course, many variations on these four basic options, from moderate to extreme.

With reference to these basic attitudes, Jung can be seen to have assumed a combination of the conservative and religious positions. (Occasionally, he would also show evidence of pragmatism, especially in his clinical writings and comments.) He instinctively distrusted the progressive-to-revolutionary advocates with their reliance on abstract ideology and reason (rationalization?) and without reference to authoritative historical precedents. Jung was conservative both with regard to his psychological theory, for which he was ever seeking to establish linkages to intellectual history and continuity with ancient authorities like alchemy and Gnosticism, and with respect to his views on society, which were traditional and bourgeois.[4] He ascribed paramount importance to connecting firmly and deeply to one's specific cultural past, whether as an individual or a collective body politic, in order to move toward the future in a developmentally fruitful and stable way. On this he was in complete agreement with Edmund Burke. He also agreed with Burke that reason by itself is not a sufficient or reliable guide to human affairs, and with the British Tory he would prefer to consult tradition when it comes to making important political decisions. He was not reactionary, however, since he subscribed to the notion that society and culture must evolve, not remain fixed and frozen in place, and he was not nostalgically committed to returning to a paradisal past. He applied the idea of individuation to social and political evolution as well as to an individual person's psychological development.[5]

In the final analysis, however, Jung gave strongest preference to the religious option, although in a modified form that one could call psycho-spiritual or psycho-metaphysical (or metapsychological). It was a type of modern Gnosticism that sought to discern underlying spiritual (i.e., archetypal) trends in history and in contemporary events and to understand the present and possible futures from this perspective and to act accordingly. Jung's metapsychological (i.e., spiritual) position subsumes all else, including his conservatism. Regrettably, Sherry does not bring this feature of Jung's thinking sufficiently into focus in his analysis of his attitude toward politics and social issues. Sherry would argue that the conservative position is more findamental and controls the metapsychological attitude, in other words that Jung's depth psychological position is fundamentally conservative. I find the opposite to be the case, i.e., that his conservative attitudes (also his vangardism, for that matter) flow from his commitment to the spiritual.

Was Jung also avant-garde? This is more difficult to answer positively since this term is normally applied specifically to artistic movements and associated with the adoption of unconventional, bohemian life-styles, but it is also a term that can be appended to marginal and counter-cultural movements. Jungians think of it as an unregulated puer attitude. Insofar as Jung was an innovative and experimental author, which he certainly was, and engaged in thinking about newly emergent and not yet fully revealed or developed forms of culture, which is also true, the term has some relevance for him. His vanguardism was of the intellectual and spiritual sort, however, and not the social. Also, since Jung did not care much for modern art, literature, or music, his avant-garde side was rather muted in a cultural sense. On the other hand, because he transgressed cultural conventions and was an early admirer of Freud, whose theories were anathema to the psychiatric world of the day and were considered to be wild and socially unacceptable; that he took an interest in spiritism and occult phenomena; that he studied alchemy deeply and brought it into his psychological thinking; that he was fascinated with flying saucers (Sherry cites this several times as an example); and that he was very adventuresome and original in his ideas about psychology and the evolution of religion and culture, Jung could be said to have had avant-garde tendencies. He certainly was not a boring, stick-in-the-mud conservative, as Sherry makes amply evident. Perhaps, too, his hermit-like life while in his tower at Bollingen could qualify as somewhat bohemian, but as he describes his feelings in *Memories, Dreams, Reflections,* this would rather qualify as an expression of his traditional and above all his spiritual side—"If a man of the sixteenth century were to move into the house, only the kerosene lamp and the matches would be new to him… Moreover, my ancestors' souls are sustained by the atmosphere of the house, since I answer for them the questions that their lives once left behind."[6]

As an advanced and innovative thinker about depth psychology and related fields, Jung lived on the margins of the general collective all of his adult life. In that sense, he lived in the vanguard, but in no way could he be compared to a true avant-gardist like the psychoanalyst Wilhelm Reich (1897-1957).

Jung is a maddeningly difficult figure to biographitize, as anyone who has ever tried to capture him in this genre will attest. His written works can be equally daunting to interpret.[7] Some of his essays are impossible to understand accurately without fully grasping the immediate historical context in which they were written and having a detailed knowledge of the conditions under which he was authoring and the audience for whom his writings were intended. They can be subtly indirect, ironic, and elliptical. This is especially true of the materials that form the backbone of Sherry's study. These are the essays, lectures, interviews and letters that pertain to the cultural and political situation in Europe in a period of intense crisis, embedded in the shadowy political world that was unfolding after WWI through the outbreak of WWII and into the ferociously anxious times of the Cold War. Sherry argues that Jung tended to align himself with conservative (mostly German) thinkers during this period and concludes his book by saying that Jung was "a cosmopolitan intellectual with conservative views on politics and society… This is not to say that he ever lost his maverick streak."[8]

In his depiction, Sherry offers us a complex Janus-faced figure, an avant-garde conservative, with one countenance looking to the past and to tradition and the other peering ahead with anticipation into an unknown future that was being created in his time. That he misses the more fundamental underlying spiritual (archetypal) factor in Jung's thinking severely limits the work, however, and leaves one with the feeling that this is a caricature that fails to capture the most outstanding feature of its subject.

JUNG AND THE GERMANS – WAS JUNG "A GERMANIC NATIONALIST"?

Now to the specifics: how did Jung, a Swiss citizen, position himself toward the neighbors to the north, the Germans, especially in the turbulent 1930's? This question lies at the heart of Sherry's concern.

One gets a sense of the scope and focus of the project by glancing at the Table of Contents. The book is divided into seven chapters, plus an important Introduction and an equally significant Conclusion: 1) Basel Upbringing (28 pages), 2) Freud and the War Years (28 pages), 3) Jung's Post-Freudian Network (34 pages), 4) The Question of Accomodation (40 pages), 5) Nazi Germany and Abroad (32 pages),

6) The World War II Years (28 pages), and 7) The Cold War Years (28 pages). The book's center of gravity is made explicit here and in short order. It is Jung and the Germans, the 1930's—a little before, a little after.

To summarize: in his brief discussion of the Basel of Jung's childhood and youth (Chapter One), Sherry sketches in elements of the prevailing cultural atmosphere in the city during the late 19th Century. He highlights the intellectual influences of two fellow Basel residents, Jacob Burkhardt (1818-1897), the historian, and Friederich Nietzsche (1844-1900), the philologist and culture critic, the first an elitist decrier of modernity and politically an arch-conservative, the second an iconoclast and representative of post-Christian nihilism and therefore of the avant-garde ("God is dead"). According to Sherry, these figures played a key role in forging the background for Jung's avant-garde conservativism, in that they were competing influences upon the young Jung's mind and set up the tension in his cultural and political attitudes. They also voiced the antisemitism prevalent in the culture.

The appearance of Freud upon Jung's intellectual horizon, immediately following his departure from Basel (considered in Chapters 2 and 3), opens the critical issue of Jung's use of the term "Jewish psychology," while the topic of Jung's attitude toward Germany and the Nazis occupies the center of the book in Chapters 4, 5 and 6. The latter chapter also details Jung's involvement with the spy operations of the Allies, headed up by Alan Dulles in Switzerland. Finally, Jung's attitude toward Soviet Communism and his position on the Cold War are discussed in Chapters 6 and 7.

As Sherry connects the dots, he descries how they reveal the patterns in Jung's avante-garde conservativism and how this position determines his attitudes toward Nazi Germany and leads to his comments on Jewish psychology. It should be noted, however, that this is an image whose features are constructed out of a strict and carefully sifted selection of Jung's capacious features as a human being and a thinker, the kind of portrait a Lucien Freud might paint of someone toward whom he had highly ambivalent feelings but also someone who fascinated him endlessly.

Whence this ambivalence? In the Introduction, Sherry tells us that he began his research "wanting to know whether this member of Sgt. Pepper's Lonely Hearts Club (top row between W.C. Fields and Edgar

Allan Poe) [i.e., Jung] was really a Secret Architect of the Holocaust" (p. 2). This starting point, even if meant only ironically, must be the source of his grave ambivalence, and the fascination. From there, he tells us, he extended his quest to include the broader issue of how Jung related to modernity and to the burning political and social issues of his day in general.

While the scope of the book may seem large on the one hand, in that it attempts to trace the cultural background and historical context of Jung's thinking about social and political issues in general, it is also very narrowly construed on the other. Sherry concentrates primarily on a selection of the essays in volume 10 of the *Collected Works*—"The Role of the Unconscious" (1918), "The State of Psychotherapy Today" (1934), "Wotan" (1936), and "After the Catastrophe" (1945)—because they contain some key reflections on contemporary events and on what was transpiring in Europe. These essays were written in what was arguably one of the most troubled and tragic period of European history, an era of paroxisms of violent political conflict and upheaval throughout all the nations of Europe, which resulted in the evil of the Holocaust and countless other horrors. In this period, Europe entered the heart of darkness and still has not fully recovered. Hence, the on-going fascination with this time. We have to keep in mind that Jung lived through the nightmare that we study today in retrospect and from a distance. How did he position himself in the midst of all this turmoil?

A basic flaw in Sherry's portrait of Jung the political man results from labelling him a "Germanic nationalist"[9] and saying that he identified himself as "a German."[10] This is not only misleading, it is incorrect. Jung was a Swiss, as Barbara Hannah makes so abundantly clear in her memoir, *The Life and Work of C.G. Jung*, and as Deidre Bair also recognizes and anchors in place in her biography, *Jung*. The adjective "Germanic" (*germanisch*) should not be confused with "German" (*deutsch*). "Germanic" applies to all the descendents of the cluster of tribes who lived east of the Rhine in Roman times, including the German-speaking Swiss but also others in surrounding countries. The Swiss, however, draw a sharp distinction between themselves and the Germans (*die Deutschen*) to the north, which is spelled out almost daily in the Swiss newspapers. A loyal Swiss, as Jung was without doubt, does not identify himself as a "German," nor would he consider the possibility of "Germanic nationalism," since this does not exist because there is no Germanic nation. Insofar as Jung would consider himself "Germanic," it would be only in the sense of descent from Germanic stock and would have nothing to do with states or nations, therefore only relevant to cultural issues and differences ("the blond beast") but not to political or nationalistic ones. The failure to make this crucial distinction blurs the lines and hobbles Sherry's narrative. In all of his statements about or to Germans, Jung was speaking self-consciously as a Swiss. He was definitely not "one of them," *die Deutschen*!

What Sherry's book does contribute to the literature is an examination of the personal and professional associations Jung had with people, organizations, and publications in the Germany of the 1920's and 1930's. This is a positive value, if understood correctly and in a broad context. In his conclusion, Sherry tells us: "While tracking down what Jung wrote about politics and race I also researched his professional activities and publishing history, which I learned were either missing from the literature or relegated to footnotes. I wanted to accurately map the German branch of Jung's intellectual and social network and decided to begin with the 1920's since that period was largely terra incognita."[11] The result amounts to a trove of new information, which although quite raw and unfiltered and also not exhaustive, will certainly be useful for further research in the future.

Linkages and Associations – a Questionable Methodology

Sherry's methodology in pursuing his investigation, which consists in highlighting a (very limited) selection of Jung's writings and utterances and linking them up with a (also very limited) selection of Jung's relationships with people and organizations and then creating out of the resulting networks an image of Jung's political and social attitudes, introduces what is for me a major problem in his portrayal of Jung's positions with regard to his chosen themes of race and politics. The meaning and significance of the associations between Jung and the other figures cited by Sherry, mostly contemporary writers and thinkers, are often vaguely established and suspiciously speculative. While suggestive, these associations are finally not really convincing. Moreover, the work begins to look like an over-determined attempt to pin opinions, attitudes, fantasies[12], and views on Jung that are not really his own. It is often not clear just how firm or straight-forward many of these connections really are. Especially within the context of Europe in the 1930's, public communications tended to be politically slanted and distorted by fear or attempts at manipulation. In some cases, secret censorship was at work or feared (which led to much self-censorship), letters were opened and suspicious ideas were reported to authorities, and writers understandably tended to disguise their real feelings and views. A kind of code developed even in personal communications, just in case someone was hacking in.[13] In other cases, one individual was trying to influence or subtly direct the other to carry out a certain policy, but indirectly. Ellipsis was a strategy—what was left out was more important than what was included. One has to read between the lines and know the players well to catch their intentions. Just because there were communications and connections, therefore, does not mean there was agreement or that the words written and published can be taken at face value. Often Jung's expressions are ironic, and if this tone is not heard his intended meaning can actually be reversed.

The selection of materials, too, is critically important because it determines the parameters of the context being considered. Also how the pieces are then stitched together is key. It is easy to create fictions, another thing to hold up a mirror to reality.

For instance, Sherry cites Oscar A. H. Schmitz ominously several times without giving the reader much information about him other than the titles of a small selection of his many books. From other sources, one learns that Schmitz (1873-1931) was "a German author, philosopher, and bohemian... [who] on Freud's recommendation ... entered analysis with Karl Abraham..."[14] and was responsible for introducing Count Hermann Keyserling, founder and leader of the Darmstadt School of Wisdom, to Jung's psychology and instigating an invitation for Jung to speak there in the late 1920's.[15] Schmitz sent Jung a copy of his book *Psychoanalyse und Yoga* in 1923, for which Jung thanked him in a letter and congratulated him on a brilliant work but strongly disagreed with positions taken in it: "Do you not find it also rather suspect to nourish the metaphysical needs of our time with the stuff of old legends?"[16] He also voiced sharp differences with Count Keyserling's Eastern philosophical approach to cultural issues. In Jung's published letters, there are a couple of other very short notes to Schmitz, none of them of any real significance. Sherry elevates this slight connection to a position of great importance, however, and states that "in the years after the war [i.e., WWI] Jung was *to grow close* to a group of German intellectuals who had fought on the war's cultural front. The most important was Oscar Schmitz who was remembered as 'this type of German-Jewish mixture who was very nationalistic and an officer in the German army in World War I. He had much national political interest as a writer also'"[17] (my italics). What this group is supposed to have shared in common was antipathy to the political left and criticism of the Weimar Republic. Was this also true of Jung? Sherry offers no evidence of this from Jung's writings nor is there any futher evidence of "closeness" between Jung and the others in this group. Sherry simply lists several of Schmitz's other many works and links him to Rudolf Eucken (a Nobel Prize winner for literature in 1908 and the author of a multitude of books on philosophy and religion), Thomas Mann (another Nobel prize winner and novelist), Max Scheler (the German-Jewish social-political thinker), Werner Sombart (a Marxist philosopher who blamed Jews for modern capitalism, then later turned racist and helped pave the way for National Socialism), and Leopold Ziegler (a many prize-winning philosopher). Sherry claims that "'The Role of the Unconscious' can be seen as Jung's contribution to this school of literature."[18] It is hard to see how Jung's essay, published in 1918 in Switzerland and famously raising his "blond beast" warning about the aggressive potential in the Germanic psyche, can have been a contribution to this school of literature. Jung did not meet Schmitz, the key figure according to Sherry, until sometime after 1923. This is like casting a single net over a great variety of fishes. The differences among this group of enormously gifted individuals are more remarkable than the likenesses. Making Jung a member of this small collection of highly disparate intellectuals, and in such a casual fashion, is simply not plausible. One would like to hear Sherry on, for instance, just how Jung's essay, "The Role of the Unconscious" (1918) and his "blond beast" thesis fits into the universe of ideas proposed by these other figures. This could be interesting, but I personally cannot find a coherent group or common philosophical premise among this collection of names, and Sherry does not help me out. He does indicate that all the others contributed to the German war effort in WWI, but surely he cannot be suggesting that Jung shared this military goal as a neutral Swiss. Most probably, Jung would not have accepted this association as defining him in any important way whatsoever. On the contrary, he emphasized his differences with Schmitz and Scheler, two other members of this group. Moreover, all of these figures are German. Jung is Swiss. This is a difference that matters especially when it comes to war and politics. This is an example, though not an especially important one, of Sherry's lumping people together without offering a convincing rationale for the linkage.

Another example of loose linkage: Sherry writes that as a student at the university in Basel Jung owned a copy of *Transcendental Physics* by Johann Zöllner (1879), in whose published reports of experiments with the American medium, Henry Slade, Jung "found inspiration for his doctoral research."[19] Sherry writes that Zöllner was a champion for the spiritualist cause in Germany in the 19th century and an outspoken antisemite who dubbed his times "the century of Jewish liberalism" and complained about the "reigning Judaization of German universities."[20] As a young student, Jung borrowed some of this language in one of his Zofingia Lectures,[21] which Sherry notes astutely but then goes on to associate this with "opinions about Jews... held by Burckhardt and many others in Basel"[22] and describes some of Burkhardt's antisemitic statements and attitudes. In this, he is trying to depict a cultural context, Basel in the late 19th century. Burckhardt was a significant cultural figure in the Basel of Jung's day, to be sure, and Sherry's speculation that his attitudes (specifically toward Jews) influenced Jung or were reflected in Jung's attitudes may have some validity, but if this is the case it is strange that Jung does not quote or reference Burckhardt in his Zofingia Lectures nor mention him in relation to views about Jews or modern culture in any of his later works. It is not at all certain that Burckhart was as important a figure for Jung's formation as Sherry argues. Again, the links that Sherry forges among these figures are weak. They do not convince me that Burckhardt, for instance, was terribly important in Jung's thinking. The confabulated context casts a shadow, but one wonders where the sun stands in the heavens in relation to the figures. Whose shadows are they?

Sherry's strained associative leaps and linkages, while perhaps somewhat informative of attitudes in the prevailing culture in which Jung grew up (in Basel) and lived (in Switzerland) and which dominated the Germany of the 1920's and '30's, end up, unfortunately, creating a thickly woven cloak of attributions that blanket rather than reveal Jung the man. They do not account for Jung's unique and most distinctive features. One should remember, for instance, that another looming figure in the Basel of Jung's youth was his late maternal grandfather, Samuel Preiswerk (1799-1871), who was a proto-Zionist and laid the groundwork for the First Zionist Congress, held in the liberal and friendly city of Basel in 1897. As Sherry notes in a footnote, Jung's family on both sides was philosemitic due to their "devotion to biblical philology."[23] Was this not also an important influence on Jung? And could it not perhaps account for his close collaboration and friendship with so many Jews in his lifetime? Sherry does not mention this possibility.

The methodology in evidence, ostensibly aimed at building context, turns out, in my opinion, to create distortions rather than offer enlightenment on the context and so obscures rather than reveals the true lineaments of Jung's attitudes on politics and society.

Jung and "Jewish psychology" – What is it?

In reading this work, I had to stop frequently and ask myself if my visceral discomfort with the portrait that Sherry was constructing was due to having to face a truth about Jung that I would find abhorent—that Jung really was an antisemite and a racist of the type he has been accused of being so often over the last seventy-five years—or if it was due rather to a perception that Sherry was being unfair to Jung by leaving out the most essential features of his personality and character. At times, his work seemed tendentious and willfully skewed; at other times, it struck me as more happily balanced and even-handed, especially in the Introduction and Conclusion, which obviously were written last and therefore offer a more worked-through vision.

To his great credit (and my immense relief and gratitude!), it turns out that Sherry is very careful to affirm (more than once) that Jung was not a racist and that he did not subscribe to a biological view of the differences among ethnic groups, nor favor one over the other, nor consider some inherently superior to others. This is the essence of racism, of which antisemitism is a specific instance. In other words, Jung was not in the Nazi racist camp. It could be argued, in my view, that he was actually a multiculturist with an appreciation for ethnic differences. But Sherry does see him skirting dangerously close at times to playing into the hands of the Nazi position when talking about the psychological differences between ethnic groups, especially in his use of the phrase "Jewish psychology," even while repeating time and again that he did not mean by this term to imply superiority or inferiority, only to indicate a difference from other ethnic psychologies. Jung would attribute this difference in psychologies to history and culture rather than to race and not elevate one over the other. Sherry also notes, albeit rather *sotto voce* to my ear, that Jung spoke positively of Freudian and Adlerian psychoanalysis during Congresses held in Nazi Germany in the 1930's, which was a very unpopular (even dangerous) opinion to voice in those venues at that time.

What disturbed me, however, was Sherry's methodological strategy throughout the book of pinning Jung's attitudes to those of others with whom he was professionally associated, without explicit statements by Jung that support this, which creates an impression of finding him guilty by association. Because the territory that this book most deeply explores—Nazism and antisemitism—is so highly charged with emotion, it is often enough to say that Jung had professional contact in the 1930's with a German named Goering, a cousin of the infamous Nazi leader, Hermann Goering, to set off all kinds of alarm bells in the mind. This makes it difficult to think and to sort out the differences between Dr. Matthias Goering, the psychiatrist who had an Adlerian analysis, and his cousin Hermann Goering, the Nazi war criminal; between Jung and Goering; between the Swiss and the Germans, and so forth. Every distinction evaporates, and all tend to become blended into one big Image of Horror. This is a gross example, but Sherry's relentless linking of Jung to writers, intellectuals, magazines, and others who were either outright Nazis or were used by Nazis in their propaganda machine, without at the same time mentioning Jung's many connections and associations with people who were utterly opposed to Nazis and Fascism, or without detailing his strong resistance to Goering's and other Nazis' pressures to make him conform to their heinous political agendas, can easily create the impression that Jung was somehow vaguely in their camp.[24] And this is of course what Jung's most vitriolic critics have been relentlessly charging since 1933 and in full throat after WWII until the present day. Sherry ameliorates this somewhat by going into considerable detail about Jung's wartime relationships with the Allied spies and operatives in Switzerland whom he assisted by giving them militarily valuable advice about German psychology.

Reading the book from cover to cover, I had the impression, too, that Sherry travelled a fair distance from his starting point, which was, as he said, to find out if Jung was indeed an "architect of the Holocaust." In his "Conclusion," Sherry shares a telling experience regarding the change in his opinion about Jung's alleged antisemitism: "In the early stages of my work people would ask, 'Well, was he or wasn't he?' At first I would respond as succinctly as possible but finally found myself replying, 'Tell me your definition of an anti-Semite and I will tell you the degree to which Jung matches it.' Things got interesting when I would point out that some of Jung's most loyal defenders were a group of Jewish followers..."[25] He does not say what his original succinct answer was, but it seems that as he studied the materials his opinion changed and the answers were not so simple. By normal definitions of the term, antisemitism was not a feature of Jung's mature cultural and political thinking, although in certain passages of his early Zofingia Lectures one does hear this sentiment in a few of his utterances, which he borrowed from other sources.

As Sherry states the case, Jung was importantly influenced by 19th century thinkers like Eduard von Hartmann, for whom "and for many others Jews were to blame for a new, materialistic spirit that they saw permeating their country's economic and cultural life."[26] From his university years in Basel onward, Jung objected to a form of modernity that dismissed the religious and mystical elements of human experience. "Jung would later criticize Freud not for being Jewish per se but for contributing to the triumph of a rationalistic, 'disenchanted' view of modern life. For Jung, Freud was an examplar of the modern, Jewish intellectual who had lost his religious faith and rejected all religion as a supersititious crutch."[27] When Jung spoke of "Jewish psychology," therefore, he was referring to Freud and his psychoanalysis and to what James Kirsch called "the Galut phenotype," the psychology of the exile ("Galut"),[28] a position held by many Jewish intellectuals after the enlightenment. Jung was not intending with this phrase to characterize all Jewish people on a "racial" basis. To say it again, because it bears repeating, this was a specific cultural, and not a racial, designation. Jung also realized that many other forces were responsible for secularist modernity, including his own Protestant tradition, and in his fourth and final Zofingia Lecture in Basel, not mentioned by Sherry, he criticized the Protestant theologian, Albrecht Ritschl (1806-1876), precisely for stripping Christian theology of metaphysics and the mystical element. He would have had the same criticism of Adolf Harnack's lectures, *Das Wesen des Christentums* (*What is Christianity?* in the English translation), published in 1900, which carried Ritschl's theology several steps further in the direction of rationalism and was considered so antisemitic that Leo Baeck (1873-1956), the notable Rabbi of Berlin (and later an associate of Jung's through their mutual connection to Count von Keyserling and the School of Wisdom in Darmstadt), was driven to write a well-received and still studied rebuttal with the title, *The Essence of Judaism* (1905). Jung had a similar critical reaction to the later demythologization project of the Protestant Biblical scholar, Rudolf Bultmann (1884-1976).

What Jung found objectionable in modernist thinkers like Freud was the distance they took from their traditional religious backgrounds, adopting instead a stance of positivistic intellectualism and a secularist identity. In this critical reaction, we can see Jung's conservatism and religious attitude in action. The move away from tradition and toward resolute secularism resulted, in Jung's view, in serious identity problems, in a psyche without ground under its feet and removed from the deeper layers of the unconscious, devoid of feeling for "ancestors" and the cultural history which they represent. Such alienation from cultural depth makes people more susceptable to disenchantment with life itself and the consequent neurotic problems that Jung saw in his analytic practice regularly. All "moderns," not only Jews, were in danger of the same malady. Jung himself was, of course, no exception. He was in the same predicament, since he too was such a modern who could no longer believe in the religion of his ancestors, and his search for the "soul," as recorded *The Red Book*, shows his suffering and his strategy for reconnecting with the ancestoral spirits. His Tower at Bollingen was an extension of this project.

One of Jung's chief Jewish defenders was James Kirsch (1901-1989), whose correspondence with Jung, dating from 1928 to 1961, has recently been published (and is reviewed in this issue of *Spring*) In an early exchange, Kirsch asked Jung if he was an antisemite, to which Jung replied emphatically: "In general, you really ought to know me well enough not to attribute to me uncritically a non-individual stupidity like anti-Semitism."[29] Kirsch accepted Jung's blunt denial of antisemitism, which corresponded to his personal experience of Jung as he had known him through his analytic relationship and otherwise, and he and Jung went on to have many further exchanges about Judiasm and Jews in a cordial and differentiated fashion. Kirsch credited Jungian psychology with making it possible for him to reconnect to his Jewish roots.

Toward the end of his study, Sherry says that it was Jung's conservatism that drew the ire of his hardest critics, who came mostly from the political left and not primarily, as is often said, from the Freudian camp. In a section of the book entitled "Jung's Critics in Switzerland and the United States,"[30] which actually should have included Jung's "Defenders" in its title, Sherry offers a detailed review of Jung's most vocal, and at times vicious, post-war critics and also of his most effective defenders. As Sherry finds, the most extreme critic was Albert Parelhoff, "remembered by Karl Shapiro as 'a caricature of a Red – slouch hat pulled down over one eye and chewing a cigar.'"[31] Parelhoff published his diatribes in a far left magazine with the astonishing title, *The Protestant*—articles with titles like "Dr. Carl G Jung—Nazi Collaborationist" and "Jung's Unclean Hands." Who knows how many minds were turned away from considering Jung's ideas by the dreadful Parelhoff. Jung's most effective defender, remarkably, was a Jewish child psychotherapist, not formally Jungian, named Ernest Harms, about whose work, Jung said, he could add very little since it was so complete and correct in its explanations of all relevant materials. This section of Sherry's book offers a vivid impression of the heated exchange of accusations and rebuttals made about Jung's activities and statements following his acceptance of the presidency of the IAAGP in 1933. The recent work by Giovanni Sorge, "Jungs Präsidentschaft in der Internationalen Allgemeinen Ärztlichen Gesellschaft für Psychotherapie. Neue Erkenntnisse,"[32] is a solidly researched study on Jung's presidency from beginning to end and shows explicitly and step by step how Jung resisted throughout his terms in office, and with increasing effectiveness, the Germans' attempts to co-opt him and bring him into the pale of collaboration, until in the end they declared him *persona non grata* in Germany and banned his work.

For his discussion of Jung and "Jewish psychology," as well as of the issue of antisemitism, I give Sherry high marks, with appreciation.

NOTES

1. Sherry, *Carl Gustav Jung: Avant-Garde Conservative* (New York: Palgrave Macmillan, 2010), p. 5.

2. Like so many others before him, Sherry relies primarily (almost exclusively) on published materials and does not present much in the way of new archival material, which other recent authors like Ann Lammers and Giovanni Sorge have been digging into with surprisingly revealing results.

3. Sherry, *Jung: Avant-Garde Conservative*, p. xiii.

4. In a letter to James Kirsch, dated 26 May 1934, Jung writes: "As a human being I am a European, as an atom of the masses I am a Swiss bourgeois, domiciled at 228 Seestrasse, Küsnacht near Zürich." Ann Conrad Lammers, *The Jung–Kirsch Letters* (London and New York: Routledge, 2011), p. 47.

5. Jung's essay "Wotan" is an example of this, also his discussion of the evolution of western culture in *Aion*.

6. C.G. Jung, *Memories, Dreams, Reflections* (New York: Vintage Books, 1961), p. 237.

7. There are many interpretations of Jung's essay, "Wotan," for instance, none of which are terribly satisfactory. Sherry's comments on this essay are completely off the mark, but addressing his misreading in detail is beyond the scope of this review. He sees the essay as Jung's "most sustained völkisch text" (p. 150), which, depending on the meaning attributed to völkisch, tends to cast the essay as one of advocacy for Nazi propaganda. That it certainly is not. To read this essay with any degree of accuracy requires a deep knowledge of Jung's language, his use of irony, the situation in Germany and Switzerland in the spring of 1936, and his basically religious/spiritual orientation toward history. It is an example of his attempting to discern the archetypal background of an actual religious and cultural movement and its possible meaning. Jung is neither advocating nor praising the eruption of Wotan in the German collective. He is reflecting, discerning, wondering in astonishment at such a collective happening in his time. Unfortunately, Sherry is more intent on pointing out the inaccuracies of Hull's translation than he is on elaborating a reading of the German original. A useful introduction to the Wotan essay can be found in Guenter Langwieler's "'Wotan' — a political myth of the German collective

unconscious," in *Cultures and Identites in Transition*, edited by Murray Stein and Raya A. Jones (London and New York: Routledge, 2010), pp. 30-40.

8. Sherry, *Jung: Avant-Garde Conservative*, p. 215.

9. *Ibid.*, p. 14.

10. *Ibid.*, p. 54.

11. *Ibid.*, p. 215.

12. Sherry makes a small but telling error when, in his enthusiasm to depict Jung's "Orientalist harem fantasy" (p. 53), he claims that Antonia Wolff was half Jewish (p. 52). This may stem from a similar erroneous identification of Ms. Wolff in the stage play, *The Talking Cure* by Christopher Hampton, where she is similarly miscast.

13. A graphic example of this is described by Ann Lammers in her scholarly investigation of the relationship between Jung and Walter Cimbal and their correspondence during the 1930's, "Professional Relatonships in Dangerous Times: C.G. Jung and the Society for Psychotherapy" (in press).

14. Wendy Swan (ed.), *The Memoir of Tina Keller-Jenny* (New Orleans, Spring Journal Books, 2011), p. 162, citing Falzeder.

15. Gerhard Adler (ed.), *C.G. Jung Letters: I 1906-1950* (Princeton: Princeton University Press, 1973), p. 39, ftn.

16. *Ibid.*, pp. 39-41.

17. Sherry, *Jung: Avant-Garde Conservative*, p. 61.

18. *Ibid.*, p. 62.

19. *Ibid.*, p. 25.

20. *Ibid.*

21. C.G. Jung, *The Zofingia Lectures* (Princeton: Princeton University Press, 1983), p. 35.

22. Sherry, *Jung: Avant-Garde Conservative*.

23. *Ibid.*, p. 222, ftn. 67.

24. Jung's clear and steady resistance to the Nazi program and to Goering's pressures is detailed in the article by Giovanni Sorge, mentioned at the end of this review, see ftn. 18.

25. *Ibid.*, p. 215.

26. *Ibid.*, p. 3.

27. *Ibid.*

28. In Lammers, *Jung-Kirsch Letters*, p. 56: "In this we are also justified to consider Freud, without distracting from his courageous

discoveries, as a figure determined by the *Galut* (the *Galut* phenotype), rather than as a timeless manifestation of the Jewish essence." This statement is embedded in a short essay that was included in Kirsch's letter to Jung of 8 June 1934.

29. Lammers, *Jung-Kirsch Letters,* p. 47.

30. *Ibid.*, pp. 197-204.

31. *Ibid.*, p. 200.

32. Giovanni Sorge, in press.

BOOK REVIEWS

Craig Chalquist, Editor. *Rebearths: Conversations with a World Ensouled.* World Soul, 2010.

REVIEWED BY LISA LYNCH

A man wakes up in the dim early light of morning from a strange dream. A woman in his dream introduces herself to him as "San Diego." The man wonders, "could this be the place of San Diego coming to him in the dark folds of his sleep?" This moment became for Craig Chalquist the beginnings of "Terrapsychology"—the deep study of the soul of a place, the earth, the landscape, history and mythology of our interrelationship with non-human life. Chalquist published the book *Terrapsychology* in 2007. As a follow-up to *Terrapsychology* Chalquist has gathered together a collection of essays in his latest book *Rebearths: Conversations with a World Ensouled* to further illustrate and elaborate his foundational exploration and development of terrapsychology. In order to distinguish terrapsychology from depth psychology Chalquist says in his introduction;

Lisa Lynch, Ph.D., is Coordinator of Integrative Studies in Psychology, Ecopsychology Concentration, and Associate Faculty, School of Applied Psychology, Counseling and Family Therapy at Antioch University, in Seattle, Washington.

> Very often, however, a depth-psychological analysis stops at the myth or motif "behind" or "below" the surface of the topic of study, as when impressions of a landscape are filed in the Great Mother Archetype category. Terrapsychology closes the circle of inquiry by looking still deeper for the place, creature or world that hosts the archetypal figure.[1]

The essays in this collection range from interesting student explorations to powerful, insightful, and transformative illustrations of encounters with places, landscapes, elements, and other forms and dimensions of this essential and profound relationship. Chalquist has organized this collection around six sections; *elements*, *places*, *bodies*, *things*, *methods*, and *ethics*. Each section is introduced with very beautiful, relevant and inspiring poems by Catherine Baumgartner:

> but how will I know the way?
> do I follow the leaves
> as they are turning?
> the bends in the grass
> the clawprints in the dust?
> there are so many signs
> all of them beautiful
> which one is for me?[2]

The voice of the poet helps to weave together the fabric of the stories and insights of each section. Her musical, vivid images open the reader to the possibilities and the potency of the stories to come.

The opening essay "Dirt" by Laurel Vogel grounds the whole of the book in her very sensual and open relationship to the land she lives on and the literal dirt that supports the life of the forest. She says as she watches an alder leaf fall "The ways in which I do belong begin to clarify."[3] This statement moves from the perception of separation to one of understanding and reverence. A moment watching a leaf fall illustrates the actual relationship and how it manifests in our perceptions and insights.

Giving a voice to this transcendent, trans-human relationship, whether through story, dream recall and active imagination is the intent and attempt by this collection of essays. Perhaps the word "deep" needs a friend, it is used as a place holder to signify the beyond, the below, the belly, and the earth that opens maw-like in canyons. The authors struggle to give names to the often unnamable, except perhaps by the poets and mystics among them. The essays mostly succeed when they focus on specifics—a dream image, a petroglyph, an erotic relationship with a Monterey Cypress, our historical use of uranium, and the love of the scent of the Midwestern prairies.

In his own essay "Tales Told by Corn," Chalquist attempts to differentiate his work in Terrapsychology with the field of ecopsychology which he has been intimately associated with. He is critical of the focus on trying to figure out the historical sources of our destroyed intimacy with nature and exclaims in an almost Franciscan lament, "Here at the edge of extinction with so many fellow creatures falling irrecoverably into the abyss, our as-yet unmanaged passions overheating the planet to its sobbing poles, we hold within fragile five-fingered hands the outcome of one of Terra's grandest experiments."[4]

Chalquist has gathered his tribe in a lovely, well-documented collection of essays and stories. I would have liked this to be separated into perhaps two volumes. The swing from personal essay to organized scholarly papers is too far to track easily the focus of this book.

I admire the contributors for not just trying to answer the questions but tending the fire and the heart of the wounded, beautiful, sensitive, appreciative voice of *Terra* through our stories, myths, dreams, and songs that she is giving us each day, each night in the bounty of our dreams and visions. Through re-enchanting and re-empowering the places our lives we are given a powerful map and a possible strategy that can inspire and invite nourishing and potent relationships. *Rebearths* is a guide, a collection of wise voices and warm hearts that offers images, stories, and reminiscent companions on our many expected and unexpected journeys through this time.

NOTES

1. Craig Chalquist, *Rebearths: Conversations with a World Ensouled* (World Soul, 2010), p. 7.
2. Catherine Baumgartner, *Rebearths,* p. 12.
3. Laurel Vogel, "Personal History of Dirt," *Rebearths,* p. 21.
4. Chalquist, "From Ecopsychology to Terrapsychology: Tales Told by Corn," *Rebearths,* p. 226.

BOOK REVIEWS

Linda Buzzell and Craig Chalquist, Editors. *Ecotherapy: Healing with Nature in Mind.* San Francisco: Sierra Club Books, 2009.

REVIEWED BY LISA LYNCH

In this collection of essays, *Ecotherapy: Healing with Nature in Mind*, the editors have collected articles and essays to illustrate what they call "applied ecopsychology." In some way this text exemplifies rather than solves one of the central issues we have struggled with in ecopsychology these many years. The practice of applied ecopsychology explores a vastness of practice and application that spans many disciplines and modalities. From shamanism to gardening; dream analysis to wilderness therapy; ecopsychology and now ecotherapy seems to scramble for a definition. That's not to say that every one of these practices can be considered as working from an informed ecopsychological perspective. But, what is that? How is dream analysis ecopsychology and not depth psychology? And, is applied ecopsychology merely a new stack of therapeutic techniques, utilizing nature as a tool for individual healing? In his essay, "Psyche as Big as the Earth," Theodore Roszak attempts to show us the depth of what

Lisa Lynch, Ph.D., is Coordinator of the Integrative Studies in Psychology, Ecopsychology Concentration, and Associate Faculty, School of Applied Psychology, Counseling and Family Therapy, Antioch University in Seattle, Washington.

he imagined an applied ecopsychology would look like, "Many therapists seem content to tinker, adjust, and above all prescribe; it is all their clients seem to expect. Going deeper takes longer and hurts more."[1] Is it the role of psychotherapy to help people feel better about what is going on in their lives and the world around them, or as Joanna Macy says, "The crisis that threatens our planet, whether seen from a military, ecological or social perspective, derives from a dysfunctional and pathological notion of the self. It derives from a mistaken understanding of our place in the order of things."[2] These quotes refer the reader back to the early days of ecopsychology where the practice of contemporary psychotherapy was called into question and challenged to broaden and question its own definitions of self and techniques of adaptation.

This collection of very short essays is a multi-dimensional look at the practices and insights of many therapists, writers, teachers, and gardeners. I am left wondering if the book would have served our needs better if there were fewer contributors and longer essays. Also, it seems the editors gleaned from a mostly Euro-American, Northern California base of authors. I do get criticism from my classes for not offering readings that are multi-cultural and come from a more environmental justice and indigenous perspective. It is true that there are mostly Euro-Americans writing and thinking about ecopsychology, but it would serve to enrich and expand the appeal of ecopsychology to tend the possibility of being inclusive and draw from a more diverse base of contributors.

What is true about the role of ecopsychology and ecotherapy is that its best application will serve both humans and our relationship to the potential threats and impending changes of a warming earth. We are heading into a vastly unknown and dangerous future. What the impacts of inevitable climate change will bring to us physically and psychologically are unknown. As Richard Heinberg says, "In the decades ahead we will be going through hell. That is an awful thing to contemplate, but the only alternative to accepting the facts is to live in denial until the reality is inescapable and our room for maneuvering is even more restricted than it has already become."[3] I honor this book and the tenacity of the editors for gathering many essays that can help those of us working in the classrooms and therapy offices, some tools, some comfort, and courage to "go deeper" and serve the earth and those who suffer with her through the inevitable changes that we all know are coming.

NOTES

1. Theodore Roszak, "A Psyche as Big as the Earth", in *Ecotherapy; Healing with Nature in Mind* (San Francisco: Sierra Club Books, 2009), p. 34.
2. Joanna Macy, "The Greening of the Self", in *Ecotherapy,* p. 241.
3. R. Heinberg, "The Psychology of Peak Oil and Climate Change", in *Ecotherapy,* p. 202.

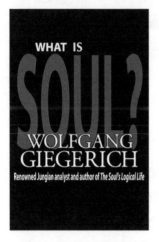